P9-CDV-767

Is the Fetus a Person?

Is the Fetus a Person?

A COMPARISON OF POLICIES ACROSS THE FIFTY STATES

Jean Reith Schroedel

Cornell University Press

Ithaca and London

Copyright © 2000 by Cornell University

First published 2000 by Cornell University Press

Printed in the United States of America

Library of Congress Cataloging-in-Publication Data

Schroedel, Jean Reith.
    Is the fetus a person? : a comparison of policies across the fifty states / Jean Reith Schroedel.
        p. cm.
    Includes bibliographical references and index.
    ISBN 0-8014-3707-5
    1. Fetus—Legal status, laws, etc.—United States—States. 2. Abortion—Law and legislation—United States—States. I. Title.

KF481.S37 2000
342.73'085—dc21

                                                                            00-025087

Cornell University Press strives to use environmentally responsible suppliers and materials to the fullest extent possible in the publishing of its books. Such materials include vegetable-based, low-VOC inks and acid-free papers that are recycled, totally chlorine-free, or partly composed of nonwood fibers. Books that bear the logo of the FSC (Forest Stewardship Council) use paper taken from forests that have been inspected and certified as meeting the highest standards for environmental and social responsibility. For further information, visit our website at www.cornellpress.cornell.edu.

Cloth printing   10 9 8 7 6 5 4 3 2 1

For my sons—Rick, Rob, and John

Contents

Tables and Figures

Tables

Figures

Tables and Figures

Preface

Usually an author can identify the point when he or she began working on a book. In this case, I cannot do that; instead I can point to several beginnings that fed into this research. Public policy scholars often write about "trigger events" that lead to major changes in the ways that issues are framed. Three trigger events—all of which occurred more than twenty years ago—have profoundly shaped my thinking about the value of fetal life and the ways that it is related to the status of women in American society. The trigger events involve the three fetal policy issues that I analyze in this study—abortion, prenatal exposure to drugs, and third-party fetal killing/battery. Together, they constitute this book's earliest beginning.

The first trigger event is a diffuse set of experiences rather than a single event. I was part of the last wave of young women to reach adulthood before the Supreme Court's decision on *Roe v. Wade*, back when getting in "trouble" meant that you either had a shotgun wedding or a back-alley abortion. What made it even more terrifying was that unmarried women, at least where I lived, could not get any form of birth control—not even from Planned Parenthood. In short, there was no way to have responsible sex. For young women, the choices were stark—protect your "virtue" or run the risk of being damned. I was lucky rather than virtuous. Fortunately for me, the sexual revolution arrived before my luck ran out. Other women were not so lucky. Having lived through that period, I am firmly committed to ensuring that women continue to have control over the reproductive decisions that so profoundly affect their lives.

The second trigger event occurred several years later and started out innocuously. A friend of mine asked me to come over to her apartment and help her take care of her brother's newborn baby. She said the baby wouldn't stop crying and she really needed a break. I remember thinking on the drive over that it was not like my friend to get upset about a crying baby. After all, she had two children and knew much more than I did about calming babies. When I arrived, she handed me the screaming baby and went into the back bedroom to try to get a few minutes of peace. In retrospect, I know that we must have gotten a few quiet spells over the next two days when her nephew slept, but I sure don't remember any. Nothing we did calmed the baby. I remember thinking he was the baby from hell, crying and flailing out at us with his little fists. What, I asked, made him like this? My friend, who had been into the "fast life," gave me one of those looks that seemed to indicate that I was hopelessly naive. Then she explained that her nephew had been born addicted to heroin. He had undergone withdrawal shortly after birth while in the hospital, but she explained that he was still missing heroin. In fact, she thought that "in his bones and being" he might miss it all his life. I will never forget the anger I felt at that moment toward the child's mother for putting him through such pain at that early age. Perhaps today, thanks to the media, we are more used to images of suffering "drug babies" and it is easier to create the emotional distance needed to shut them out of our thinking. Just add it to the long list of seemingly insurmountable social problems and get on with our lives. I, however, cannot do that. I keep remembering that long weekend with the crying baby who could not be soothed.

Even though the third trigger event also occurred more than two decades ago, my recollections of it are as vivid as those involving the baby born addicted to heroin. It was a beautiful spring evening and I was driving home. My three-year-old son was also in the car. A few blocks from home, while stopped at an intersection, I looked down a side street and noticed a man using a metal pipe to beat a woman. The woman was trapped half in and half out of the car. The man was standing outside, trying to push her back into the car. He was flailing at her, lifting the pipe up in the air and bringing it down on her. My first instinct was to jump out of my car and attack him. A split second later, I remembered that my son was with me. Instead I drove home and called the police. After listening to my story, the police dispatcher had only one question— "White or colored?" I remember screaming at her that it didn't matter what color the people were, that I was afraid the man was going to murder the woman. While I was on the telephone, two male friends had gone out to try to stop the assault. By the time I got back there, they had succeeded in pulling the man off the woman. He was screaming obscenities at them and saying he was "gonna smash that bitch good." Only then, when I went over to see what I could do to help the bleeding woman, did I realize that she was pregnant. I will never forget what happened when the police arrived a few minutes later. The two officers did not even speak to the injured woman. Instead they spoke briefly with the man and then let him leave. I was outraged. Why had they let the man go? He could have killed the woman. One of the officers then explained that the woman was a prostitute and the man was her pimp and that these things go on all the time and we shouldn't worry about what happens to trash like the woman. The sense of outrage that I felt that day has not dissipated.

Without these early experiences, I might not have realized that it was important to jointly analyze three fetal policy issues—abortion, prenatal drug exposure, and third-party fetal battering/killing—and that leads to a second, more conventional set of beginnings. In 1991, Deborah Stone sent me an article that she had written about fetal protection policies in industry. After reading the piece, I casually suggested that what she really needed to write a paper about was fetal battering. I explained that acts of violence against women increased during pregnancy and this was a really important policy issue but that no one seemed to care. Then I went on to compare the absence of concern about fetal battering with the media frenzy about "crack babies." Stone's response was, "Why don't you write about it?" At the time I said that was impossible; I was in the midst of finishing up a book about executive-congressional relations and didn't have the time to take on an entirely new area of research. But the seed was planted. I kept thinking of the woman I had seen beaten so many years earlier. I ended up dragooning Paul Peretz into coauthoring an article exploring how "fetal abuse" became defined as women's lifestyle choices that adversely affect fetal health while equally pernicious male actions were ignored. After the piece was published in the *Journal of Health Politics, Policy and Law*, I thought I would be able to get back to concentrating on my primary research agenda. I was mistaken.

Research projects have a way of taking on a life of their own. After Paul Peretz and I were asked to participate in a symposium on policy responses to drug use by pregnant women, I realized that there was a lot more that needed to be written about the subject. I still, however, was thinking of doing research for a series of articles. That did not change until 1996. Midway through teaching a policy clinic on fetal policy-making at Claremont Graduate University, I realized that the interconnections between the three policies were far too complicated to be analyzed in articles. I still tried to avoid taking on a fetal policy book project. Repeatedly, I told myself that I had far too many research commitments and could not realistically take on so massive a project. But when I woke up at 3:00 A.M. and couldn't sleep because I was blocking out book chapters in my head, I realized that I could not avoid it.

The seven students in the policy clinic (Pamela Fiber, Christina Fletcher, Dennis Falcon, Jane Greathouse, Charmaine Jackson, Dana Newlove, and Karla Salazar) and my research assistant, Daniel Jordan, did an incredible job. This project could not have been completed without their meticulous work. They spent months in law libraries and on Lexis/Nexis digging out fetal case and statutory laws in the fifty states. These laws constitute much of the primary data set analyzed in this project. The students also made significant contributions to the history and public policy sections. I thank them for their efforts. A couple of the students chose to continue working on fetal policymaking after the class ended. Christina Fletcher wrote a very fine master's paper on fetal personhood in civil law, which I cite in several places. Pamela Fiber also must be singled out. She made very important contributions to the sections on legal scholarship and took on the herculean task of checking citations. Many thanks to her. I would also like to thank another graduate student, Bruce Snyder, for helping me understand the intricacies of "compelling state interest." He also is a wonderful copy editor. Tanya Corbin, my current research assistant, has been great about handling last-minute queries. This project was truly a collective effort and could not have been completed without the deep commitment of these students.

There are many others, without whom this project would not have reached fruition. Financial support for this research was provided by the G. E. Bradshaw Foundation and the Fletcher Jones Foundation. From the beginning (or at least one of the beginnings), Deborah Stone has been of great assistance. Vivian Brown and Karen Devor Sherman provided important insights about the problems of pregnant addicts. Brown has been in the forefront of developing drug-treatment programs designed to meet the real-world needs of women addicts. I thank them. The staff at the Claremont College's Honnold Library, especially Mary Martin and Adam Rosenkranz, have been incredibly helpful. At this point, I am amazed that the library staff don't bar the door every time they see me coming. I would also like to thank Barbara Harris, Daniel Mazmanian, Karen Torjesen, Tammi Schneider, Janet Ferrell Brodie, Jay Jostyn, Craig Volden, George Monsivais, and Joseph Bessette for their useful comments. Peter Agree from Cornell University Press also has been incredibly supportive from the first time we discussed the project. My thanks also go to Susan Barnett, Nancy Winemiller, Trudi Calvert, and all of the other people at Cornell University Press. It has been a pleasure working with them.

Because fetal policy issues are so highly politicized, I must make one point absolutely clear: at no point did I attempt to manipulate the evidence or data to achieve a predetermined outcome. In fact, the conclusions that I reach in the final chapter are radically different from those that I anticipated at the start of the book project. Also, given that this work is likely to be somewhat controversial, it is important that only I be held responsible for it. While the people I thank in these pages contributed enormously to the project, the interpretations and conclusions are mine alone. The question of whether students in the policy clinic were pro-life or pro-choice on abortion never came up in the class. To this day I do not know where many of them stand on the issue. The class did, however, discuss at length the importance of striving to be as objective and unbiased as possible in one's research. As to the many other people who commented on the manuscript or in other ways contributed to this endeavor, their views on abortion span the entire spectrum. Some are strongly pro-choice. Others are equally adamant pro-life proponents, and still others fall in the middle or reject the pro-choice/pro-life labels entirely.

The politicized nature of fetal policymaking also poses another problem for researchers. State laws in this area are constantly in flux. It is unlikely that another policy area changes as rapidly as this one does. What this means is that everything written on the topic is out of date before it is even published. Unfortunately, this project is no exception. After updating my data analysis several times, I realized that it was impossible to be fully current. That being said, I have endeavored to make this book as up to date as is possible, given the time lags inherent in publishing. The material in the first five chapters has been updated through January 1998, as compiled by Lexis. In the final chapter, I discuss the most significant subsequent developments (or at least those through November 1, 1999).

I also acknowledge the support provided by Paul Peretz. Thank you for being intellectually cantankerous and personally supportive. Finally, I want to thank John Alexander Peretz for being his wonderful six-year-old self. He constantly serves as a reminder of what truly is important in this world.

CHAPTER 1

Introduction

Because our parents were human, we are human . . . after conception, life in the womb is in this respect no different than life outside the womb.

> Alan Keyes, the first African American Republican presidential candidate,
> "Alan Keyes on Abortion and Euthanasia"

As a captive samaritan a pregnant woman no longer has the option to withhold the donation of her body. Rather the fetus has already intruded upon her body, "taken it," so to speak, thereby serving its own survival and developmental needs.

> Eileen McDonagh, "From Pro-Choice to Pro-Consent in the Abortion Debate," 255

In the Bible the fetus is referred to as a sacred "fruit" or "seed,"[1] but more recently less positive descriptions, such as a nonconsensual "trespasser,"[2] also have been used to describe the fetus. These radically different perceptions of the fetus have triggered a polarized and strident debate over its moral and legal status in American society. Without a doubt, the sharpest public disputes over the value of fetal life have revolved around the question of the conditions, if any, under which abortion should be legal.[3] The October 23, 1998, murder of an upstate New York physician who performed abortions demonstrates the passions aroused by this debate. Dr. Barnett Slepian was the fifth New York or Canadian physician to be shot in his home by a sniper using a high-powered ri-

[1] See, for example, Zechariah 8:12. "For the seed shall be prosperous; the vine shall give her fruit, and the ground shall give her increase, and the heavens shall give their dew; and I will cause the remnant of this people to possess all these things" (*Holy Bible*, King James Version 1966). According to Olasky (1992a, 33), there are more than forty biblical references to human life beginning at conception.

[2] In the contemporary period, this position is most clearly articulated by Eileen McDonagh (1996). The first scholar to make this argument was a sixteenth-century Jesuit, Thomas Sanchez. Like many medieval thinkers, Sanchez believed that a human soul did not enter the embryo until forty days after conception for males and eighty days after conception for females. Because the embryo had no soul during this early stage of its development, Sanchez believed that a woman could abort it on the grounds that the fetus was an invader and the doctrine of self-defense allows a person to fight off invaders. For a discussion of early religious thinking, see Davis 1985, and Melton 1989.

[3] Although public opinion polls consistently show strong public support for abortion as a legal option, most polls also indicate that a majority of Americans support some restrictions on access to abortion. Even the *National Right to Life Convention Handbook,* in its section titled "Pro-Life Majorities," quotes polls showing that only a small fraction of the public favors a complete ban on abortion; not surprisingly, the handbook emphasizes the strong support for restrictions on abortion such as parental consent laws and opposition to government funding for abortions for poor women (1994, 106–7).

1

fle since 1994.[4] Slepian's name was listed among those of roughly two hundred other physicians and sixty clinics along with gruesome photos of aborted fetuses on the antiabortion Christian Gallery Web site. The day after his murder, Slepian's name was still on the list, but a line was marked through it to show that he was no longer performing abortions. Eleanor Smeal, president of the Feminist Majority Foundation, charged that the shootings were part of an "organized campaign of domestic and international terrorism aimed at denying a woman's right to choose" (Goldman 1998, A1).

Yet the question of whether the fetus is or is not a person is a central concern in other public policy domains, most notably policies concerning pregnant women whose substance abuse could harm the fetus and those dealing with whether third parties (usually husbands or boyfriends who physically assaulted the pregnant woman) can be charged with the crime of murder if their actions result in the death of the fetus. Because the status and value of the fetus is at the core of all these policies, it is crucial to analyze broadly the politics of fetal personhood and not simply examine those dealing with abortion. The purpose of this research is to study the question of fetal personhood in the context of *all* state criminal statutes that have the potential to accord personhood status to the fetus. Because the question of fetal "personhood" involves public order in criminal law, as opposed to the settling of private disputes among citizens as occurs in civil law, criminal law is a more appropriate venue to examine. Moreover, only in criminal law are the coercive powers of the state used to their fullest extent to enforce the law. For these reasons, the focus of this research is on the three main areas of criminal law that concern fetal "personhood"—abortion statutes, the prosecution of pregnant women for potentially harmful conduct against the fetus, and third-party actions that inflict harm on the fetus. Nevertheless, significant developments in civil law are considered in light of their impact on criminal law regarding the fetus.

In particular, this book explores inconsistencies within and across states concerning the legal status of the fetus. Questions such as whether pregnant women's behaviors that could harm the fetus are treated more harshly than are third-party (typically male) actions that cause harm to fetuses are examined.

---

[4] Probably the most heinous act of violence was the January 29, 1998, bombing of a Birmingham, Alabama, abortion clinic, which killed an off-duty police officer and critically injured a nurse. Although bombings of abortion clinics are relatively common, this was the first that resulted in a fatality. Other deaths have been caused by shootings. On July 29, 1994, Paul Hill, an antiabortion activist, murdered Dr. John Bayard Britton and his volunteer escort Jim Barrett in the parking lot of a Pensacola, Florida, abortion clinic. Britton was working at the clinic because another abortion provider, Dr. David Gunn, had been killed while working there. On December 30, 1994, Shannon Lowney and Leanne Nichols, receptionists at the Brookline, Massachusetts, Planned Parenthood Clinic, were also murdered by a "pro-life" activist (National Abortion Federation Annual Report 1994, 1). Other acts of nonlethal violence directed against abortion providers and clinics continue to be common. In fact, acts such as the January 16, 1997, bombing of an Atlanta abortion clinic that injured six people did not warrant front-page newspaper coverage. See, for example, Harrison and Healy 1996; Bragg 1997; and Sverdlik 1997.

Also, are the actions of physicians, who are professional and usually male, less likely to be criminalized, and, even if criminalized, are the "crimes" punished less severely? Moreover, to what extent do criminal laws that accord the fetus personhood reflect a broader regard for human life (both born and unborn)?

Framing the Issue of Fetal Personhood

Technically, the human organism is not labeled a fetus until it has reached the fourth month of its development. Up to that point, it is considered an embryo or a fertilized ovum (female egg). In the contemporary debates over fetal personhood, however, these distinctions blur, and the term "fetus" is applied to all stages from conception. In this research I follow the conventional usage in the literature unless a reference is solely to the very early stages of the human organism's development, when "embryo," "fertilized egg," or "fertilized ovum" will be used.

Because the debate over whether the fetus is or is not a person has taken place primarily in the context of abortion, the interests of the fetus increasingly have come to be viewed as separate from and contrary to those of the pregnant woman. Pro-life advocates proclaim that it is a mother's duty to "insure that the fetus is born with a sound mind and body" (*Smith v. Brennan* 1960), and thus a mother should take all necessary measures to protect the unborn child in her womb.[5] Conversely, pro-choice advocates assert that a woman's constitutional rights to privacy, bodily integrity, and equal protection under the law should not be abrogated simply because she is pregnant.[6] They believe that any expansion of fetal rights causes a commensurate decline in the rights of pregnant women and, by extension, all women. The fear is that women will eventually be reduced to nothing more than "fetal containers" (Annas 1986, 13–14).

Change and Continuity in Visualizing the Fetus

Until the 1990s, the parameters of the debate over fetal personhood had not changed significantly over the past twenty-five hundred years. In fact, Aristotle (384–322 B.C.) developed a three-part framework of fetal development that

[5] See also *Grodin v. Grodin*, 301 N.W.2d 869, 870 (Mich. 1980), where the court held that a child was entitled to damages from anyone who wrongfully interferes with her "legal right to begin life with a sound mind and body." The court held that the mother was not immune to a suit brought by a child charging that maternal negligence caused harm in utero. Depending on the circumstances, the mother could be held liable for damage that occurred after conception.

[6] To a large extent, activists on both sides of the abortion debate have used language in a manner designed to further their political goals. Because the labels that one uses to describe abortion opponents and proponents have become so value laden, I have chosen to use the terms "pro-life" and "pro-choice"—the terminology used by each side to describe itself—rather than become caught up in an endless dispute over the significance attached to the particular words used in this research.

still influences our thinking. He believed that the fetus assumed a "vegetable" stage at conception, followed by an "animal" stage, and culminating in the final "rational" stage. Although the duration of the stages is different, a similar framework was followed by the Supreme Court in *Roe v. Wade* (1973). Like Aristotle, it divided fetal development into three stages, each of which implicitly moved it closer to being considered a full human being. The Court held that during the first trimester, the fetus had no independent status separate from the woman and the state could not restrict abortion. During the second trimester, the state could regulate abortion, but only for the purpose of protecting the woman's health. Only in the third trimester could the state impose restrictions to protect fetal life.

As indicated by the *Roe v. Wade* decision, human progress and technological change over the last two and a half millennia had little effect on the Supreme Court's thinking about fetal development. The Court is probably not alone; the view that the fetus moves sequentially toward full humanity is intuitively appealing. Most people believe that a couple of cells containing human genetic material are less of a "person" than a five-month-old fetus, which in turn is less of a "person" than a week-old infant.

In the past quarter-century, ideas about fetal development have shifted dramatically. Through advanced prenatal technology, such as ultrasounds[7] and fetoscopes,[8] the fetus can be observed while in the mother's womb, encouraging right-to-life supporters to portray it as a "tiny person," instead of as a "fetus" or an "embryo." Very different connotations are associated with the terms "fetus," "embryo," and "person." The first is defined as "the offspring in the womb from the end of the third month of pregnancy until birth" as opposed to "embryo," which is applied to the human organism during the first trimester. In contrast, "person" is defined as "an individual human being, especially as distinguished from a thinking or lower animal; an individual man, woman, or child" (*Webster's Deluxe Unabridged Dictionary* 1983, 679, 1338). The implications of the linguistic shift are profound. As Cynthia Daniels noted, "As the fetus is animated and personified in public culture, the power of the state to regulate the behavior of women—both pregnant and potentially pregnant—is strengthened. Women's rights as citizens are potentially made contingent by fetal rights" (1993, 2).

Recent technological advances have also changed the medical and legal communities' perception of the fetus. As a "tiny person," or a "uterine capsule," the fetus may be a medical and legal entity independent from the mother (Boling 1995, 10). A separate medical field, fetal embryology, treats fetal patients, and pro-life lawyers advocate the legal definition of the fetus as "per-

[7] Ultrasound technology uses sound waves that are bounced off the dense parts of the body of the fetus, transmitting reproduction of the body to the technician.

[8] The fetoscope is a miniature camera mounted on a device that is surgically inserted into the pregnant woman's body, where it photographs the fetus.

son" entitled to equal protection under the law as guaranteed by the Fourteenth Amendment.

Although it has not responded to these societal changes by formally overturning *Roe v. Wade*, in more recent rulings, such as *Webster v. Reproductive Health Services* (1989) and *Planned Parenthood of Southeastern Pennsylvania v. Casey* (1992), the Supreme Court has ruled that states may enact laws that accord personhood or nearly personhood status to viable fetuses. These rulings and the tightening of state abortion statutes have generated little attention, perhaps because a complacent public believes *Roe* guarantees abortion rights or because sentiment regarding fetal life has truly changed. After all, most of the technologies that allow fetal images to be viewed in utero have emerged only during the last quarter of a century.[9]

The Debate over Fetal Personhood

Contemporary fetal rights advocates assert that there is no fundamental difference between a day-old single-cell embryo and a twenty-five-year-old man. Each has the requisite forty-six chromosomes that determine a person's unique genetic identity.[10] As John C. Wilkie, the founder of the National Right to Life Committee (NRLC), said, "Contained within the single cell who I once was is the totality of everything I am today" (Reprinted in Tribe 1990, 117). A right-to-life pamphlet, *Language of Illusion: The Abortion Slogans*, argues:

> Calling human beings "embryos" or "fetuses" serves the same purpose as calling them "adolescents" or "adults." These scientific terms are used to indicate where a person is in his or her development. They were never meant to imply that the unborn child is not human. As the "infant" is different from the "adolescent" in terms of development and dependence, so the "fetus" is different from the "infant." Yet all are genetically human, and therefore persons. (Garton 1984)

[9] Although medical journals previously published "pictures" of fetal life, the first mass exposure to these images occurred in a 1965 *Life* magazine article, followed by another article using the same images in 1972. In 1983 a PBS program ran a series called "The Miracles of Human Life," in which a camera attached to a fetoscope presented live images of the fetus in the woman's womb. Public exposure to "pictures" of fetuses has increased dramatically in the past decade. Physicians routinely give expectant parents sonograms of their unborn child, labeling it "baby's first picture." In a similar vein, books about pregnancy include "pictures" of the fetus at different gestational stages. For a discussion of the history and impact of fetal imaging, see Stabile 1992, and Condit 1995.

[10] A well-known antiabortion pamphlet, *Did You Know*, makes this argument when it tells the reader: "You were once a fertilized ovum. A fertilized ovum? Yes! You were then everything you are today. Nothing has been added to the fertilized ovum who you once were except nutrition" (Reprinted in Tribe 1990, 117).

Pro-life activist and 1996 Republican presidential candidate Alan Keyes equates a woman's right to have an abortion with the right of whites to hold blacks as slaves before the Emancipation Proclamation: "You cannot have the right to do what is wrong" (Alan Keyes 1999b). Many American right-to-life publications describe legalized abortions as "the American Holocaust."[11] References to the suffering of concentration camp victims and Holocaust imagery figure prominently in publications of a Palm Springs, California, organization called the Center for Documentation of the American Holocaust.

In contrast, women's rights advocates believe that the interests of the fetus cannot be separated from those of the woman. Just as the fetus and the woman are biologically united during pregnancy, so should their interests be viewed as unitary, and the woman should be empowered to make decisions for both (Gallagher 1987; Johnsen 1989). To them, the distinction between a day-old one-cell embryo and a twenty-five-year-old man is patently obvious. Mary Warnock (1987, 11) writes:

> It could, I suppose, be said that any human being, child or adult, was "nothing but a collection of cells." But of humans in general (or indeed other animals) such a description would be paradoxically reductionist. Of the post-fertilization embryo, however, such a description would be justified. It is a collection of special, that is, of human cells, but a collection of cells, nonetheless.

Women's rights advocates further assert that an embryo neither looks like a human being nor contains the totality of a person's subsequent humanity because cell division continues throughout the gestational period. Indeed, in the early stages it is impossible to distinguish between embryos that will become a single human being and those whose cells will subdivide into twins, triplets, or even larger numbers of human beings (Warnock 1987, 11).

A legal decision such as *Roe v. Wade* cannot resolve such an important issue about which opinions differ so profoundly. Ultimately one's views about fetal personhood are determined by moral beliefs, not case law. These moral perceptions do not arise in a vacuum but rather are socially constructed over time. For these reasons, it is imperative to understand the origins of our thinking about the moral and legal status of the fetus. Because fetal status cannot be

---

[11] See, for example, the 1995 issue of *HLI Reports*, a publication of Human Life International. Two of the four pages of the report are devoted to large, full-color photographs of aborted fetuses deposited in Washington, D.C., area trash dumps. Another page includes a 1945 black-and-white photograph of Nazi concentration camp ovens and the following statement: "The determination to ignore, the will to forget, the fierce struggle to suppress the truth—these curious aspects of the human mind formed a troubling part of the story of the Nazi holocaust. Survivors of that holocaust have expressed an equally fierce determination to remember. A museum dedicated to the holocaust has recently been opened on the Mall in Washington so that we will remember and decide firmly: 'Never Again.' But the museum looks out on the 14th Street Bridge, the route to Lorton (a waste disposal site). How many discarded and ignored bodies have been carried past the museum in garbage trucks? Those corpses state quietly, 'Again.' "

isolated from that of the person carrying it, it is equally crucial also to consider whether our laws reflect status relations and gender power relations, as well as moral perceptions about fetal personhood.

Legal Status of the Fetus

For more than two centuries, changes in abortion laws have triggered broader changes in the American legal system's view of the fetus. In the contemporary period the debate concerning fetal "personhood" and fetal "rights" has spilled beyond the edges of the abortion conflict into other policy areas. The recent targeting of pregnant substance abusers for criminal prosecutions to protect the fetus is an obvious example. Since 1985, women have been prosecuted in two-thirds of the states for "fetal abuse," a crime that does not exist in any state's criminal statutes (Paltrow 1992; Center for Reproductive Law & Policy 1996; Jos, Marshall, and Perlmutter 1995).[12] District attorneys have used a wide range of existing criminal statutes (child abuse, child neglect, contributing to the delinquency of a minor, delivering drugs to a minor, assault with a deadly weapon, and homicide) to prosecute pregnant addicts for exposing their fetuses to drugs in utero. Because none of these statutes was designed to apply to fetuses, prosecutors have argued that the unborn are essentially identical to born children (i.e., persons entitled to equal protection under the law).[13]

The passage of statutes criminalizing third-party killing of a fetus is a less-publicized example of treating the fetus as a legal entity distinct from the pregnant woman. Because the vast majority of third-party fetal killings occur when men (typically husbands or boyfriends) kick, beat, knife, or shoot their pregnant partners, such cases provide a particularly useful counterexample to abortion and prenatal drug exposure, both of which involve the actions of women toward their fetuses. Roughly, half of the states, by criminal statute or case law, define the killing of a fetus as "murder," "manslaughter," "feticide," or some lesser criminal offense (Lexis 1998). Maximum punishments range from eleven years' imprisonment to the death penalty (Lexis 1998). By separating fetal killing from the killing of or assault on the pregnant woman, these

---

[12] For a discussion of how unconscious patriarchal biases limited the definition of "fetal abuse" to maternal behaviors, see Schroedel and Peretz 1994.

[13] On July 15, 1996, a state high court for the first time upheld a woman's conviction for prenatal child abuse. On a 3–2 ruling the South Carolina Supreme Court held that a viable fetus is a "child" or a "person" under state law and entitled to legal protection, reinstating an eight-year prison sentence given to Cornelia Whitner, whose son tested positive for cocaine after he was born. See *Whitner v. State* (1996). In the past, high courts in Florida, Kentucky, Ohio, and Nevada had ruled that the fetus was not a "child" or a "person," thereby absolving women of child abuse liability for in utero exposure to illegal narcotics. Most cases involving prenatal child abuse are not appealed to state supreme courts because convicted women typically accept plea bargains or serve the time mandated for child abuse.

states implicitly or explicitly accord the fetus independent value. While the value may be less than that accorded a born human being, it is substantial and more than is given to nonhuman life. After all, no state punishes the killing of a dog or cat with an eleven-year prison term, much less the death penalty.[14]

Conventional Approaches to Studying Fetal Personhood

Despite the enormous social implications, little academic research directly addresses the question of fetal personhood. Although it is debated in law journals, the subject is typically limited to particular court rulings that do or do not regard the fetus as a person.[15] Social science research has deficiencies of a different sort. Because they are trained to tackle issues empirically rather than normatively, social scientists have generally not directly confronted the thorny question of whether and under what conditions the fetus is a person. A discussion of fetal personhood without confronting moral (i.e., normative) questions, however, ignores a forest for the trees. Social science is further limited by its fixation on empirical questions related to abortion that only tangentially address the issue of fetal personhood.[16]

To some extent, the failure to consider the moral ramifications of fetal personhood is a result of the ahistoricism of most legal and social science scholarship. Comprehension of contemporary moral issues is difficult without an understanding of cultural history. Little systematic research has addressed the broad question of fetal personhood. This book is designed to remedy these weaknesses in the existing literature and expand our general understanding of the politics of fetal personhood.

The Research Design

This research has three broad and interrelated aims. First, because most of the existing scholarship on fetal personhood fails to consider the impact of a shared cultural history on contemporary developments, the initial focus is on

[14] Although states differ somewhat in the punishments meted out to individuals convicted of cruelty to animals, the range is relatively narrow for first offenses, varying from fines of up to $400 in Colorado (Colorado Revised Statutes 18–9–202, 1997) to a one-year prison sentence in Kansas (Kansas Statutes Annotated 21–4310, 1997).

[15] Although there are many examples of legal scholarship assessing the impact of particular court rulings on the question of fetal personhood, most of the court decisions that provoke this type of analysis deal with either abortion or substance abuse during pregnancy. See Olsen 1989 and Rubenfeld 1991 for excellent examples of this literature.

[16] For example, some scholars (Cohen and Barrilleaux 1993; Wetstein 1996) have attempted to model interstate differences in public opinion regarding abortion, while others (Halva-Neubauer 1990; Strickland and Whicker 1992) have examined conditions under which states enact new abortion restrictions (e.g., waiting periods, parental and spousal notification, and public funding). This research is only marginally related to the question of fetal personhood because it focuses on a single policy area (abortion) rather than on all of the relevant fetal policies and their inherently moral nature.

developing a comprehensive history of ideas and policies regarding fetal protection. This history examines both the moral and legal underpinnings of existing American laws and practices and shows how cultural interpretations of the fetus have changed over time. The second aim is to compile and analyze case and statutory laws in the fifty states that relate to fetal protection. The focus will be on identifying and analyzing patterns with particular attention to the impact of gender and power relations on laws dealing with fetal status. Because the previous research has studied fetal policies in isolation from one another, it has been impossible to identify and examine systematically the patterns of policymaking within and across states. The final aim is to examine more broadly the relationship between state fetal policies and the role of the states in protecting society's most vulnerable citizens. Just as the issue of fetal personhood is relevant to all three aims, so too is women's economic, political, and social status.

Conflicts between those who consider the fetus to be a "child—not a choice" and those who continue to accord it less status than born life have polarized American society since *Roe*. Pro-life activists have used fetal imaging to build support for their position that abortion is murder. For example, pro-life activists held Christian funerals for 54 aborted fetuses, each of whom was given a Biblical name and placed in its own small coffin before being buried in a Riverside California, cemetery (Cicchese 1998; Gorman 1998; Times Wire Services 1998).

Unable to compete with the stark visual power of these fetal images, pro-choice advocates have tried to shift public attention away from the fetus and toward the protection of women's rights. Rather than vainly attempting to analyze fetal policymaking in isolation from the claims of the activists on each side, this book examines the logical underpinnings of the arguments put forth by the two sides. Again, the aim is to uncover patterns and inconsistencies in the positions held by the competing groups.

Both pro-life and pro-choice activists have attempted to construct policy narratives to bolster their cultural interpretations. According to Deborah Stone, cultural narratives are commonly used to build support for a particular policy or interpretation of events.

> Definitions of policy problems usually have a narrative structure; that is, they are stories with a beginning, middle, and an end, involving some change or transformation. They have heroes and villains and innocent victims, and they pit the forces of evil against the forces of good. The story line in policy writing is often hidden, but one should not be thwarted by the surface details from searching for the underlying story. Often what appears as conflict over details is really disagreement about the fundamental story. (1997, 138)

The heroes, villains, and innocent victims in the stories crafted by pro-life and pro-choice activists are obvious. In the pro-life narrative, antiabortion activists are clearly the heroes and unborn children are the innocent victims. Evil, money-grubbing abortionists and feminists are the villains. For example, in the antiabortion video *The Silent Scream*, which purports to show a twelve-week-old fetus being aborted, the narrator claims that the mob controls many abortion clinics—a patently false claim. A woman choosing an abortion is cast more ambivalently. Should she be viewed as a quasi-innocent victim or as a self-centered ogre? In stories that depict the woman as duped or manipulated by groups such as Planned Parenthood, she is cast as a victim, but in other stories she is depicted as a full-blown villain. In the debates over whether Congress should ban "partial birth" abortions,[17] for example, pro-life advocates argued that women frivolously choose late-term abortions, citing a teenager who supposedly got an abortion so she would fit into a prom dress.[18]

In the pro-choice narrative, the hero and villain roles are reversed. The heroes are pro-choice activists, feminists, and abortion providers while the villains are the right-to-life forces. The former are viewed as staunch defenders of women's rights, including the right to bodily integrity. Abortion providers are depicted as courageous individuals, willing to risk their lives to ensure that women have the option to obtain safe, legal abortions. The villains are portrayed as religious fanatics bent on restoring male dominance over women in all realms of life. The pregnant woman seeking an abortion is cast as the innocent victim, forced to run a gauntlet of crazed protesters to exercise her right to choose. For obvious reasons, the fetus is rarely mentioned in this narrative. In both narratives the conflict is presented as a stark struggle between the forces of good and the forces of evil.

Assessing the Validity of the Narratives

Policy disagreements rooted in conflicts over fundamental values are usually irreconcilable. In the past quarter-century, policymakers at all levels of government have been forced to grapple with an increasing number of these "morality policy" issues.[19] When emotions run high over such issues, assessing the validity of the competing claims is difficult. According to Christopher Mooney and Mei-Hsien Lee (1996, 1–2), disputes over morality policies are less likely than other policies to be resolved by appeals to "argumentation, analysis, and evidence" because they involve the "fundamental legal sanction of what is right and wrong."

[17] The term "partial birth" abortion was coined by pro-life groups to describe an "intact dilation and extraction" abortion. In this procedure, the physician delivers all of the fetus except for its head, then drills into the skull and suctions the brain tissue, causing the head to collapse. The fetus dies and is then completely removed from the woman. The gruesomeness of the procedure is far better symbolized by the term partial-birth abortion than by the medical term "intact dilation and extraction" abortion.

[18] In April 1996 Catholic bishops ran a newspaper ad stating that young women obtain late-term abortions because they cannot fit into prom dresses. A year later they admitted that this was a fabrication (Rivenburg 1997).

[19] For examples of scholarly research on morality policies, see Moen 1984 and Haider-Markel and Meier 1996.

Probably no contemporary morality policy has triggered more intense conflicts than abortion. Other fetal policies (e.g., those dealing with prenatal substance abuse and third-party killings) have not polarized the public, albeit for
very different reasons. Public support for sanctions against prenatal substance
abuse is widespread, while very little attention has been paid to third-party fetal killings.

Enhanced fetal status in a single policy area (such as abortion) may be expected to be transferable, creating the political momentum necessary to give
greater status to the fetus in other relevant policy areas,[20] but policymakers often enact policies that undercut one another. The lack of coherence of most
policies across related areas is caused by lobbying of competing interest groups
advocating very different policy outcomes. When a group fails to achieve its
policy aims in one arena, it may try to repackage the same proposal and gain
the support of a different set of key decision makers. Although this strategy
makes perfect political sense, the end result may be a lack of consistency in
policies across related areas. For example, radically divergent governmental
policies with regard to tobacco, which on the surface appear illogical, make
perfect political sense. The tobacco industry has been very successful in getting
support from the agriculture committees in Congress for the continuation of
governmental subsidies to tobacco growers, while at the same time the health
industry and consumer groups have gotten bans on television advertising of tobacco products and health warning labels on cigarette packages. But this political logic does not apply to policymaking regarding fetuses. After all, no interest groups advocate the use of narcotics by pregnant women, nor are there
interest groups mobilizing to support individuals who commit acts of violence
against pregnant women and their unborn children.

Because fetal policy is not politically incoherent, I next examine patterns
of fetal policies that policymakers might be expected to generate in accor-
dance with each of the pro-life and pro-choice narratives. I begin by considering policies that flow from the pro-life position. Douglas Johnson, the legislative director of the largest pro-life organization, the NRLC, states that
its guiding principle is that "every innocent human being has a right to
life"(Johnson reprinted in Cassidy 1996, 154).[21] If pro-life forces truly have

---

[20] Fletcher (1996) found a strong correlation between a state's abortion laws and its fetal tort
laws. Over the past fifteen years, the right to "personhood" in civil law has been a singular ac-
complishment of the pro-life camp, primarily through judicial rulings and statutory enactments
that allow parents to pursue wrongful death claims on behalf of nonviable fetuses and the enactment of bans on claims for wrongful life and wrongful birth. Fletcher found that states that restricted access to abortion were also far more likely to have civil laws enhancing fetal status than
were states that did not restrict abortion.

[21] By defining its role as defending innocent human life, the National Right to Life Committee
avoids the problem of having to take a position on whether all human life, innocent or not, is
worth protecting. This means that the NRLC explicitly opposes abortions and euthanasia but
avoids taking a stance on issues such as the death penalty that divide large portions of the movement.

as their overarching goal providing the fetus with personhood and legal protection equal to that of a born person, then states whose laws reflect a pro-life stance toward abortion would be expected to have policies that make fetal well-being their top priority and do so consistently across the range of fetal policies. One also would generally expect such states to have policies that protect and nurture human life (e.g., support adoption, provide prenatal care, and the like).

Conversely, if pro-life positions with regard to abortion are simply a smoke screen for broader attacks on women's rights, these states will not necessarily have enacted other policies consistent with the pro-life philosophy. Although they may support criminal actions against pregnant drug users because these policies target women for punitive actions, there is no reason to expect them to support benign policies such as adoption or prenatal care or to treat third-party killings as murder. Pro-choice (and more broadly women's rights) proponents believe that most "fetal protection" policies are hypocritical because their real purpose is the subjugation of women, not a defense of the fetus.

The validity of the cultural narratives told by fetal rights proponents and women's rights proponents can be assessed empirically. The two sides' underlying moral imperatives are quite different, generating a distinct set of testable propositions. If the pro-life movement is fundamentally about the protection of society's most vulnerable "persons," the following set of propositions should be upheld.

> Proposition 1a: Antiabortion states treat the fetus as a "person" in other areas of the law, regardless of the gender and status of the individual responsible for harming it.

> Proposition 2a: Antiabortion states are more likely than other states to adopt policies to combat prenatal drug use and third-party killings.

> Proposition 3a: Antiabortion states are more likely to support a wide range of policies that improve the health and well-being of society's weakest and most vulnerable "persons."

Conversely, if the women's rights position is correct, the following set of alternative propositions should be upheld.

> Proposition 1b: Antiabortion states do not consistently treat the fetus as a "person" in other areas of the law.

> Proposition 2b: Differences in abortion laws are a function of women's political, social, and economic status, which is generally lower in antiabortion states than in pro-choice states.

> Proposition 3b: Antiabortion states are not more likely to support a wide range of policies that improve the health and well-being of society's weakest and most vulnerable "persons."

Because the propositions represent strong characterizations of each side's position and do not allow for multiple motives and policy ambiguities, neither set is likely to be fully supported. Yet they allow us to identify patterns of policy enactments, measure the relative impact of the different motivations, uncover inconsistencies in the policymaking, and consider possible explanations for those inconsistencies.

An Empirical Analysis of Fetal Status

I have developed a comprehensive data set to test these propositions, containing all criminal laws relating to fetal personhood status. For each state, the case law and criminal statutes that apply to the fetus have been classified according to whether they accord the fetus no independent value, some independent value but less than personhood status, or full personhood status. The data set also includes variables designed to measure the different stages at which the fetus is legally relevant, the specific categories of prosecution for harming the fetus, and the penalties for such offenses. The case and statutory laws are current through January 1998 (Lexis). I also have developed other variables that attempt to measure the degree of value accorded fetal life in each state. Although some measure the access to and prevalence of abortion, others examine such topics as the relative importance accorded the fetus in civil laws and whether a state has drug education and treatment programs for pregnant addicts.

The data set also includes variables designed to measure potentially relevant interstate demographic factors, as well as political support for fetal personhood such as the degree of support for pro-life positions in the state legislature and governor's office, support for the Democratic and Republican Parties, and public support for pro-life positions. Finally, I have developed indicators of levels of prenatal care, well-being of children, and the political, social, and economic status of women. The variables are discussed in Chapter 5.

Such wide-ranging data facilitate comparisons across all fifty states and across the different types of criminal law and permit empirical tests of the alternative propositions generated by the narrative stories crafted by fetal rights proponents and advocates of women's rights. These propositions are simply extensions of each side's justifications for treating or not treating the fetus as a person. For example, fetal rights advocates believe their position accords with their deeply held regard for human life and consider the fetus to be fundamentally similar to a born child. If state laws consistently reflect this reverence for both born and unborn human life, they not only should accord the fetus full "personhood" status but also should provide significant prenatal care and a wide range of services to already born children, especially those who are the most needy and vulnerable.

Organization of the Book

The division of material into two sections, Part I, "Background and Overview" and Part II, "Interpreting the Patterns," is somewhat arbitrary. The major themes raised in the first part are explored in more depth in the second. The chapters in Part I introduce the major themes of the research and provide the historical framework needed to understand contemporary legal developments, while the chapters in Part II discuss developments since *Roe* and present the empirical results of the study of state criminal law and prosecutions. Although each chapter continues from the preceding ones, a reader with specific interests could read selectively.

Chapter 2 presents a history of the development of Western moral and legal thinking about the status of the fetus. It focuses on when, where, and under what conditions early philosophers, clerics, and legal scholars assigned personhood status to the fetus, with particular attention to those whose views have most shaped our contemporary beliefs. Because most of the thinking about fetal personhood has taken place in the abortion context, this history will focus far more on abortion than on any of the other relevant policy areas.

The primary aim in Chapter 3 is to trace the broad contours of fetal personhood as expressed in abortion law in the fifty states. The chapter begins with an explanation of the morality policy framework that is used in the empirical analysis. Because abortion policymaking pits two groups with fundamentally different moral views, it is an excellent example of a contested morality policy issue. The conflicts between pro-life and pro-choice groups are reflected in each state's abortion law, which identifies at what gestational point, if any, and to what extent, the fetus is a "person." Restrictions on an adult woman's access to abortion are considered separately from those that limit a minor's legal ability to terminate a pregnancy because the latter do not have the same legal personhood status as do adults.

The focus in Chapter 4 is on state policy responses to prenatal substance abuse and third-party fetal killings. Again, the aim is to identify broad legal patterns. Although the question of fetal personhood is central to each issue, the patterns of political mobilization are quite different than those regarding abortion. Because both drug abuse by pregnant women and third-party acts of violence against pregnant women are universally condemned, the public is not split over whether such actions are morally justified. Yet just as occurs with abortion policymaking, state lawmakers and judges are forced to confront the same issue of fetal personhood directly or indirectly. The criminal statutes or case law define whether a crime has occurred and, if so, what punishment is appropriate.

In Chapter 5, I examine the status of the fetus in the laws of individual states, across policy areas, and in geographic sections of the country to determine whether the patterns of the laws support the fetal rights narrative or give more credence to the women's rights narrative. For example, are pregnant women's actions that potentially harm the fetus treated more harshly than are third-party (generally male) actions that cause harm to the fetus? If so, what does this tell us about the status of the fetus and that of men and women in our society? The primary goal is to explain the differences within states and across different fetal policies; statistical measures as well as regression modeling are used. For example, why does Washington consider the fetus a person when a third party kills it but not in its abortion statutes? Conversely, why does nearby Montana criminalize performing an abortion, punishable by up to ten years in prison, but ignores third-party fetal killings?

Finally, Chapter 6 not only summarizes my findings but also provides an update on developments in 1998 and the first half of 1999. In addition, I explore the broader ramifications of our constitutional form of government on fetal personhood. I consider the implications of fetal personhood on traditional jurisdictional divisions between the state and federal governments. Given the inconsistencies across policy areas and across states and the moral and constitutional implications of the rights at stake, a strong case can be made for a uniform federal statute defining the personhood status of the fetus. If Alan Keyes's assertion that the fetus is a person from conception is correct, then his comparison of the current patchwork of state fetal laws to those that allowed slavery in some states but not others is compelling. Conversely, if a day-old embryo is not the equivalent of a twenty-five-year-old man, then the current patchwork system of state laws might be considered more acceptable—at least for the purpose of protecting fetal well-being. After all, the regulation of morality is part of the state's traditional "police power." It is far less acceptable, however, to allow enormous differences in states' willingness to infringe on women's fundamental rights to protect an entity that may or may not be a legal "person."

I also consider the constitutional implications of full fetal personhood. Would it require that abortions be outlawed in all situations? Would abortions be justified when the mother's life was threatened by carrying the baby to term? What about pregnancies caused by rape or incest? Would the common practice of "selective reduction"—abortion of one or more fetuses when fertility drugs cause too many embryos to attach to a woman's uterus to carry safely to term—be prohibited? Would contraceptives that do not prevent conception but stop the fertilized ovum from attaching to the uterine wall, such as the IUD and some birth control pills, be allowed? The type of line drawing involved would make current attempts at "balancing" the rights of the mother against those of the fetus look like child's play.

CHAPTER 2

Fetal Personhood through the Centuries

The value accorded fetal life is socially determined, inextricably linked to the status of women in any particular society. Reproduction is one of the means by which a society can increase its future labor force and provide a form of insurance to care for the elderly. Women's biological ability to give birth to children also has been viewed as a manifestation of God's divine plan for the "weaker sex," as well as a justification for excluding them from the public sphere. Historically, the political and social constraints relating to pregnancy and childbirth were based on superstition, functionality, and moral philosophy. Although medical technology and scientific "evidence" have reduced these ideas to anachronisms, women's status continues to be linked to their ability (potential or actual) to bear children.

Similarly, our thinking about the value of fetal life is an outgrowth of moral and philosophical beliefs that can be traced back more than two thousand years. This chapter examines the evolution of thinking about fetal personhood and the extent to which the legacy of early philosophers still affects current moral beliefs and legal views about the fetus. I show how ancient philosophical and theological thought regarding the existence of a "fetal soul" has contributed to American beliefs about the fetus. In some ways the discussion may appear to be less about the fetus than about abortion politics. It is important to recognize, however, that most of the debates surrounding fetal status have been triggered by questions of whether a woman should have a moral or legal right to terminate an unwanted pregnancy. Only in recent decades have the health, well-being, and legal rights of the fetus been considered independently from those of the pregnant woman. Cynthia Daniels explains some of the reasons why the fetus's status has changed:

During the 1980s a number of cultural, political, legal, and technological developments converged to bring the fetus into public consciousness as an independent and autonomous being. In law and in popular culture, the fetus was treated as physically separate from the pregnant woman and was personified—granted interests, concerns, and needs which may conflict with the pregnant woman's. (Daniels 1993, 9)

The Moral and Legal Dimensions of Fetal Status

Considerations of fetal status have always revolved around two distinct dimensions: a moral nexus and a legal one. Early Western philosophers and Catholic theologians focused primarily on moral questions dealing with the exact point at which a fetus became a human being. The initial disagreements were over the issue of "ensoulment"—the moment when a person's soul entered his or her body. Eventually, quickening (the start of detectable fetal movement in the womb) replaced ensoulment as the determinant of moral status as a human being.

Fetal status has always been an issue in debates over abortion. It was discussed by Catholic theologians when questioning whether abortion was a venial sin or a mortal sin[1] during the Middle Ages and is equally important in contemporary disagreements between members of the National Right to Life Committee and their adversaries from the National Abortion Rights Action League (NARAL).

The Early Moral Discourse

Early Western philosophical and religious thought focused on questions related to the formation of the soul. The Greek mathematician Pythagoras (ca. 582–ca. 500 B.C.) and the physician Hippocrates (ca. 460–ca. 377 B.C.) believed that the soul formed at conception, so they opposed abortion at any point (Rubin 1994, 3). Aristotle (ca. 384–ca. 322 B.C.) disagreed, however, and developed a systematic theory to explain the relationship between the soul and the fetus. Aristotle believed that personhood was attained gradually, as the fetus increasingly takes on human form. The process occurs sequentially, in three stages: the "vegetable phase," the "animal phase," and finally, the "rational phase" (Davis 1985, 41). The "vegetable" stage runs from conception until the entry of the soul into the body, forty days after conception for males and eighty days for females. "Ensoulment" begins the "animal" stage, which continues until birth. In Aristotle's view, the fetus had to assume a human shape before it could be considered "fully human"—a phenomenon that occurred at the actual moment of birth (Melton 1989).

Aristotle's beliefs about abortion grew directly out of his moral views about ensoulment. Although he believed that abortion was an acceptable way to

---

[1] The Catholic Church considers any willful thought, action, or omission that goes against the word of God to be a sin. There are two categories of sin: mortal and venial. Mortal sins are offenses so heinous that they merit everlasting punishment. Venial sins are less serious offenses that can be expiated through acts of penance (McBrien 1995, 26).

limit family size and reduce the societal threats of overpopulation and poverty, he supported its use only before ensoulment occurred. Many contemporaries were even stronger proponents of the need for abortions. For example, Plato (ca. 428–ca. 348 B.C.) argued that "abortion be demanded" for women over forty years of age. In general, abortion was thought to be beneficial to the state, a virtue higher than any rights of the woman or the unborn (Fowler 1987, 16).[2]

The Christian Church's Opposition to Abortion

Abortion was commonly practiced across the Mediterranean in the pre-Christian Roman Empire. As the empire declined and Christianity gained strength, however, views about its moral acceptability changed. The first criminal sanctions against women who had abortions were introduced during the reign of Severus (A.D. 193–211), although the earliest known Christian prohibition against abortion is found in the *Didache*, written in the first century (ca. A.D. 80). "You shall not kill the fetus by abortion or destroy the infant already born" (Rubin 1994, 3; Melton 1989, xvii).[3] The *Didache* is said to have considered abortion a sin as grave as those listed in the Ten Commandments (Davis 1985, 63).[4]

Despite the *Didache*'s prohibition of abortion, most early Christians accepted the Aristotelian view that abortion was acceptable and the fetus was a part of the pregnant woman. Not until the second century did Tertullian (ca. A.D. 160–ca. 230), a church representative trained in rhetoric and law, challenge the prevailing view that the fetus was an "appendage" of the mother. Although Tertullian acknowledged that the fetus needed the mother's blood to survive, he argued that "dependence on the woman does not render the fetus part of the woman" and that abortion was murder (Gorman 1993, 33). Tertullian did believe abortion was morally justified when the life of the mother was threatened by continuing the pregnancy (Davis 1984, 4). Despite the questions raised by Tertullian, Aristotle's theory about ensoulment would remain a part of the Roman Catholic Church's canon throughout the Middle Ages.

Although the church opposed abortion after ensoulment, the debate over the exact moment when the soul entered the body raged for hundreds of years. Although early Roman Catholic canon law adopted Aristotle's forty- and eighty-day benchmark, it was not universally accepted. St. Augustine (ca. A.D.354–ca. 430) reasoned that because it was impossible to determine the

---

[2] For a general history of abortion practices, see Fowler 1987.

[3] The *Didache* is a compilation of the early Christian church's regulations of office, rituals, and moral codes. The Catholic Church considers it to be the first catechism (Coutinho 1998).

[4] In the Old Testament, abortion was not labeled a sin because the fetus was not considered to have a soul.

moment of conception necessary to calculate the forty- and eighty-day time periods for ensoulment, abortion was not homicide until the fetus was fully formed—animation (Melton 1989). Eventually the church leaders reached the same conclusion and decided to denounce abortions of formed but not unformed fetuses (Davis 1984, 41–42; Rubin 1994, 3). Although differences between the thinking of the Roman Catholic Church and the Eastern Orthodox Church were profound by the time of Augustine, both branches of Christendom opposed abortions of formed fetuses. Basil of Cappadocia, a leader of the Greek church, believed that the punishment for abortionists should be the same as for murderers (Davis 1984, 4–5).

In time, the church fathers decided there were two moral gradations of sin attached to the act of abortion. An abortion performed to conceal the sin of fornication or adultery was considered a lesser moral offense than one committed specifically to kill the fetus (Melton 1989). The underlying intent was the determining factor in deciding the degree of sin attached to the abortion act.

During the Middle Ages, Thomas Aquinas (ca. A.D. 1225–1275) asserted that there was a period of time after conception when the fetus did not have a soul and that fetal life began at animation (Engelhardt 1983; Davis 1984). Animation, "the only feature of the ensoulment doctrine that remained undisputed in canon law of the late medieval period," marked the point at which the church decided that the fetus was a human being and after which abortion was unequivocally murder, punishable by excommunication or severe penance (Davis 1984, 42). Preanimation abortions were viewed as attempts to conceal sins of fornication or adultery, while postanimation abortions were considered conscious attempts to kill the fetus. The legal system followed the lead of the church in assessing the degree of culpability associated with committing an abortion. Fines were levied if the abortion occurred before the fetus possessed a soul (before animation), but an abortion performed on a fetus that possessed a soul (animation and beyond) was a capital crime (Rubin 1994, 3–4; Davis 1984, 41–42).

Papal doctrine on abortion underwent several shifts during the late Middle Ages. In 1588, Pope Sixtus V ruled that abortion was homicide, regardless of the stage at which it was performed, but only three years later Pope Gregory XIV declared that abortion was not categorically homicide. Pope Gregory did not waver in his belief that it was always a sin—the question was the degree of sinfulness and of punishment (Melton 1989). In 1854, Pope Pius IX transformed papal doctrine regarding the fetus when he declared that the Virgin Mary was "from the moment of her conception, specially preserved from the stain of original sin." Theologians interpreted his statement to confer "immediate ensoulment" to all fetuses, an idea that encouraged many religious leaders to question the traditional view that preanimation abortions were less sinful than those performed later. Perhaps, it was argued, abortion should never be performed, lest a person inadvertently commit the sin of murder on a fetus believed not to be ensouled. Finally, in 1869, Pope Pius IX clarified the church's position, declaring that "the fetus, although not ensouled, is directed to the forming of a man. Therefore, its ejection is anticipated homicide." From this point onward, the Catholic Church strongly denounced abortion at any stage of fetal development (Melton 1989). The development of Christian beliefs about the humanity of the fetus is summarized in Table 2.1.

The Impact of Moral Beliefs on Legal Developments

The influence of early religious theology is clearly evident in traditional British common law, which English colonists brought to the New World. Early Christian moral precepts distinguished between degrees of sin associated with early- and late-term abortions, and the Reformation churches largely incorporated the Roman Catholic perspective. Although Martin Luther never mentioned abortion in all his religious writings, his views about original sin and the belief that the human soul existed before birth make it reasonable to speculate that he accepted Roman Catholic precepts about the humanity of the fetus and against abortion (Davis 1984, 5). John Calvin described the fetus as "already a human being" and explicitly denounced the taking of fetal life as a "monstrous crime" (Davis 1985, 5).

All of the Protestant sects regarded postquickening abortion as a major moral transgression (Brodie 1994, 39). According to Carol Karlsen (1989, 141), Puritans believed that any attempt to terminate a pregnancy was a serious sin. Not only were they concerned about the moral implications of fetal killing, but they considered abortion to be a human attempt to usurp God's decision-making power over life and death. Puritans also often associated abortions with the practice of witchcraft (Karlsen 1989, 141). The well-known Protestant minister Benjamin Wadsworth argued in 1712 that abortion was "murder in God's account" (Olasky 1992b, 30).

The Influence of British Common Law on the American Legal Tradition

The religiously based distinction between early- and late-term abortions was incorporated into British common law.[5] Abortion was legal before "quickening," the stage in pregnancy when fetal movement begins (approximately the fourth month). During the mid-seventeenth century, postquickening abortion was considered a crime in all the colonies, and some localities enacted laws that made it more difficult for women to obtain abortions at any stage of their pregnancies. For example, New York City in 1716 passed an ordinance making it illegal for midwives to help women obtain abortions (Olasky 1992b, 31).

According to Marvin Olasky (1992b, 30), one of the earliest prosecutions for abortions occurred in 1629, when an unmarried servant woman was charged with the crime of obtaining an abortion. The woman was acquitted

[5] For a detailed discussion of the British common law tradition and abortion, see Mohr 1978.

Table 2.1. Christian doctrinal perspectives about fetal life

Source	Date	Doctrine
Old Testament	early A.D.	Abortion was not condemned as a "capital" offense because the fetus was not regarded as having a soul.
New Testament	early A.D.	No specific reference to abortion.
Didache	ca. 80	Abortion was considered a sin akin to violating the Ten Commandments.
Epistle of Barnabas	ca. 138	"You shall not slay the child by abortion."
Pedagogue by Clement of Alexandria	ca. 150–ca. 215	Abortion was compared with homicide.
Apology by Tertullian	ca. 160–ca. 230	"For to prevent its [fetus's] being born is an acceleration of homicide."
St. Basil	ca. 374	"Whoever purposely destroys a fetus incurs the penalty of murder [whether] it is formed or not formed."
St. Augustine	4–5th century	The use of birth control, sterilization, abortion, and infanticide was condemned.
Roman Catholic Church	5–12th century	A distinction was made between formed and unformed fetuses. Abortion of a formed fetus but not of an unformed fetus was condemned.
Si Aliquis	10th century	Both contraception and abortion are murder.
Decretum by Gratian	1140	"He is not a murderer who brings about abortion before the soul is in the body."
Jesuit, Thomas Sanchez	1550–1610	If the fetus was not ensouled and the woman died without completing the abortion, then the act was lawful because the fetus was an invader (based on the doctrine of self-defense).
Pope Sextus V	1588	All abortion is homicide.
Pope Gregory	1591	Papal edict rescinded doctrine that all abortion is homicide. Penalties should be assessed only for aborting ensouled fetuses.
Church Dogma	1588–1869	There was popular observance of the Immaculate Conception of Mary. The growing importance of the view that Mary was born free from the "stain" of original sin led many to question the ensoulment doctrine that held that the soul entered the fetus at forty or eighty days after conception. There was a growing sense that all abortions should be prohibited.

(continued)

Table 2.1. (continued)

Source	Date	Doctrine
Pope Pius IX	1869	The distinction between formed and unformed fetuses was eliminated, and any abortion was subject to the penalty of excommunication.
Canon Law—new code	1917	All references to forty- or eighty-day ensoulment were removed.
Casti Connubii	1930	Pope Pius adopted the Augustinian principle that the lives of the mother and fetus are equally sacred and may not be destroyed for any reason.
Mater et Magistra	1961	Pope John Paul XXIII stated that whatever is opposed to life in any form violates God's will.
Humanae Vitae	1968	Pope Paul VI held that "any direct interruption of the generative process already begun, and above all, directly willed and procured abortion even if for therapeutic reasons are to be outlawed as a means of regulating birth." Two exceptions were abortions to deal with an ectopic pregnancy and for treating a cancerous uterus. In these situations, the death of the fetus is a "secondary effect" of removing the fallopian tube or the cancerous uterus to save the life of the woman.

Sources: Davis 1985; Melton, 1989.

because it could not be definitively proven that she had been pregnant and aborted the fetus. The 1652 prosecution of William Mitchell is typical of cases involving a male defendant. Mitchell, who forced his pregnant maidservant to take poison to induce an abortion, was found guilty of performing an abortion and fined five thousand pounds of tobacco (Olasky 1992b, 30).

Convictions for abortion were rare (Brodie 1994, 39). In Middlesex County, Massachusetts, between 1633 and 1699, for example, there were only four convictions for abortion-related crimes (Thompson 1986, 10–11). A survey of the colonial records indicates that while both men and women were prosecuted for abortion-related crimes, officials typically targeted women who were either unmarried or had been abandoned by their husbands (Olasky 1992b, 30).

Following independence, British common law traditions, including the quasi-legal doctrine of quickening and the "born alive" rule, were incorporated into the American legal system. The born alive rule of jurisprudence held that non-abortion-related acts causing fetal injury could not be prosecuted unless there was proof of a live birth and that the acts at issue were responsible for the injury or death. The limited medical knowledge of the period made a determination of the exact causes of miscarriages and stillbirths extremely difficult. The born alive rule at least allowed doctors and criminal prosecutors to establish with certainty that a child's death did not result from problems during delivery or from unknown causes while in the womb.

Abortion Practices in Early America

Until the 1830s, reproductive decisions were rarely part of the public discourse, so any conclusions about actual practices are speculative (Brodie 1994, 39, 87). The historical record on the frequency of abortion in early America is mixed. Abortion was considered a sin, and few individuals were convicted of abortion-related crimes. But despite the current medical understanding that self-induced abortions are difficult to perform, knowledge about these procedures was widely disseminated by the early seventeenth century (Brodie 1994, 42).[6] Folk medicine practitioners included among abortifacients fourteen of the most potent plants that grow in this country (Brodie 1994, 44). Home medical manuals typically provided information about abortifacients in two sections: one detailing measures to release "obstructed menses" and another that listed things that might cause unintentional abortions. The most popular home medical manual of the period suggested the use of bloodletting and hot baths, the ingestion of iron and quinine solutions, and the use of a potent purgative (black hellebore) to restore regularity. The section on actions to avoid during pregnancy because of the risk of abortion included violent exercise, sharp blows to the abdomen, reaching too high, and falling down (Mohr 1978, 6–7). A health manual suggested that otherwise healthy young women afflicted with "what you call the *common cold*"—a euphemism for missing a menstrual period—take hot baths, engage in bloodletting, and drink a concoction of calomel and aloe (a standard abortifacient recipe) (Mohr 1978, 7).

Women often were deemed "irregular" rather than pregnant before the first fetal movement. Because menstruation can be delayed for reasons other than pregnancy, many women and their physicians felt that measures to remove blockages obstructing menstrual flow were appropriate (Mohr 1978, 4). In fact, physicians of the era feared that blocked menstrual flow could cause serious injuries and even death (Brodie 1994, 11–12).

In the 1830s and the next several decades the dissemination of information about contraception and abortion increased dramatically. Robert Dale Owens's popular pamphlet *Moral Physiology*, first published in 1831, taught

---

[6] According to Brodie (1994, 42–44), many families kept copies of popular texts containing herbal remedies for a range of medical complaints. For example, Nicholas Culpepper's *English Physician* and *Complete Herbal* recommended more than a dozen plant concoctions that were believed to bring on a woman's menstrual cycle, including pennyroyal, sage, common groundpine, bistort, gladwin, brake fern, calamint, and honeysuckle. Culpepper believed that adding tansy to wine would cause menstruation. Brodie also discovered evidence that colonial folk medicine incorporated Native American traditional remedies, including abortifacients, for gynecological problems.

men the skills needed to practice the withdrawal method of birth control. In response to the many problems associated with that method, A. M. Mauriceau[7] wrote a book descriptively titled: *The Married Woman's Private Medical Companion Embracing the Treatment of Menstruation or Monthly Turn during Their Stoppage, Irregularity or Entire Suppression,* PREGNANCY *and How* IT MAY BE DETERMINED: *With the Treatment of Its Various Diseases, Discovery to* PREVENT PREGNANCY: *Its Great and Important Necessity Where Malformation on Inability Exists to Give Birth. To Prevent Miscarriages or Abortion When Proper and Necessary. To* EFFECT MISCARRIAGE *When Attended With Entire Safety,* CAUSES AND MODE OF CURE OF BARRENNESS OR STERILITY (Brodie 1994, 64). Beginning in the 1840s, douching became a very popular method to prevent pregnancy or terminate an early pregnancy. The use of a douching syringe to inject various solutions into the uterus was commonly recommended to induce abortions.

Fetal Status in Antebellum America

Documents gleaned from county legal files, as well as slaveholders' financial records, provide more evidence of antebellum America's view of the fetus. County registrars' records indicate that a free woman's duties did not change significantly during pregnancy, although she was to be accorded a higher level of "deference and protection." Although not required to do so by law, many slave owners assigned less strenuous work to their female slaves during pregnancy. Antebellum legal rulings pertaining to the fetus were based on economic rationales rather than moral considerations, but it is possible that moral considerations figured into the treatment of pregnant women, both slave and free.

The Legal Safeguards Accorded Pregnant Women

Legal documents indicate that society's "deference and protection" accorded pregnant nonslave women was sporadically incorporated into common law practices. Laurel Ulrich (1982, 136–37) uses examples from the Essex County Record to illustrate the degree of "protection" given to pregnant women. In one case, after a man accidentally hit a pregnant woman with a ladder, the woman's husband succeeded in suing him for damages to cover expenses during the period of time that his wife was unable to work, as well as the cost of a consultation with a midwife. But women were expected to take precautions to protect themselves and their potential offspring while pregnant. In another case, a woman lost her suit for damages because the judge believed she had not adequately protected her fetus. The woman charged that a neighbor's verbal attacks and threats caused her such psychological distress that her

---

[7] Mauriceau is a pseudonym for Joseph Trow, the brother of Ann Trow Lohman. Lohman was the actual name of the infamous New York abortionist Madam Restell (Brodie 1994, 64).

baby was stillborn. The suit was dismissed, however, because the woman had been seen carrying a bucket on her head, which, according to folk belief, constituted a threat to fetal health. A pregnant woman was expected to take precautions to ensure the health of her unborn child. Even the minimal legal protection of pregnant women typically involved economic compensation to a woman's husband for the loss of her labor rather than compensation to the woman for the loss of the unborn child. Moreover, even that "protection" and "deference" could be negated if the woman's behavior was inconsistent with the norms and folk beliefs of the era.

The common law governing damages for injuries to pregnant women and their unborn children highlights the curious legal status of ostensibly "free" women. The law considered a free woman to be either a person or chattel, depending on the circumstances. Judith Wegner (1988, 6–7) explains the distinction: "*Personhood* means the complex of legal entitlements and obligations that largely define an individual's status in society. The converse of *person* in this sense is *chattel*—an entity lacking powers, rights, or duties under the law." The free woman's personhood status was a legal hybrid. To the extent that common law practices held a pregnant free woman responsible for taking reasonable precautions to protect her fetus from harm, she was considered a person. At the same time, however, she was chattel, lacking legal ownership rights over her own reproductive functions (i.e., her husband, not she, was compensated for damages).[8]

The pretense of "deference and protection" disappeared with respect to slave women in the antebellum South. Slaves were pure chattel, valuable economic commodities, and fecund slave women had a particularly high market value. For economic more than moral reasons, slave women were typically given time off from work both before and after giving birth because it reduced infant and maternal mortality rates (Woloch 1984, 175–84). For example, according to the records from one Georgia plantation, pregnant slaves were given more sick days and lighter work than other slaves, and the more "humane" regime on this plantation resulted in lower infant mortality rates and fewer miscarriages (Campbell 1984).[9]

The Limited Value of Fetal Life

Nothing in any of the records from the early nineteenth century indicated that fetuses were valued because of their intrinsic humanity. These little human organisms certainly were not viewed as persons in the way that contem-

---

[8] For further information about how "free" women's legal status in patriarchal societies is anomalous, see Wegner 1988.

[9] Campbell (1984) offers no conclusions about the motivations of the slave owner whose records he studied. Although slavery was an institution whose one "rational" justification was economic, it is possible that this slave owner (and others) may have been motivated by some degree of altruism. Nevertheless, a person whose economic livelihood is derived from slave labor and the sale of excess slaves raised on his plantation is probably not a great humanitarian.

porary pro-life advocates view them. Fetuses and their mothers, both free and slave, were valued for their actual and potential economic worth. While men may have loved their wives and future offspring and a few slave owners might have held some regard for slave women and their future progeny, the absence of those sentiments from the formal records, such as court records, implies that they were not critical. The common law did make distinctions, such as between pre- and postquickening fetuses, but it is unclear whether this demonstrated increased regard for evolving fetal life or simply reflected the fact that a postquickening fetus was more economically valuable than a pre-quickening one.

Changes in Nineteenth-Century Legal Doctrine

During the first half of the nineteenth century, the annual number of abortions increased sharply for a variety of reasons, including urbanization, increased mobility, more prostitution,[10] and higher rates of pregnancy outside of marriage (Olasky 1992b, 31; Rubin 1994, 12; Mohr 1978, 17). Moreover, economic constraints during the early nineteenth century forced families to use abortion as a means of "conscious fertility control." Thus prequickening abortions were widely accepted (Mohr 1978). James Mohr explains that although postquickening abortions were criminal, punishment was not comparable to that for individuals convicted of murder.

> After quickening, the expulsion and destruction of the fetus without due cause was considered a crime, because the fetus itself had manifested some semblance of a separate existence: the ability to move. The crime was qualitatively different from the destruction of a human being, however, and punished less harshly. Before quickening, actions that had the effect of terminating what turned out to be an early pregnancy were not considered criminal under the common law in effect in England and the United States in 1800. (Mohr 1978, 3)

In 1812 the Massachusetts Supreme Court became the first appeals court in the nation to decide whether a prequickening abortion was a crime. The court ruled in *Commonwealth v. Bangs* that "an abortion early in pregnancy would remain beyond the scope of the law." Although the precedent was binding only in Massachusetts, other states adopted it until the middle of the nineteenth century. In fact, *Commonwealth v. Bangs* was taken "so much for granted" that cases involving prequickening abortions were rarely heard before 1850 (Mohr 1978, 5–6).

---

[10] At least part of the increase in abortion rates came from a sharp increase in prostitution from 1830 to 1860. Without reliable means of contraception, many prostitutes were forced to rely on abortion. Olasky (1992b, 31) estimates that approximately sixty thousand abortions during those years were performed on prostitutes.

Criminalizing Abortion to Protect Women

In 1821 Connecticut became the first state to enact a criminal abortion statute, outlawing administering poison as an abortifacient after quickening. The intent was not to criminalize the act of killing a fetus but to halt the common practice of using poisons as abortifacients (Mohr 1978).[11] In 1830, the law was amended to include the use of instruments to induce abortion after quickening, again ostensibly to protect the woman's health (Mohr 1978; Rubin 1994). Missouri and Illinois, in 1825 and 1827, respectively, made it illegal to prescribe poison to terminate a pregnancy; neither specified the point in a pregnancy when the administration of poison became illegal. In 1828, New York passed the strictest statute of the period prohibiting all types of abortion after quickening. By 1841, ten out of the twenty-six states had enacted antiabortion statutes.

All of these early laws were created to protect women from unsafe abortion practices (Rubin 1994, 14) rather than to preserve fetal life, although they did capture some of the concern that Americans felt about terminating fetal life. Under the common law born alive rule the fetus did not have any legal rights until it existed outside of the womb and nothing in these state laws contradicted that position. Although reflecting some social ambivalence, these laws did not represent a significant legal shift toward according the fetus some degree of legal personhood.

Despite the statutory language criminalizing abortion, juries found it difficult to convict individuals of abortion-related crimes. The antiabortion crusader Herbert Storer discovered that between 1849 and 1858 Massachusetts prosecuted thirty-two abortion cases but was unable to convince juries to return a guilty verdict in any of them (Brodie 1994, 254). Moreover, in other states where a handful of individuals were convicted, nearly all cases were subsequently reversed by higher courts on appeals. Between 1840 and 1860 there were nine appeals by individuals convicted under the new restrictive abortion laws. In seven, the courts cited the common law tradition in ruling that pre-quickening abortions were not a crime (Smith-Rosenberg 1985, 219).

The Movement to Criminalize Abortion

In the mid-nineteenth century, several political and social movements coalesced around a campaign to criminalize abortions performed at any point in a pregnancy. Although physicians were the most important organized group, the

[11] Brodie (1994, 44) explains the reasoning behind the use of poisons as abortifacients: "Taking poisons to kill the invading ill humor was an established part of medical theory in the eighteenth and nineteenth centuries, so it should not be surprising that women tried such poisons as aloes, oil of savin, oil of tansy, oil of cedar, oil of pennyroyal, cottonroot compound, or teas made of rue, tansy, and nightshade to abort an unwanted pregnancy."

first wave of feminists, antivice crusaders, and early proponents of eugenics also played significant roles. Each group had its own reasons for wanting to ban abortions. Most scholars (Mohr 1978; Chavkin 1990b; Rubin 1994) believe that physicians were primarily driven by economic motivations, a desire to wrest control of this portion of the medical "market" from abortionists, midwives, and local healers. But the doctors publicly appealed to broader concerns such as maternal health (Rubin 1994).

Noneconomic motivations were predominant among the other groups. Early feminists supported antiabortion legislation because they wanted to stop men from using abortion as an excuse to abandon responsibility for their partners' pregnancies (Gordon 1977). The antivice crusaders were morally opposed to abortion, as well as all forms of contraception (Mohr 1978, 196–97; Rubin 1994, 27). The 1873 passage of the Comstock Act, which made the distribution of written materials about contraception and abortion through the mail a federal crime, was the most important contribution of the antivice movement to criminalizing abortion (Mohr 1978, 196–97).

Eugenicists wanted to ban abortions because they believed that the decreasing birthrate among white Anglo-Saxon women was leading to "race suicide" (Rubin 1994). Nativist beliefs gained support during the second half of the nineteenth century as the country grappled with the problems of assimilating large numbers of Catholic immigrants from southern Europe. The high birthrates among immigrants, coupled with declining rates among native-born women, led to fears about race suicide.

Despite the involvement of early feminists, much of the rhetoric in the drive to criminalize abortion had a distinctly antifeminist character. The most prominent physician in the antiabortion campaign, Herbert Storer, also was deeply committed to keeping women out of the medical profession (Reagan 1997, 11). Storer strongly supported traditional roles for women and argued against women having "undue power in public life . . . undue control in domestic affairs . . . or privileges not her own" (Storer reprinted in Reagan 1997, 11). When a doctor wrote to the leading medical journal, the *Journal of the American Medical Association*, asking whether he was justified in performing an abortion on a sixteen-year-old rape victim, the editor warned that "pregnancy is rare after *real* rape, and that the fright may easily cause suppression of menstruation and other subjective symptoms. . . . The enormity of the crime of rape does not justify murder" (*Journal of the American Medical Association*, August 6, 1904, 413, reprinted in Reagan 1997, 65).[12]

[12] In the Senate race in Arkansas in 1998, Fay Boozman, the Republican nominee, justified his support for banning abortions even in cases of rape on the grounds that women who are truly rape victims secrete a hormone that prevents them from becoming pregnant. Although this comment can be taken as an indication of how deeply embedded misogynist beliefs are in the American culture, an important difference is that Boozman's comment was widely denounced. Moreover, the Democratic candidate, Blanche Lincoln, defeated Boozman by a wide margin.

Although the antiabortion drive garnered support from disparate groups, physicians were the dominant force in the campaign. Beyond the general social respect accorded doctors, a key reason for their effectiveness was the formation of the American Medical Association (AMA) in 1847. Between 1850 and 1880 the AMA's efforts contributed to the passage of forty antiabortion statutes, most of which made it a crime to abort a fetus of any gestational age (Mohr 1978). The new laws permitted the prosecution of abortionists (and, in some cases, anyone who supplied materials for an abortion) and in some states their patients. Those convicted of abortion-related offenses could receive fines, prison sentences, or both (Mohr 1978). Indeed, by the end of the century, all but six states gave physicians complete control over the access to legal abortions, typically by allowing for "therapeutic exceptions" in their antiabortion statutes. These exceptions effectively gave physicians almost unlimited discretion to decide when an abortion was necessary (Luker 1984).

By 1910 every state had laws banning abortion, but medical exceptions provided a loophole that primarily benefited wealthy women with private doctors. Physicians believed that a number of medical conditions and diseases warranted therapeutic abortion, such as "hyperemesis gravidarum," or excessive vomiting and nausea, which if untreated was believed to lead to severe dehydration and possibly fatal starvation (Reagan 1997, 63). Private physicians often diagnosed typical morning sickness as hypermesis gravidarum, a medically justified reason for therapeutic abortions. Even after treatments were developed to control the nausea and vomiting that many women experience during pregnancy, physicians continued to justify therapeutic abortions to guard against excessive vomiting that might lead to death (Reagan 1997, 63). Poor women from cities and farms across the country, unable to afford the "discreetly interpreted legal exception," turned to much more dangerous and unregulated alternatives (Segers and Byrnes 1995, 2). Some poor women were able to obtain abortions from midwives, who typically charged roughly half the amount that doctors did (Reagan 1997, 74). Others had to rely on home remedies.

Although most physicians ceased their antiabortion mobilization once states had enacted criminal abortion statutes, doctors directly competing with nonphysician abortion providers continued to wage a political campaign to pass even stricter laws. Leadership for this second antiabortion drive came from the AMA's Section on Obstetrics and Gynecology (Reagan 1997, 82).[13] Between 1890 and 1920 new laws were passed forcing midwives to stop performing abortions, driving them underground. Despite these new laws, prosecutors were unable to convict many black market abortionists. Leslie Reagan (1997, 116–17) found that between 1902 and 1934 the number of convictions for per-

[13] At the 1893, 1906, 1908, and 1911 national meetings of the American Medical Association, the heads of the Section on Obstetrics and Gynecology spoke on the need to suppress nonphysician abortion providers (Reagan 1997, 82).

forming illegal abortions in Chicago never exceeded two a year, but arrests fluc-
tuated in response to political pressure by the Chicago Medical Association.

Moral Considerations in the Nineteenth-Century Crusade

Although the morality of taking fetal life was not a principal theme in the
antiabortion campaign, some participants in both the antivice and physicians'
campaigns voiced moral opposition to abortion (Brodie 1994, 259–72). For
example, the AMA's national convention in 1859 passed a resolution declaring
that the fetus was a "living being" with civil rights at all stages of gestation,
but the organization subsequently dropped this argument. Some northern
physicians compared abortion to slavery and warned that divine retribution
would be exacted from those involved in either enterprise (Olasky 1992a,
120). For example, Dr. P. Haskell of Maine described both abortion and slavery as grievous sins that could bring "the penalty which a Just God, the
avenger of the blood of innocents, will mete out to us." About the consequences of abortion, he wrote, "Whether we be innocent or guilty, we shall all
suffer, as a people, as a profession and as individuals, just as we have all suffered and are now suffering for the curse of American slavery" (Reprinted in
Olasky 1992a, 120). Despite these concerns, none of the physicians emphasized the moral issues related to fetal personhood in the public campaign
(Petchesky 1985, 79–80).

The paucity of religious leaders,[14] especially Catholics, in the antiabortion
campaign contributed to this absence of moral discourse. Although Catholic
bishops in New York, Boston, and Baltimore denounced abortion as a sin, the
church was not a major participant and did not excommunicate abortionists
(Olasky 1992b, 32). A handful of Protestant ministers also spoke out against
abortion, but only one Protestant denomination formally opposed the practice
(Olasky 1992b, 32).[15] The limited involvement of the religious community is
one of the most striking differences between the nineteenth-century antiabortion campaign and the contemporary movement. Over time, religious and
moral arguments became even less important in the abortion debate as the

---

[14] It is, however, important to recognize that religious convictions played a role in mobilizing
some leaders of the antivice crusade. Anthony Comstock was a deeply committed Christian, who,
while in the Union army, led prayer meetings and distributed religious tracts to his fellow soldiers
(Brodie 1994, 259). An antiabortion crusade orchestrated by the *New York Times* in 1870 was an
outgrowth of the conservative Christian beliefs of its editor, Louis Jennings. In an editorial, Jennings wrote that the "perpetration of infant murder ... is rank and smells to heaven" (Reprinted in
Olasky 1992a, 153).

[15] The General Assembly of the "Old School" Presbyterian Church adopted a resolution denouncing abortion as a "crime against God and nature." Although no other Protestant denomina-
tions adopted similar antiabortion positions, several Congregationalist churches in the Northeast
and the Great Lakes regions became involved in the drive to criminalize abortions (Davis 1984,
5–6).

medical community's hegemonic control over legal abortion and childbirth in the early twentieth century became complete.[16]

Changes in the Legal Status of the Fetus in Civil Cases

Although the moral argument about fetal status was not a major theme in the late nineteenth century, the fetus gained legal rights in some areas of civil law. By this time some form of fetal personhood was well established in civil cases involving property and inheritance rights, and attempts were made to expand those rights to other areas of tort law.[17] These developments in civil law influenced aspects of criminal law. For example, the use of the quickening doctrine and the born alive rule spread from civil cases to criminal cases involving third-party feticide, marking an important change in criminal law that accorded at least partial personhood status to some fetuses. Also for the first time, in the late nineteenth century criminal and civil courts slowly became more concerned with the value of fetal life, although this was not explicitly stated. In all other respects, however, fetal rights in civil and criminal law have evolved very differently (Klasing 1995).[18] Some of the most important legal developments in criminal and civil law related to the personhood status of the fetus are summarized in Table 2.2.

Fetal Rights in Property Law

In property law, the fetus was first accorded inheritance rights in the Roman Empire. As long as the fetus was conceived before the death of the testator (usually the father) and subsequently was born alive, its inheritance rights were equal to those born before the testator's death. According to William Curran (1983, 59–61), the fetus was not a legal subject under Roman law but was a potential person whose property rights were secured after birth. The "right" of the fetus to inherit property was based not on its personhood status but as a means of fulfilling the testator's wishes (Nelson, Buggy, and Weil 1986, 738).

British common law generally followed Roman precedents. A baby born alive within forty weeks of his or her father's death had the same right to in-

[16] For a detailed discussion of abortion practices and the social climate in the early twentieth century, see Luker 1984.

[17] *Black's Law Dictionary* defines a tort as "a personal or civil wrong or injury, including action for bad faith breach of contract, for which the court will provide a remedy in the form of an action for damages" (1990). The primary goal in tort action is to provide compensation to the damaged party (Podewils 1993).

[18] Today, although thirty-seven jurisdictions recognize the fetus as a "person" in tort law, most states "refuse to extend protection of the criminal law to the fetus" (Klasing 1995).

Table 2.2. The American legal tradition and fetal rights, 1776–1900

Date	Legal status of the fetus
1776	British common law with its distinction between prequickening and post-quickening abortions was incorporated into American law. The former were legally permissible, but the latter were a criminal offense.
	The "born alive" rule from British common law was applied to non-abortion-related acts resulting in fetal injuries or death. Unless there is proof of a live birth and that the acts in question caused the injury or death, a person cannot be prosecuted for harming the fetus.
1812	In *Commonwealth v. Bangs*, the Massachusetts Supreme Court held that pre-quickening abortions were legal. Other states invoked it as precedent.
1821	Connecticut became the first state to enact a criminal abortion statute. The law made it a crime to administer an abortifacient after quickening.
1825	Missouri passed a law making it a criminal offense to prescribe poison for terminating a pregnancy. The statute did not specify the point in a pregnancy when the use of an abortifacient became illegal.
1828	New York passed a criminal abortion statute that made all postquickening abortions illegal. (By 1841 ten states had passed criminal abortion statutes.)
1830	In *Marsellis v. Thalimer* a New York court used the "born alive" rule to deny inheritance rights to a stillborn child.
1835	Missouri revised its criminal manslaughter statutes to include the killing of a "quick" fetus. (Nine additional states enacted similar laws before 1900.)
1884	*Deitrich v. Northampton* established the legal precedent that a fetus has "no separate existence" from the mother and therefore cannot sue to obtain damages for injuries sustained in utero. This precedent defined the parameters in fetal personhood tort cases for more than sixty years.
1894	Frank Williams's manslaughter conviction for the killing of a "quick" fetus was upheld in *Williams v. State*.

herit property as any previously born siblings (Glantz 1976, 37; Andrews 1986, 393),[19] based on the general rule that favors a testator's intent. To keep property within a particular bloodline, fetuses were given the "right" to inherit but only if they were born alive within ten lunar months (i.e., were the child of the deceased).

American courts have incorporated British common law practices with regard to fetal inheritance rights. For example, in *Marsellis v. Thalimer* (1830) the born alive rule was used to deny inheritance rights to a stillborn child. In 1959 the New York Court of Appeals in *In re Peabody* (1959) stated: "The

[19] See *Burdett v. Hopegood*, 24 Eng. Rep. 485 (1718) and *Wallis v. Hodson*, 26 Eng. Rep. 472 (1740) for examples of early common law cases that accorded property rights to fetuses.

common law rule of equity . . . does not justify the conclusion that the fetus is a 'person' before its birth. On the contrary . . . a child *en ventre sa mere* is not regarded a person until it sees the light of day." American Bar Association (1994, 2–108) simply codified the common law practices: "Relatives of the decedent conceived before his death but born thereafter inherit as if they had been born in the lifetime of the decedent."

The Changing Legal Status of the Fetus in Tort Law

Dietrich v. Northampton (1884) established an important precedent that defined the parameters of fetal personhood tort cases for more than sixty years. In *Dietrich* a woman tried to hold the city of Northampton, Massachusetts, liable for the miscarriage of her fetus after she fell as a result of a defect in a public highway. The court ruled that the unborn child could not sustain life outside the mother and therefore did not have the legal right to action. Justice Oliver Wendell Holmes's reasoning that the fetus had "no separate existence" was adopted by other supreme courts, resulting in the denial of prenatal civil injury cases across the nation (Klasing 1995; McDowell 1994; Daniels 1993).

State courts throughout the United States continued to follow *Dietrich* as the benchmark for all prenatal injury cases well into the twentieth century. In *Drobner v. Peters* (1921), a woman was denied a claim for compensation for the death of her infant after she fell into a hole and delivered prematurely. Although the infant was born alive and did not die until eleven days later, the New York Court of Appeals ruled that the defendant owed no duty of care to an unborn child, apart from the duty to avoid injuring the mother. The court held that the fetus's simply being born alive was not sufficient to invoke liability under the common law born alive rule. The plaintiff had to prove causation, a difficult task given the medical knowledge at the time. Echoes of *Dietrich* could be heard in *Lipps v. Milwaukeee Electric Railway & Light Co.* (1916), where the court cited the born alive rule and held that "since a non-viable child cannot exist separate from its mother, it must, in the law of torts, be regarded as part of the mother, and hence . . . not an independent person to whom separate rights can be given" (reprinted in McDowell 1994, 166).

Throughout the first half of the twentieth century, state courts adhered to a very strict interpretation of common law tort recovery for the fetus. The validity of claims for prenatal injuries to a fetus required that the child was born alive, living separately from the mother, and that the death was caused by an external force while in the womb (Klasing 1995). Given the level of technological sophistication, it was extremely difficult for a plaintiff to meet the standard and win damages for injuries sustained by a fetus. Courts maintained that strict standards were necessary in fetal injury cases to protect against "fictitious claims" (Klasing 1995).

Tort law regarding fetal rights changed dramatically in *Bronbrest v. Kotz* (1946), which broke with *Dietrich* and legitimized "limited fetal rights" in civil cases beyond property and inheritance. The court ruled in favor of a plaintiff who sought to pursue damages for prenatal injuries caused during delivery. In *Dietrich* the infant died as a result of injuries less than an hour after delivery, but in *Bronbrest* the infant did not die. Following *Bronbrest*, tort law in every state confers legal standing on those who were injured in utero, providing they satisfy the live birth and viability standards (Condit 1995, 34). Some courts have even held that legal personhood in fetal injury cases begins before viability (Condit 1995, 34–35).[20]

The Criminalization of Third-Party Fetal Killing

The civil law debates over extension of the limited fetal personhood rights in property and inheritance law to negligence cases involving fetal deaths or injury affected developments in criminal law. An unintended consequence of the nineteenth-century bans on abortion was greater protection of fetal health. By the middle of the nineteenth century, criminal courts in several states extended at least a limited degree of personhood to fetuses that were killed by third parties. A couple of cases applied common law precepts,[21] states were more likely to amend existing criminal statutes to make them applicable to third-party fetal killings. Until 1965 all of the changes in criminal law extended manslaughter statutes to cover fetuses. Legal records indicate that Missouri (as early as 1835) was the first state to revise its manslaughter provisions, and Michigan revised its manslaughter statute to include the killing of a viable fetus eleven years later. Three additional states (Mississippi, Iowa, and New Hampshire) revised their manslaughter statutes before the Civil War. Alabama, Florida, Tennessee, and Oklahoma included viable fetuses in their manslaughter statutes before 1900, and were followed by Nevada and Washington.

The legal records of prosecutions for the killing of fetuses under these revised manslaughter statutes are difficult to find because legal records from the period are not well preserved, especially in frontier areas of the country. Also, cases of fetal killing normally are tried in local courts, and records for cases that are not appealed to higher courts are kept for only a limited period of time. Despite these difficulties, I was able to identify two cases tried before 1900. In the first the defendant, Frank Williams, was convicted in 1892 under Florida's revised manslaughter statute, which prohibited the "willful killing of an unborn quick-child by an injury to the mother of such child which would be deemed murder if it resulted in the death of such mother, and shall be deemed manslaughter" (*Williams v. State* 1894). Williams was convicted and sentenced to life in prison.

[20] As early as 1956, a Georgia court accepted the plaintiff's contention that the age of the fetus was irrelevant to a fetal injury case. See *Hornbuckle v. Plantation Pipe Line*, 212 Ga. 504 (1956).
[21] See *Abrams v. Foshee*, 3 Iowa 274 (1856); *Evans v. People*, 49 NY 86 (1872); and *State v. Winthrop*, 43 Iowa 519 (1876).

In the second case, the defendant was found guilty of manslaughter even though the "willfulness" of the killing was not proven. The Alabama court held that "malice could be implied" from the "intentional beating of a pregnant mother resulting in the death of her infant after its birth" (*Clarke v. State* 1898), a standard of implied malice subsequently adopted by courts in different parts of the country.[22] Although these statutes do not necessarily grant full personhood status to the fetus, they demonstrate a state interest in preserving fetal health and well-being.

The Movement to Reform Abortion Laws

For much of the first half of the twentieth century, abortion was not part of the public discourse, principally because the medical community's campaign during the nineteenth and early twentieth centuries had transformed the debate into a medical one (Luker 1984, 41). Through its monopoly on the technological expertise to decide when and if an abortion was necessary, the medical community succeeded in preventing other groups (clergy, lawyers, and women) from challenging its "right to control abortion" (Luker 1984, 43). Ironically, the first challenge to the nineteenth-century abortion bans came from within the medical profession.

By the 1950s medical advances had rendered obsolete the maternal health rationale for allowing abortions. Although some doctors broadened the definition of "medical necessity" so they could continue to provide abortions for their patients, others morally opposed abortions unless there was a real medical necessity. Because technological advancements had found means other than abortion to protect the health of pregnant women, the divisions between the two groups of physicians (broad constructionists and strict constructionists) became greater. No longer could broad constructionists cite medical necessity for performing abortions without harsh criticism from their strict constructionist colleagues (Luker 1984, 55–57).

One of the ways that the medical community dealt with this internal conflict was by authorizing hospital therapeutic abortion boards to decide which abortions were medically necessary. Although this forced strict constructionists to confront the power of an entire hospital rather than a single physician, the boards were very conservative in their interpretations of medical necessity and often instituted abortion quotas, which increased conflict. Not only were few abortions approved, but critics charged that the boards discriminated against poor women. As a result, the legitimacy of the boards was questioned by segments of the medical profession and by outsiders (Luker 1984, 55–57).

[22] For example, in 1941, William Passley was convicted and given a life sentence under a Georgia state foeticide statute for attempted murder. Passley tried to kill his pregnant wife (whose pregnancy was at the quickening stage) by beating her entire body, including her abdomen, with a stick, resulting in the death of the fetus. See *Passley v. State*, 194 Ga. 327, 21 S.E.2d 230 (1942).

Critics charged that the primary effect of the strict antiabortion laws and practices was to force women to obtain illegal abortions rather than legal ones (Blake 1977, 46; Rosenberg 1991, 353–55)[23] and that the high number of women's deaths and maimings caused by illegal abortions constituted a serious public health problem. Because there are no reliable records on the numbers of illegal abortions before *Roe*, all numbers must be considered estimates. Most studies indicated that approximately one million women annually underwent illegal abortions before 1973, but others argue that the number was far higher (Rosenberg 1991, 353; Graber 1996, 42).[24] Regardless of the actual number of illegal abortions, it is clear that a significant number of women died or were injured as a result of botched abortions performed by untrained and illegal abortionists (Petchesky 1985, 50; Tribe 1990, 41). Many deaths caused by illegal abortions were attributed to other, nonstigmatized causes, yet the official numbers of women's deaths from abortion-related causes were high.[25] According to Cass Sunstein (1993, 278) 5,000 to 10,000 women may have died annually as a result of poorly performed abortions before *Roe*. In addition, public health officials estimated that 350,000 women annually were injured by illegal abortionists (Graber 1996, 43). Some hospitals admitted so many women patients suffering from injuries caused by incompetent abortionists that special wards were created to treat them. Many of these women were suffering from a serious and often fatal uterine infection (sepsis) caused by unsterile medical instruments and practices. In the mid-1960s, a single Chicago hospital admitted nearly 5,000 women a year for problems caused by septic abortions (Graber 1996, 43). In 1969, 23 percent of all New York City hospital admissions for pregnancy-related reasons were due to complications caused by illegal abortions (Institute of Medicine 1975).

These problems led the American Law Institute (ALI) in 1959 to recommend reforms to the nineteenth-century abortion laws. According to the institute's guidelines:

1. Unjustifiable Abortion—A person who purposely and unjustifiably terminates the pregnancy of another other than by live birth commits a felony of the third degree or where the pregnancy has continued beyond the twenty-sixth week, a felony of the second degree.

[23] For a detailed discussion of the research on the prevalence of illegal abortions before *Roe v. Wade*, see Rosenberg 1991.

[24] Generally speaking, pro-life scholars downplay the numbers of illegal abortions while those on the pro-choice side tend to choose higher figures. The propensity of pro-life scholars to have lower estimates lends credibility to the relatively higher figures cited by Graber, a pro-life scholar, who believes that the estimated annual number of illegal abortions plus the annual number of legal abortions performed pre-*Roe* (i.e., medically approved therapeutic abortions) is comparable (Graber 1996).

[25] Rosenberg (1991, 353) cited government figures showing that deaths resulting from illegal abortions accounted for 18 percent of maternal deaths in 1930, almost 21 percent in 1962, and 16 percent in 1969.

2. Justifiable Abortion—A licensed physician is justified in terminating a pregnancy if he believes there is substantial risk that the continuance of the pregnancy would gravely impair the physical or mental health of the mother or that the child would be born with grave physical or mental defect, or that the pregnancy resulted from rape, incest, or other felonious intercourse. Justifiable abortions shall be performed only in a licensed hospital except in the case of emergency when hospital facilities are unavailable.

3. Physicians' Certificates; Presumption from Non-Compliance—No abortion shall be performed unless two physicians, one of whom may be the person performing the abortion, shall have certified in writing the circumstances which they believe to justify the abortion. (Rubin 1994, 80)

Although disagreement within the medical community persisted for nearly a decade, it was not until Sherrie Finkbine's case gained notoriety in 1962 that pro-reform groups actively mobilized to change abortion laws. The host of the popular children's television program *Romper Room* had been given an anti-nausea drug, thalidomide, early in her fifth pregnancy. A couple of months later, thalidomide was identified as the cause of an epidemic of severe birth defects throughout the world. Finkbine's physician and the local hospital agreed that an abortion was justified in her situation. On the day the procedure was to be performed, however, the local newspaper printed a front-page story about "the Romper Room lady" getting an abortion, and the hospital canceled it. The Finkbine case heightened the split between strict constructionist and broad constructionist doctors and polarized the public as well.

The case also brought the issue of fetal personhood to the forefront of the abortion debate. As Kristin Luker (1984, 80) pointed out, "The fundamental disagreement about whether or not an embryo represented a 'real' person or merely a potential person, a disagreement that had existed beneath the surface for at least a hundred years, was finally forced into the open by the Finkbine case." As interest in the Finkbine case died down after several years, the country was hit with a rubella measles epidemic. Thousands of pregnant women exposed to measles sought therapeutic abortions to prevent giving birth to deformed babies. Improved technology and the combined impact of the Finkbine case and the rubella epidemic forced physicians to grapple with the morality of elective abortions of fetuses they knew were deformed. Broad constructionists had little problem, but strict constructionists could not accept the idea of sacrificing the fetus "for its own good" (Luker 1984, 80).

The Impetus for Reform

In 1964 California enacted the first liberalized abortion reform law in more than one hundred years. Although the law did not actually lift any existing restrictions, it provided legal support for a broader interpretation of medical necessity, allowing broad constructionists to perform abortions without facing criminal charges.[26] The law dramatically reduced the number of abortion-related complications. For example, the number of women admitted to the Los Angeles County/University of Southern California Medical Center for abortion-related complications fell nearly 75 percent (Seward, Ballard, and Ulene 1973).

In 1966 Mississippi became the first state to adopt an abortion reform law modeled on the ALI guidelines, although the statute severely restricted abortion to situations in which carrying a pregnancy to term threatened a woman's life or was the result of rape. Over the next nine years, thirteen more states revised their criminal abortion laws to conform to the ALI guidelines,[27] and those acting later tended to be more permissive than their predecessors (Mooney and Lee 1995, 609–610). Even after enacting ALI reforms, the states still banned most abortions; the more "liberal" states allowed exceptions for cases of rape, incest, and fetal deformity and to protect the woman's physical or mental health. Mary Segars and Timothy Byrnes (1995) argue that while the reforms minimally increased a woman's right to choose an abortion, they significantly reduced the legal liabilities of physicians. But that situation was about to change.

During the 1960s, several important national pro-choice organizations, including the Society for Humane Abortions and the National Association for the Repeal of Abortion Laws (NARAL), were created. They joined forces with other interest groups such as the National Organization for Women (NOW) and the AMA to lobby for reforms.[28] The AMA sought to expand the number of states enacting limited reforms similar to the ALI model, but NARAL and NOW, which favored repealing the bans, saw their efforts rewarded in 1970 when four states (Alaska, Hawaii, New York, and Washington) repealed their abortion bans and legalized abortion as an elective medical procedure. These victories marked the high point of pro-choice legislative lobbying because their successes also mobilized pro-life forces in states subsequently targeted by pro-choice activists.

Pro-Life Mobilization

The term "right to life" was used by antiabortion activists to describe their beliefs as early as 1963 (Cassidy 1996, 139), although significant mass mobilization did not begin until later. The first permanent community-based pro-life group was established in 1967 when New York antiabortion activists mo-

[26] For a brief history of the politics surrounding the liberalization of California's abortion laws in the 1960s, see Russo 1995.

[27] The reform ALI states were Arkansas, California, Colorado, Delaware, Florida, Georgia, Kansas, Maryland, Mississippi, New Mexico, North Carolina, South Carolina, Oregon, and Virginia.

[28] According to Ginsburg (1989, 39–40), the National Association for the Repeal of Abortion Laws led the effort to unite the very liberal groups that had spearheaded the early pro-choice movement and more conservative groups, such as Church Women United and the Young Women's Christian Association, which provided broader political and social legitimacy for the campaign.

bilized against efforts to reform the state's abortion law (Cassidy 1996, 139). Although eventually defeated in their attempt to halt liberalization in New York, pro-life groups expanded rapidly in the late 1960s, as mass-based pro-life organizations sprang up in New York, Virginia, Minnesota, California, Florida, Colorado, Michigan, Illinois, Ohio, and Pennsylvania. The Minnesota Citizens Concerned for Life (MCCL), one of the largest of the state pro-life groups, had ten thousand members in the early 1970s before *Roe* (Halva-Neubauer 1995, 29).

In Pennsylvania, antiabortion organizations bucked the national trend toward a loosening of abortion restrictions in the late 1960s and early 1970s and managed to get the state legislature to pass a bill in 1972 banning all abortions not necessary to preserve the life of the woman. Even though the bill was vetoed by Governor Milton Shapp, pro-life groups in Pennsylvania have continued to be a powerful political force (Nossiff 1995, 16).

The contemporary pro-life movement is predominantly a religious movement. Most of the early activists were Catholic, and the Catholic Church occasionally helped establish local pro-life groups, the strongest of which developed in heavily urban and Catholic states. According to Catholic doctrine, anyone who has an abortion or assists in the performance of an abortion is subject to excommunication. Even though Catholics predominated in the early years, some leaders were Protestants (Cassidy 1996, 139). The first national right-to-life organization, Americans United for Life (AUL), which was founded in 1971, receives backing from both conservative Protestants and Catholics (Center for Reproductive Law & Policy 1998b). Although conservative Protestants, like their Catholic counterparts, are opposed to abortion because they believe the fetus is a human being, they consider abortion to be part of a larger social evil—the "shift from a God-centered society to one based on secular humanism, in which satisfying individual desires is elevated above all else" (Center for Reproductive Law & Policy 1998b, 9).

In the early 1970s pro-life forces mounted strong opposition to attempts to reform nineteenth-century state abortion statutes. For example, pro-choice forces in Michigan launched a referendum campaign in 1972 to enact provisions granting unrestricted access to legal abortion in the first twenty weeks of pregnancy. One of the founders of the National Right to Life Committee led a drive against the measure, and it failed (Segers and Byrnes 1995, 4). Efforts to weaken or repeal abortion bans in North Dakota, Iowa, and Minnesota were also defeated in 1972 (Segers and Byrnes 1995, 4).

Challenging Abortion Bans in the Courts

After pro-choice lobbyists failed to weaken or repeal abortion bans in several states, the leadership deemphasized the campaign for changes in state laws and began searching for legal test cases to challenge the constitutionality of state laws that banned abortion. Pro-choice organizations recognized the need to find sympathetic women able to generate public support for abortion rights. In this sense, they viewed the legal struggle as part of a much broader political and public relations battle to win the hearts and minds of the American public. The two abortion cases that reached the Supreme Court in 1972 had just such a pair of sympathetic women. The women, using the pseudonyms Jane Roe and Mary Doe, gained popular support for their plight and for "other similarly situated" women. Jane Roe, an unmarried woman, claimed that her pregnancy was caused by rape. The Texas abortion ban included an exception only "for the purpose of saving the life of the mother." Jane Doe was a married woman, suffering from serious mental illness and with three children, two in foster care and the other up for adoption. Although her doctor believed that having another baby would damage her already fragile health, Doe was unable to get approval from the hospital abortion panel as required by Georgia law (Goldstein 1979, 273–74).

In its 1973 *Roe v. Wade* decision, the Supreme Court on a 7–2 vote ruled that the right to privacy contained in the Fourteenth Amendment "is broad enough to encompass a woman's decision whether or not to terminate her pregnancy" and overturned the Texas abortion ban, which had not been revised since its adoption in the nineteenth century. The second decision, *Doe v. Bolton* (1973), which overturned the relatively more liberal Georgia abortion statute that permitted ALI therapeutic exceptions, has received far less attention. Much of its relative obscurity is owing to the Supreme Court's much narrower decision. The opinion in *Doe* simply invalidated the requirement that abortions be performed only in a hospital after a woman obtained approval from the hospital's abortion board and two outside physicians. It did not address the broader issue of whether a woman's reproductive choices are covered by the Fourteenth Amendment.

The Court's intent in *Roe* to defuse the abortion issue backfired. While the decision's formal and most immediate effect was the invalidation of abortion statutes in forty-six states,[29] it also "triggered the rapid development of the right-to-life movement in the United States and lulled abortion rights supporters into a false sense that women's access to abortion was secure" (Segers and Byrnes 1995, 5).

Pro-Life Activism after *Roe*

The Catholic Church was a leading force in the creation of a mass-based national right-to-life movement, organizing the NRLC in 1973, five months after the *Roe v. Wade* decision. The NRLC was formed by Monsignor James

[29] Twenty-eight states responded to the *Roe* decision by repealing their restrictive abortion laws: Connecticut, Maine, New Jersey, Pennsylvania, Rhode Island, Iowa, Illinois, Indiana, Kansas, Minnesota, Missouri, North Dakota, Nebraska, Ohio, South Dakota, Florida, Georgia, Kentucky, Maryland, North Carolina, South Carolina, Tennessee, Virginia, Idaho, Montana, Nevada, Oregon, and Wyoming. Seventeen others with pre-*Roe* abortion bans chose not to repeal their laws. If *Roe* is ever overturned, those laws will again be in effect.

McHugh, acting on behalf of the National Conference of Bishops (Cassidy 1996, 140).

Nationally pro-life groups mobilized their constituencies to support a variety of initiatives, including an unsuccessful attempt to pass a constitutional amendment banning abortion,[30] more fruitful efforts to prohibit the use of federal Medicaid money to pay for abortions,[31] and massive country-wide fund-raising drives to generate money for pro-life congressional candidates. In 1979 Richard Viguerie, the conservative political operative who first used computerized mass mailings as a fund-raising technique, launched "Stop the Baby-killers," a campaign to defeat liberal pro-choice members of Congress. Organized under the auspices of the Americans for Life Political Action Committee, the campaign was most notable for its incendiary language. Its first fund-raising letter used the words "babykiller" and "murderer" forty-one times (McKeegan 1992, 24). State and local groups divided their time between traditional political activities, such as lobbying and working to elect pro-life state legislators, and acts of civil disobedience to close abortion clinics.

According to Clyde Wilcox (1989), in the decade and a half after the *Roe* decision, pro-life groups were better organized and funded than their opponents. Luker (1984) found that local pro-life activists committed twice as much volunteer time to the cause as pro-choice activists. The advantages in resources and commitment enjoyed by activists is a direct outgrowth of *Roe*, which mobilized pro-life activists but demobilized pro-choice forces, who were lulled into a false sense of security by interpreting the ruling as a guarantee of a woman's right to abortion. Pro-life organizations and politicians continually sought to find new ways to undermine *Roe*. When their constitutional amendment failed, many pro-life activists renewed efforts to pass federal and state laws that would slowly erode abortion rights. Although national pro-life groups after *Roe* focused on changing the composition of the courts, traditional coalition building, lobbying, and electoral politics remained a priority of some organizations (Cassidy 1996, 149).

Juridical Implications of *Roe*

Roe raised serious questions about whether abortion policies would be decided at the state or federal level. The opinion seemed to indicate that the Court would decide fundamental issues related to a woman's right to have an abortion without specifying where day-to-day abortion policies would be de-

[30] The National Right to Life Committee at its December 8, 1973, board meeting designated as its top programmatic priority the development of a national campaign to pass a human life constitutional amendment (Cassidy 1996, 144).

[31] Since 1976 a version of the Hyde Amendment, named after its primary congressional sponsor Representative Henry Hyde (R-Ill.), has been either attached to every appropriations bill that covers Medicaid funding or passed as a joint resolution of the House and Senate. According to Berkman (1995), Representative Hyde was inspired to introduce the amendment after reading *The Vanishing Right to Live*, a book written by longtime antiabortion activist Charles F. Rice. The constitutionality of the amendment was upheld in *Harris v. McRae*, 448 U.S. 297 (1980).

cided. As Segers and Byrnes wrote, "*Roe* had left so many questions unanswered that it stood as an open invitation to states to regulate and litigate" (Segers and Byrnes 1995, 6).[32]

The Court's opinion in *Roe* incorporated two major concepts. The first recognized that a woman's decision to have an abortion was the product of a privileged doctor-patient relationship, protected by her constitutional right to privacy. It stated:

> This right of privacy, whether it be founded in the Fourteenth Amendment's concept of personal liberty and restrictions upon state action, as we feel it is, or, as the District Court determined, in the Ninth Amendment's reservation of rights to the people, is broad enough to encompass a woman's decision whether to terminate her pregnancy. (Section 8, *Roe v. Wade* 1973)

The second acknowledged that the state may have a legitimate interest in protecting the health and well-being of the fetus. The Court made it clear, however, that the fetus was not legally considered a person:

> The Constitution does not define "person" in so many words, Section 1 of the Fourteenth Amendment contains three references to "person." The first, in defining "citizens," speaks of "persons born or naturalized in the United States." The word also appears both in the Due Process Clause and in the Equal Protection Clause. "Person" is used in other places in the Constitution. . . . But in nearly all these instances, the use of the word is such that it has application only postnatally. None indicates, with any assurance, that it has any possible pre-natal application. All this, together with our observation, supra, that throughout the major portions of the 19th century prevailing legal practices were far freer than they are today, persuades us that the word "person," as used in the Fourteenth Amendment, does not include the unborn. (Section 9, *Roe v. Wade* 1973)

Roe v. Wade's Balancing of Competing Rights

The Court's decision was in many ways an uneasy compromise between competing rights. Had the Court declared that a woman's right to privacy was absolute, the matter would have been settled. Instead, it also recognized a state interest in "potential life." Hence *Roe* presented the Court with the problem of balancing one value (the individual's right to privacy) against another (the right of the state to enact laws to protect the health, safety, and morals of its citizens). In the past the Court had held that certain rights under the Constitution are "fundamental" but also recognized the need to balance one set of fundamental rights against other fundamental rights.[33]

---

[32] Although *Roe* left many questions unanswered, that is consistent with the Court's usual practice, especially in its first venture into a new area. One of the major criticisms of Supreme Court opinions is that they are "too legislative" (i.e., too detailed). See, for example, McDowell 1988.

[33] For different interpretations of the difficulty in balancing competing rights, see Rossum and Tarr 1995; Moore 1996; Epstein and Walker 1992.

To resolve the dilemma, the Court tried to devise a working balance between the interests of the individual and the state's traditional "police power,"[34] aiming to establish a legal standard for this and future cases. The Court effected the balance by dividing fetal development into three trimesters. The Court held that during the first trimester the abortion decision be left entirely to the woman and her doctor. It recognized a state's right to intervene during the second trimester only to promote the mother's health, reconciling the state's police power and the woman's right to privacy. Only in the third trimester did the Court allow the state to regulate abortions in order to "promote its interest in the potentiality of human life" (Sect. 11, *Roe v. Wade* 1973), using fetal viability as the rationale for state intervention (Daniels 1993; Glink 1991; Hornick 1993; Losco 1988; and McDonagh 1994a,b).

The Court's opinion in *Roe* seemed to suggest an exacting level of judicial scrutiny by requiring states to prove a "compelling state interest" to justify restricting a woman's privacy rights. The Court placed a heavy evidentiary burden on the states, requiring them to make decisions on a case-by-case basis. Thus, whatever limitations *Roe* appeared to place on states would actually be determined only after a period of state action and litigation.

Paradoxical Aspects of the Trimester Framework

Although the Court's decision in *Roe v. Wade* has generated massive amounts of scholarly and popular attention, I wish to highlight a very important and paradoxical aspect of the case. By adopting the trimester framework for weighing the interests of different parties affected by abortion decisions, the Court simultaneously returned to a very old philosophy and developed a new legal standard regarding fetal personhood. The implications of this paradoxically new and old way of conceptualizing fetal personhood have been enormous.

First, the most interesting historical aspect of the trimester framework is its similarity to the three-part conception of fetal personhood developed by Aristotle twenty-five hundred years earlier. Aristotle believed that during the first stage of development—the "vegetable" stage—the fetus had no independent status. When the soul entered the body, the fetus entered the second stage—the "animal" stage—which lasted until the fetus assumed a fully human shape and was able to live separate from its mother. Aristotle believed that the fetus then entered into the final stage—the "rational" stage—but unlike the Supreme Court in 1973, he believed that it did not adopt a human shape or reach viability until it was born.

Second, the legal implications of the Court's three-part framework for bal-

---

[34] The "police power" of states has been described by the Supreme Court as the "power to govern men and things within the limit of [their] own dominion" in *License Cases*, 5 U.S. 504 (1847) and as "the power of the state to establish all regulations that are reasonably necessary to secure the health, safety, good order, comfort, or general welfare of the community" (*Atlantic Coast Line Co. v. Goldsboro*, 232 U.S. 548 [1914]).

ancing the privacy rights of the woman against the interests of the state in protecting "potential life" changed the conception of maternal-fetal relations. Until *Roe*, the legal system supported the biological unity of woman and fetus
and viewed their interests as identical. Even when courts had found some degree of legal personhood in the fetus in civil law or, to a lesser extent, in criminal law, they had assumed that the interests of the woman and fetus at least
coincided. In *Roe*, however, the Court's trimester framework established a
precedent that viewed the interests of mother and fetus as adversarial. As I
show in the next section, this precedent inappropriately spilled over into other
aspects of the maternal-fetal relationship.

Expansion of Fetal Rights

While *Roe* established that a woman's right to privacy extended to the decision to have an abortion, the subsequent abortion cases established a permissible zone within which states could pursue their interests. These rulings granted
states greater latitude in the use of their police power to protect the fetus. As
the Court made clear in 1973, the constitutionally protected rights of the
woman are to be balanced against the state interest in the health and welfare
of the fetus (Trindel 1991; Peak and Del Papa 1993).

While women's rights advocates hailed *Roe* because it invalidated state
abortion bans, fetal rights advocates were not totally defeated. *Roe* recognized
the possibility of a compelling state interest in preserving fetal health in the
third trimester of pregnancy, during which time a state may legally restrict a
woman's access to abortion to protect the fetus. Moreover, because the Court's
rationale for allowing restrictions during the third trimester was its recognition of that time as the earliest point of viability, pro-life forces had a legal basis for pushing the point of compelling interest to earlier in the pregnancy as
medical advances made it possible for fetuses to survive before a gestational
age of seven months. Further, as states demonstrate a greater interest in the
protection of fetal health, the fetus itself gains greater admission to personhood and a claim as a separate entity.

Since *Roe*, the moral and legal debates have focused on the struggle to balance the woman's constitutionally protected right to privacy against an expanded set of fetal rights. Fetal rights advocates view the state as a guardian of
the fetus, with a compelling interest in protecting potential life and fetal
health. Most support the principle of moral and legal equivalence with respect
to fetal personhood. Women's rights supporters emphasize the need to protect
a pregnant woman's fundamental rights to both privacy and liberty. They believe that enhancing the legal status of the fetus diminishes a woman's rights,
creating a continuous "slippery slope" of state intervention into women's lives.

The conflict over abortion has spilled over into other policy areas, most notably governmental responses to the problem of prenatal drug exposure. Re-

gardless of the specific policy, the fundamental dilemma remains balancing the rights of the fetus and the rights of the pregnant woman. Recent Supreme Court decisions have emphasized the state's interest in fetal welfare. While *Roe*, perhaps unwittingly, began the balancing act between the woman and the fetus, subsequent cases permanently fixed it in the legal debate.

The Expanding Parameters of Compelling State Interest

In *Planned Parenthood Association v. Ashcroft* (1983), the Court for the first time considered the possibility that fetal viability could be a compelling state interest. *Webster* (1989) further recognized fetal viability as a means to increase the state's regulation of a woman's reproductive decisions by advancing the argument that the state's compelling interest in protecting life begins at viability and not arbitrarily at the third trimester.[35] Justice William Rehnquist, writing for a three-member plurality, asserted that compelling state interest predates viability, encompassing potential life.[36] But because previous Supreme Court rulings had used viability, Missouri was required to begin treating the fetus as a person from that point onward rather than from conception. The Court did allow Missouri to require doctors to determine whether fetuses of twenty or more weeks' gestational age are viable.

Three years later, in *Planned Parenthood v. Casey* (1992), the Court further indicated an acceptance of the view that the state's interest in fetal health predates viability. *Casey* did not formally overturn *Roe*, but a badly fractured Court held that a state's interest in fetal health allowed it to limit previability abortions as long as those restrictions did not place an "undue burden" on the women. A plurality of three justices (Souter, Kennedy, and O'Connor) reaffirmed *Roe*, while at the same time allowing restrictions that did not violate the undue burden abortion standard. They argued that the "essential holding of *Roe*" had three parts: women have a right to abortion before a fetus becomes viable, the state can restrict that right after viability as long as continuing the pregnancy does not threaten the woman's life or health, and the state

[35] The Bush administration, as well as the state of Missouri, asked the Court to reconsider the standard that it applied to abortion in *Roe*. During the intervening sixteen years, the composition of the Court had changed enormously. All five of the justices who retired during the Reagan and Bush years—Potter Stewart, Warren Burger, Lewis Powell, William Brennan, and Thurgood Marshall—had been part of the seven-person majority in *Roe*. Their replacements—Antonin Scalia, Anthony Kennedy, Sandra Day O'Connor, David Souter, and Clarence Thomas—shifted the ideological center of the Court dramatically to the right.

[36] The most controversial aspect of the Missouri statute was its preamble, which declares, "the life of each human being begins at conception" and that "unborn children have protectable interests in life, health, and well being" (Missouri Revised Statute @ 1.205.1 1986). In *Webster*, the Court used the fact that Missouri state law treats unborn children as persons in tort and probate law to hold that it could apply this principle to abortion decisions, subject to restraints imposed by the Constitution and Supreme Court precedent. Because previous Court interpretations have never upheld the principle of fetal personhood from conception, the preamble is simply an assertion that the principle applies in other fields of the law and does not hold at this time in abortion cases.

has a compelling interest in protecting both the woman's health and potential life from conception.

Although the Court already had fully developed the "strict scrutiny" level of review in other areas of constitutional law, the justices did not choose to invoke it in *Casey*.[37] Because the *Casey* language pertaining to undue burden places the evidentiary requirements on the person challenging the state action, the Court seemed to be applying ordinary levels of constitutional scrutiny rather than "strict scrutiny." Under ordinary levels of constitutional scrutiny a state action is presumed to be constitutional until proven otherwise. In contrast, strict scrutiny, which is triggered whenever a state action discriminates against a suspect classification (e.g., race or national origin) or abridges a fundamental right under the Constitution (such as the right to travel), the evidentiary burden is shifted to the government. According to *Casey*, the party challenging the action has to show that the restriction does not impose an undue burden, which indicates that the Court is applying ordinary scrutiny. The Court, however, is considering fundamental rights, which usually would trigger strict scrutiny.

The Court Shifts Its Focus from the Woman to the Fetus

The cumulative impact of *Roe* and the subsequent abortion cases is twofold: first, they established that a woman's right to privacy encompasses the decision to have an abortion and second, they found that states may claim a "compelling interest" in protecting fetal health and well-being from the point of viability. Since the *Roe* decision in 1973, the Court has said that it would balance the woman's rights against state interests in the health and welfare of the fetus (Trindel 1991; Peak and Del Papa 1993).

In subsequent cases, the Court's primary concern has seemingly shifted from the woman, her rights, and her experiences as the pregnancy matures, to the rights of the fetus and its well-being. This shift reached its high point in *Casey*, in which a plurality of justices argued there was a compelling state interest in the fetus from conception. The majority opinion, however, held that any restriction before viability must not impose an undue burden on the woman. Although the abortion cases fall short of granting legal personhood to the fetus, states have continued to enact laws recognizing a growing sphere of fetal rights.

Although many states have enacted restrictions on abortion since 1973, only a few have enacted bans that would become effective if *Roe* is overturned. The pro-life movement sought to sway "middle ground" Americans, who have misgivings about abortion but do not want to eliminate it as an option. One of the movement's most effective strategies for shifting public senti-

[37] Under strict scrutiny, the government would have to establish a compelling state interest and that the government had no less intrusive alternative to the challenged action. This is also referred to as the requirement that the policy or action be "narrowly tailored."

ment is to focus on the most horrible abortion procedure—the intact dilation and extraction abortion. By characterizing the procedure as "partial birth abortion" and publicizing gruesome descriptions of it, pro-life groups hope to shift the opinion of these middle ground Americans. For example, a national pro-life newspaper included the following account by Brenda Pratt Schafer, a registered nurse.

> I stood at the doctor's side and watched him perform a partial-birth abortion on a woman who was six months pregnant. The baby's heartbeat was clearly visible on the ultrasound screen. The doctor delivered the baby's body and arms, everything but his little head. The baby's body was moving. His little fingers were clasping together. He was kicking his feet. The doctor took a pair of scissors and inserted them into the back of the baby's head, and the baby's arms jerked out in a flinch, a startle reaction, like a baby does when he thinks that he might fall. Then the doctor opened the scissors up. Then he stuck the high-powered suction tube into the hole and sucked the baby's brains out. Now the baby was completely limp. I never went back to the clinic. But I am still haunted by the face of that little boy. It was the most perfect angelic face I have ever seen. ("What the Nurse Saw," 1996, 20)

Pro-life activists hope to use these images to create their own slippery slope that slides toward a complete ban on abortions and a constitutional amendment defining the fetus as a legal person. Patricia Kuivenen, executive director of the Right to Life chapter in Dayton, sums up the problem and the challenge for both sides. "If you can convince people that [abortion] is bad at twenty weeks, it is not such a big step to get them to understand that it's bad at sixteen weeks or at twelve weeks" (Healy 1996, A1).

Applying the Adversarial Lens to the Other Fetal Policy Areas

Over the past two decades the question of fetal personhood has been an issue in two other areas of criminal law—prenatal drug exposure and third-party fetal killing/injury. Although roughly half of the states have made the killing of a fetus a criminal offense,[38] virtually all of the public attention and the preponderance of legal scholarship have focused on the need to prosecute pregnant women whose substance abuse could potentially harm their fetuses. One reason for the emphasis on the problem of prenatal drug exposure is that it *appears* to conform to the adversarial legal framework created by *Roe* and the other abortion cases, while the third-party fetal killing and battering cases do not.

[38] The first statutes criminalizing third-party fetal killings were passed in the mid-nineteenth century. Initially, generic manslaughter statutes simply incorporated the killing of a fetus (usually postquickening), but more recently, states have chosen to include in their homicide and manslaughter statutes a special category of crimes, such as feticide, killing the unborn, or battery of a fetus. Convictions for these crimes carry maximum sentences from eleven years' imprisonment to the death penalty.

Regardless of the context, most of the legal debates over fetal personhood have emphasized the balancing of the state's compelling interest in the fetus against the pregnant woman's constitutional rights. When applied to other fetal policies, the spill over from the abortion cases can lead to poor policy decisions. In particular, the adversarial maternal-fetal framework posited in the *Roe* decision is an inappropriate lens for viewing the relationship between pregnant women and their fetuses in the other two areas of criminal law, prenatal drug exposure and third-party fetal battering/killing.

Although on the surface, the pregnant addict and the fetus seem to have competing interests, that is not the case. Because a pregnant addict abuses herself as well as her fetus when she takes illegal narcotics, the woman and the fetus have a joint interest—ending the addiction—rather than competing interests. The spillover from *Roe*, however, an adversarial maternal-fetal relationship, has been applied to this policy area without giving adequate thought to whether it will improve fetal health and well-being. The adversarial issue also is not useful in cases involving third party fetal battering/killing because there the interests of the fetus and the pregnant woman are identical. Each has an interest in preserving her health and punishing her assailant.

Even though fetal personhood is a central issue in third-party fetal injury/killing cases because defendants usually argue that the fetus is not legally a person and, therefore, they have committed no crime, these cases typically do not generate much legal debate. Legal scholars appear to have little interest in cases involving fetal personhood when the rights of the fetus are not pitted against those of the pregnant woman. The spillover from *Roe* seems to have created intellectual blinders, ignoring cases that do not fit the adversarial maternal-fetal framework. Even cases that appear to break new legal ground by extending fetal rights do not generate much scholarly interest. For example, in a remarkable 1984 case, a New York family court held that the fetus was a person and entitled to be covered by a protective order. The court issued an order prohibiting an allegedly abusive man from coming near or harming his estranged pregnant wife, the fetus, and two born children. Despite the unusual nature of such a ruling and the court's explicit statement that it reached this decision at least in part because there was no conflict with the pregnant woman's privacy rights, this case has sparked very little interest in legal circles.[39]

The Problem of Substance Abuse by Pregnant Women

Although the public only recently awoke to the problem of "fetal abuse," substance abuse by pregnant women is not new. The United States has always had drug addicts (and some have always been pregnant women), and society's view of drugs has always been schizophrenic (or at best ambivalent). Before

[39] See *Gloria C. v. William C.*, 124 Misc. 2d 313, 476 N.Y.S.2d 991 N.Y. Fam. Ct. (1984).

1800 opium extracts were prescribed by physicians to treat cholera and para-sites, and by the middle of the nineteenth century patent medicines with opium and cocaine had become "popular—if unrecognized—items in the every day life of Americans" (Musto 1987, 3). Items as common and diverse as soft drinks and hay fever remedies contained cocaine.[40] Opium was even used in cough syrup for babies. Although the use of narcotics cut across all social classes, most patients taking opiate-based prescription drugs were middle- and upper-class women (Ashbrook and Solley 1979, 17). Less affluent women, un-able to afford the services of physicians, relied on patent medicines containing opium or cocaine (Helmer and Vietorisz 1974, 17).[41]

Still, no one believed there was a narcotics problem until opium smoking in the late 1870s became associated in the public's mind with Chinese immigrant laborers (Helmer and Vietorisz 1974, 3–4). Much of the ensuing anti-Chinese hysteria was fueled by stories about Chinese men using opium to lure "nice" girls into sexual relations (Ashbrook and Solley 1979, 19). One nineteenth-century observer of the opium smoking scene described the seduction of "nice" girls: "Many females are so much excited sexually by the smoking of opium during the first few weeks that old smokers with the sole object of ruin-ing them have taught them to smoke. Many innocent and over-curious girls have thus been seduced" (Kane 1882, 8).

During the public campaign against opium smoking, the media also began to publicize the problem of "negro cocaine fiends" (Helmer and Vietorisz 1974, 9–13). A popular mass circulation magazine reported that most of the rapes of white women in the South were perpetrated by "cocaine-crazed" black men (*Literary Digest*, March 28, 1914, 687 reprinted in Musto 1987, 283), and the American Pharmaceutical Association in its 1901 drive to eliminate the use of nonprescription narcotics described African Americans and women as particu-larly susceptible to addiction (Musto 1987, 19). In 1902 the American Public Health Association's Committee of the Acquirement of the Drug Habit also identified women in general and African Americans in the South as having the worst problems with cocaine addiction (Musto 1987, 17).

Despite the general perception to the contrary, some women were prose-cuted before 1985 for the use of narcotics while pregnant. In 1969 a New York trial court ruled that a parent's narcotics addiction created a presumption of child abuse sufficient to warrant the removal of the child from the home.[42] A few years later another New York trial court held that withdrawal symptoms in a newborn constituted prima facie evidence of prenatal neglect.[43] In 1977 a California woman was charged with felony child endangerment when her

[40] The government report in 1908 listed over forty soft drinks that contained cocaine (Kebler 1908, 372–73).
[41] By the end of the nineteenth century the patent medicine industry had gross annual earnings of more than eighty million dollars (Coombs, Fry, and Lewis 1976, 124).
[42] See *Matter of John Children*, 306 N.Y.S.2d 797 (Fam. Ct. N.Y. County 1969).
[43] See *Matter of Vanessa F.*, 351 N.Y.S.2d 337 (Sup. Ct. N.Y. County 1974).

twins were born addicted to heroin and suffered withdrawal a few hours after being born. An appellate court unanimously ruled that the child endangerment statute did not apply to fetuses and the woman was acquitted.[44] A Michigan appellate court, applying a different statute, reached the opposite conclusion in 1980.[45]

Policy Responses to the Problem of Prenatal Drug Exposure

Fetal rights advocates (Schierl 1990; Mathieu 1995) argue that the state has a duty to mitigate the high public cost of providing for drug- and alcohol-affected children, a concern sufficiently compelling to justify intervening in the lives of pregnant women. According to one widely reported early study, as many as 375,000 drug-affected infants are born every year (Chasnoff 1989, 208). The financial costs of providing for infants whose physical and mental development is impaired by in utero exposure to drugs can be very high. The hospital bills for neonatal narcotics withdrawal treatment can reach $28,000 or more per infant (Jessup and Roth 1988, 378). Although the long-term costs of providing ongoing assistance to these children are uncertain, one study places the per capita expense for those with congenital abnormalities at $100,000 or more (Boyd 1990, 4). The prospect of such outlays has even led some fetal rights advocates (Parness 1985) to argue that pregnant women should be prohibited from engaging in otherwise legal behaviors that place the fetus at risk.

Although women's rights advocates agree that substance abuse during pregnancy can cause medical and developmental problems for the fetus, they disagree about the scope of the problem. No one knows how many infants are exposed prenatally to illegal drugs, and the estimates vary enormously. For example, estimates of the number of infants exposed annually to cocaine while in utero vary from 30,000 to 100,000 (Behrman, Larson, Gomby, Lewit, and Shiono 1991a, 10). The 375,000 figure often cited by fetal rights proponents is based on an early small pilot study of dubious generalizability (Ooms and Herendeen 1990, viii).

Assessing the scope of the problem is made even more difficult because only a fraction of fetuses exposed to drugs while in utero will be adversely affected (Chasnoff, Griffith, MacGregor, Dirkes, and Burns 1989; Chasnoff, Griffith, Freier, and Murray 1992). Physicians find it difficult, if not impossible, to determine the causes of particular medical and developmental problems. Because adverse birth outcomes can be caused by many different factors, distinguishing the effects of prenatal substance abuse from those other social and environmental conditions makes it extremely difficult to assign a specific causal event

[44] See *Reyes v. Superior Court*, 75 Cal. App. 3d 214, 141 Cal. Rptr. 912 (1977).
[45] See *In the Matter of Baby X*, 293 N.W. 2d 736 (Mich. Ct. App. 1980), where the court ruled that an infant who experienced narcotics withdrawal during the first twenty-four hours after birth was "neglected."

to any particular prenatal harm (Kandall 1991; Boling 1996; Daniels 1996). In fact, these other social and environmental factors may be as much or more responsible for adverse outcomes than is prenatal substance abuse.[46] Assuming that causality is established still leaves uncertainty with respect to the duration of adverse effects. Although some infants have chronic and acute medical problems that are evident at birth and will continue to harm them throughout their lives, others can be treated at birth and lead normal lives, while still others will continue to have relatively mild but long-lasting physical or developmental problems (Behrman, Larson, Gomby, Lewit, and Shiono 1991a, 10–11).

Women's rights advocates are also opposed to policies that single out pregnant substance abusers women for punitive sanctions on the grounds that they actually work against the desired aim of enhanced fetal welfare. Nearly all of the medical and drug-treatment professionals who work closely with pregnant addicts believe that criminal sanctions actually deter them from seeking the prenatal care and substance abuse treatment needed to ensure healthy birth outcomes (Berrien 1990, 247; Roberts 1991, 9; Poland, Dombrowski, Ager, and Sokol 1993, 201). Most research indicates that incarceration is a very poor choice if fetal health is the goal. Correctional institutions in the United States have not adopted the guidelines for minimum obstetrical and gynecological care promulgated by the American College for Obstetricians and Gynecologists (Barry 1996). All of the relevant medical associations (the American Medical Association, the American Academy of Pediatrics, the American Nurses Association, the American Public Health Association, and the American Society of Addiction Medicine) have issued statements opposing the incarceration of pregnant addicts. Less than half of all state prisons for women have written policies governing the care of pregnant inmates (Woolredge and Masters 1993, 198). Studies have found that pregnant addicts in prison have higher rates of miscarriage and birth abnormalities than addicts on the street (Barry 1985, 1989; McCall, Castell, and Shaw 1985; Shelton and Gill 1989).

Finally, women's rights advocates believe that policies that single out pregnant addicts for criminal sanctions are based on two flawed assumptions about the reasons why pregnant addicts use drugs. The first is that pregnant addicts need to be coerced into treatment (i.e., they are "bad" mothers who do not care about their children and must be forced into doing what is best for them).[47] Instead, studies have found that pregnancy is a powerful motivation for female addicts to seek treatment (Moss 1990, 283; Ooms and Herendeen 1990, 5; Walker, Eric, Pivnick, and Drucker 1991, 8). The second is that preg-

---

[46] Studies indicate that pregnant women who consume alcohol but have otherwise healthy diets have far lower rates of fetal alcohol syndrome babies than do women who drink and have poor diets. Drinkers with poor diets, however, have a 70 percent higher chance than normal of giving birth to children with fetal alcohol syndrome (Bingol, Schuster, Fuchs, Iosub, Turner, Stone, and Gromisch 1987).

[47] As one prosecutor put it, "Many drug users are led to the road to recovery in handcuffs" (Dinsmore 1992, 10).

nant addicts committed to ending their addiction can get drug-treatment. In fact, very few drug treatment centers accept pregnant addicts and those programs generally have long waiting lists (Feig 1990, 16; Moss 1990, 288; Paltrow 1991, 85; Romney 1991, 341). The National Institute on Drug Abuse (NIDA) (1992, 35) found that only one-fourth of addicts receiving treatment in 1990 were female and only 4 percent of the women in treatment were pregnant at the time of admission. In its 1990 assessment of drug-treatment needs, the Institute of Medicine identified treatment for pregnant women as the most pressing (Institute of Medicine 1990, 233–34).[48] Rather than expanding the number of drug-treatment slots for pregnant women, funding for programs that target pregnant addicts has been reduced by budget cuts at the state, local, and national levels (Wilson 1994; Chavkin 1996).

Instead of policies that call for additional sanctions against pregnant substance abusers, women's rights proponents favor increasing the number of drug-treatment slots for pregnant addicts. Although additional research is needed on the long-term effects of in utero exposure to narcotics during the early stages of prenatal development, studies have found that birth outcomes were dramatically improved when substance-abusing women entered treatment programs midway through their pregnancies. For example, one study assessing the effects of cocaine use during pregnancy found that babies born to women who had used the drug during only the first trimester had similar rates of birth complications to those of a drug-free control group of women. Women who used cocaine throughout their pregnancy, however, had higher rates of preterm delivery, low-birth-weight babies, and intrauterine growth retardation than did the control group (Chasnoff, Griffith, MacGregor, Dirkes, and Burns 1989).

Fetal Abuse Becomes a Crime

Despite the policy arguments against targeting pregnant addicts, fetal rights proponents favor charging them with a range of criminal offenses, including possession of controlled substances, delivery of controlled substances to a minor, and manslaughter for the death of the fetus as a result of drug use. For example, John Robertson (1983, 442) argues that child abuse statutes should apply to the fetus, and pregnant women who jeopardize their fetus's health should be held criminally liable. Despite the difficulties in using some of these statutes, "enduring" criminal law justifies the prosecution of women's conduct that could harm the fetus. Although no states have passed laws making substance

[48] A related problem is that very few drug-treatment centers allow women to keep their children with them (McNulty 1990, 301). The NIDA survey found only 0.1 percent of all addicts in treatment had access to child care at their centers (NIDA 1992, 45), forcing a woman to place her children in foster care if she wants to get treatment. One study (Horst 1991, 35) found that pregnant addicts considered the availability of child care to be the most important factor in determining whether they would enter a treatment program.

abuse during pregnancy a separate offense, at least thirty-four have prosecuted women for "fetal abuse" since 1985 under a variety of criminal statutes including those pertaining to child abuse, child neglect, delivery of drugs to a minor, and child endangerment (Paltrow 1992; Jos, Marshall, and Perlmutter 1995; Center for Reproductive Law & Policy 1996; Lexis January 1998).

Prosecutors and law enforcement officials are confused about the most effective strategy for pursuing criminal convictions against pregnant substance-abusing women. The use of child abuse statutes and of the laws prohibiting the delivery of drugs to minors are difficult to sustain. In the past the high courts in Florida, Kentucky, Nevada, and Ohio have overturned the convictions of women who had taken drugs while pregnant and as a result had been found guilty of committing child abuse.[49] In 1996, however, the South Carolina Supreme Court ruled that a woman could be prosecuted for child abuse if she takes drugs while pregnant. In *Whitner v. State* (1996), the court said that a viable fetus is a "child" or a "person" in South Carolina and is thereby entitled to legal protection.[50]

One of the most troubling aspects of these efforts to prosecute women for exposing their fetuses to narcotics is that not all drug-using pregnant women are equally likely to be prosecuted. Despite studies showing that white and nonwhite women are equally likely to abuse narcotics while pregnant, most of the women prosecuted for these offenses have been racial minorities (Chasnoff, Landress, and Barrett 1990, 1204; Paltrow 1992). Moreover, prosecutors across, and even sometimes within, states differ in the degree to which they single out pregnant women for criminal charges related to fetal abuse. For example, in 1992 South Carolina led the nation with at least thirty cases, yet the vast majority occurred in the city of Charleston, and nearly all of the women were African American (Paltrow 1992; Jos, Marshall, and Perlmutter 1995). These figures raise troubling questions about race discrimination and equal protection under the law.

A Comparison of Responses to Fetal Abuse and Fetal Battering

An examination of high-profile fetal abuse cases demonstrates that sex discrimination influences the decision of police to arrest and prosecutors to file

[49] In 1990 the Boyd County grand jury indicted Connie Welch on charges of criminal child abuse for her use of narcotics while pregnant. Welch was found guilty, but the verdict was overturned by the Kentucky Supreme Court in 1993. Because the state legislature did not intend that fetuses be covered by the criminal child abuse statutes, Justice Liebson speaking for the majority stated, "It is with great sadness and disappointment that I am forced to conclude that in Kentucky the majesty of the law is unable or unwilling to protect innocent unborn children from harm caused by the conduct of another human being" (*Commonwealth of Kentucky, Morant v. Connie Welch*, 864 S.W.2d [1993]).

[50] The South Carolina Supreme Court reinstated an eight-year sentence given to Cornelia Whitner, whose son tested positive for cocaine immediately after his birth. Whitner's son is now eight years old and appears to have suffered no ill effects from her use of drugs while pregnant (Times Wire Services 1996, A12).

charges against women for their use of harmful narcotics during pregnancy. The first such case related to prenatal substance abuse involved a California woman, Pamela Rae Stewart Monson, who was prosecuted in 1986 for failing to provide necessary care to her "pre-born child." According to prosecutors, Monson failed to follow her doctor's instructions to avoid taking illegal drugs or to engage in sex during the latter part of her pregnancy. When the baby was born with severe brain damage and died shortly after birth, Monson was arrested under California's criminal child support statute that requires parents to care for their children. Even though Monson was beaten throughout her pregnancy and the medical evidence indicated that the baby's injuries were consistent with those caused by a severe beating,[51] the prosecutor never considered charging her husband with a crime (Johnsen 1989, 208–10; Berrien 1990, 244–46; McNulty 1990, 33; Pollitt 1990, 416; Schroedel and Peretz 1994, 354). In another well-known Wyoming case, a pregnant woman went to the hospital because she had been beaten by her husband and feared that the fetus might have been harmed. Instead of arresting the husband for battery, authorities charged the woman with fetal endangerment because she drank a beer before coming to the hospital (Pollitt 1990, 416; Paltrow 1991, 88).

In short, pregnant women could be prosecuted for fetal abuse even when their male partners had beaten them and the fetal injuries were clearly caused by physical assaults. Women could be prosecuted even without clear evidence that the fetus had been harmed by their substance abuse. Men were prosecuted only for the most egregious acts of violence and only when fetal injuries were attributable solely to them. Finally, the press has publicized the purported harms caused by in utero narcotics exposure far more than those caused by third-party acts of violence against pregnant women (Schroedel and Peretz 1994, 336–39).

The fetal abuse prosecutions have contributed to the general expansion of fetal rights. The public as well as district attorneys appear to support according greater status to the fetus. Surveys have assessed support for limits on the behaviors women can engage in while pregnant, and although they have not framed questions specifically about fetal personhood, they have found that Americans consistently and overwhelmingly support criminal prosecution of women who use illegal drugs while pregnant. But it is also clear that not all crimes against the fetus are treated similarly. Both race and sex appear to be significant determinants in prosecutions for harming (or potentially harming) the fetus.

---

[51] A report from the surgeon general indicated that two to four million American women are battered every year and that domestic violence is the leading cause of injury to women between fifteen and forty-four years of age (Novello, Rosenberg, Saltzman, and Shosky 1992, 31–32). Domestic abuse not only can cause injuries to the fetus but it also affects other conditions that can cause poor birth outcomes. For a summary of this research, see Schroedel and Peretz 1994.

Summary

Although people no longer conceptualize the ensoulment of the fetus, most intuitively accord greater status to the fetus as it matures. Just as pregnant women in the eighteenth and early nineteenth centuries believed the prequickening use of abortifacients was an acceptable way to restore menstrual regularity, today an abortion during the first trimester is viewed more favorably than a later one.

The trimester framework that the Court established in *Roe v. Wade* is remarkably similar to the three-stage framework created by Aristotle twenty-five hundred years ago. Even though the fetus can be viewed through ultrasound technology and photographed with fetoscopes, many people still think it progresses through the same three distinct stages of development. Perhaps it is simply that most people feel that a two-day-old embryo is quantitatively and qualitatively different from a twenty-five-year-old man. Yet a key difference between Aristotle's three-stage framework and the Court's trimester approach is that the former was a philosophical construct rather than a legal framework. By creating a scheme that balances the interests of the woman against those of the fetus (as mediated throughout the state), the Court fundamentally altered the way maternal-fetal relations are viewed. In short, the Court created a new legal framework for considering fetal rights. Rather than viewing the biological unity of woman and fetus as having coinciding interests, it viewed their interests as being adversarial. Although the adversarial lens is not appropriate for viewing the other two fetal issues (prenatal drug exposure and third-party fetal killing/injury), the legal community and policymakers seem to be able to conceptualize fetal interests only if they are pitted against those of the pregnant woman.

As we have seen, the status of the fetus and of women has varied greatly over time. To some extent the changes in fetal status are the result of greater understanding of biological development. The same cannot be said about women. In the United States even into the twentieth century, women have been denied full personhood status. The history of African American women's treatment as chattel during slavery is well documented, but less attention has been paid to the ways that ostensibly free women have been treated as chattel when it comes to controlling their own reproductive capacities. Although a woman (not simply her husband) can now collect civil damages if a third party's negligent actions cause a miscarriage, both the courts and much of the public continue to act as though a pregnant woman is not fully capable of making decisions about appropriate behavior during pregnancy.

Despite the tendency to focus on the rights of the pregnant woman and the putative rights of the fetus, it is important to remember that abortion cases raise other important constitutional questions. Do state governments have the authority to determine abortion policies and, more generally, to regulate fetal life?

If so, should state governments actually exercise that power? Such questions may frustrate those who believe that arcane arguments over federalism and states' rights are red herrings designed to deflect attention from the issues of fetal personhood and women's fundamental rights. As the preceding discussion illustrates, however, from the colonial period to the twentieth century, states have used statutory and case law to regulate abortion and other actions that could harm the fetus without interference from Congress or the federal courts, suggesting that states' rights and federalism are anything but red herrings.

CHAPTER 3

Abortion Policymaking in the States

The Policy Framework

Despite extensive formal research, the field of public policy still lacks a unifying theory and an analytical paradigm to structure and guide its intellectual development.[1] David Robertson and Dennis Judd (1989, 4) point out that scholars have made significant progress in explaining policy processes and outcomes but that "the object of our study, 'public policy,' is very difficult to define with precision." Thomas Dye (1987, 2) simply suggests that "public policy is whatever governments choose to do or not to do." Theodore Lowi's definition of public policy resembles Dye's, but he chooses to emphasize the coercive aspects of the state.[2]

Public policy can be defined simply as an officially expressed intention backed by a sanction. Although synonymous with law, rule, statute, edict, and regulation, public policy is the term of preference today probably because it conveys more of an impression of flexibility and compassion than the other terms. But no citizen, especially a student of political science, should ever forget that *policy* and *police* have common origins. Both come from "polis" and "polity," which refer to the political community itself and to the "monopoly of legal coercion" by which government itself has been defined. Consequently, all public policies must be understood as co-

[1] There is no consensus among scholars on a single approach to the study of public policy. Over the past thirty-five years scholars have studied policymaking from a variety of different intellectual frameworks, including, but not limited to, classical organizational theory, public choice economics, sociology, and public administration (Easton 1965; Laswell 1971; Kingdon 1984; Garson 1986; Dye 1987; Robertson and Judd 1989; Jenkins-Smith 1990; Hayes 1992; Baumgartner and Jones 1993; Schneider and Ingram 1993; Stone 1997).

[2] The notion of state-sanctioned coercion is a necessary component of Lowi's (1964) policy typology. In his classic article, Lowi argued that policy proposals can be categorized according to whether they are distributive, regulatory, or redistributive, but a few years later (1972) he added a fourth category, constituent policies, to his categorization scheme. He posits that each policy type engenders a distinctly different pattern of political mobilization and conflict.

ercive. They may be motivated by the best and most beneficent of intentions, and they may be implemented with utmost care for justice and mercy. But that makes them no less coercive. (Lowi 1988, x)

The use of force, usually implied rather than explicitly exercised, is required to achieve citizen compliance. When the public is either apathetic or supportive, state coercion is not readily apparent. Conversely, when a policy engenders strong opposition from significant sectors of the populace, governmental force is far more visible. Because most policymaking entails bargaining and compromise among participants with different opinions about the best way to solve a particular problem, or even different conceptions of what exactly the problem is, change tends to be incremental (Lindblom 1959; Hayes 1992). Governmental coercion is rarely needed to gain citizen compliance to implement incremental policy change.

Moreover, a "politics of compromise" predominates as long as policy disputes do not become battles over fundamental moral values and citizens' policy preferences have the normal bell-shaped distribution. It is far easier to reach compromise, for example, over the placement of a sewer line than over whether a high school health clinic should be allowed to provide condoms to sexually active teens. Unlike economic disputes, differences over morality are usually irreconcilable (Lowi 1988; Mooney and Lee 1995, 1996).

Many of the regulatory policies enacted over the past forty years have involved "the exercise of legal authority to modify or replace community values, moral practices, and norms of interpersonal conduct with new standards of behavior" (Tatalovich and Daynes 1988, 1).[3] For example, in the civil rights movement of the 1960s, black protesters and their allies (mostly white northerners) engaged in a protracted struggle to change the community norms and standards of behavior that had characterized black-white interactions in the South since Reconstruction, and the national government ultimately had to use force to gain citizens' compliance with the provisions of the 1964 Civil Rights Act and the 1965 Voting Rights Act.

Morality Policy as Social Regulation and the Redistribution of Values

Although Raymond Tatalovich and Byron Daynes use the term "social regulatory policy" for policies that involve the regulation of community values, "morality policy" is more common (Meier 1994; Mooney and Lee 1995, 1996; Haider-Markel and Meier 1996). Morality policies are regulatory because their aim is to regulate human behavior, but they also resemble redistributive policies. Rather than the mandated economic redistribution of traditional redistributive policies, morality policies involve the redistribution of

---

[3] Some scholars, particularly those influenced by Max Weber, consider these conflicts to involve primarily disputes over social status. For example, see Gusfield 1963 and Moen 1984.

values (Ripley and Franklin 1988, 145; Lowi 1988, xii; Meier 1994, 1). Mooney and Lee (1996, 3) describe morality policy as "redistribution with attitude" because the enactment of such policies "validates certain basic values and rejects others." Disputes over morality policies involve fundamental core values, which makes achieving a universally acceptable compromise extraordinarily difficult.

The recent scholarly research on morality policymaking, as well as the popular media's focus on the "cultural wars," could lead one to the incorrect assumption that these conflicts are a new phenomenon. Disagreements over morality policies have been a part of American politics since the country's inception. For example, the Constitutional Convention in 1787 nearly deadlocked over the question of slavery. In the nineteenth century there were sharp divisions, not only over slavery but also over female suffrage and temperance. All are policy issues that can be characterized as attempts by one sector of society to use the coercive apparatus of the state to enforce its moral values on the entire country.

More recent political disputes that fit this category include school prayer (Moen 1984; Murley 1988), drug policies (Meier 1994), pornography (Daynes 1988), sodomy laws and gay rights (Nice 1988; Haider-Markel and Meier 1996), and the death penalty (Nice 1992; Mooney and Lee 1996). But probably no contemporary social policy has generated the intense value-laden conflict that abortion policy has, making it an archetype of morality policymaking in the current era.[4] According to James Hunter and Joseph Davis (1996, 106), the conflict over abortion is at the center of all the current disputes over morality policies because it "raises core philosophical questions about the nature of human life and human community."

Applying the Morality Policy Framework to Fetal Policies

At first glance, the entire range of fetal policies seems to fit the morality policy typology very well. The question of moral values (e.g., is the fetus a person?) is central in all three of the fetal policies under consideration, and the question of the legality of abortion, absolute or qualified, has triggered intense conflicts characteristic of morality policy disputes. Hunter (1994, 30) has even argued that *Roe v. Wade* created a legitimacy crisis that threatens public acceptance of the law.

For more than two decades, individuals and groups opposed to abortion have protested and engaged in civil disobedience. Some antiabortion activists argue that acts of violence such as bombing clinics and attacking abortion providers are morally and religiously justified by the need to save the lives of

---

[4] Luker (1984) was the first scholar to apply a morality policy framework (but not the particular terminology) to the study of abortion policy. See also Goggin 1993; Tatalovich 1988; Tatalovich and Daynes 1993; and Mooney and Lee 1995.

unborn children. For example, the four people charged and convicted in the 1984 bombing of a Pensacola abortion clinic were devout Christians who modeled their actions on those of Gideon in the Old Testament.[5] They equated their bombing of the abortion clinic with Gideon's destruction of Ba-al's temple, where infants were sacrificed in a religious ritual. Just as Gideon was judged a righteous man for violating the laws of his community to end the killing of innocents, the Pensacola bombers believed that their actions would be deemed righteous.[6] Morality policies provoke reactions that include not only civil disobedience but actual violent resistance. Certainly the dispute over abortion pits different groups against one another on the basis of deeply held moral convictions. Whether acts such as clinic blockades are justified as "civil disobedience" necessary to protect innocent human life or condemned as "terrorism" against women depends on one's moral framework (Hunter and Davis 1996, 109).

The problem is that the politics surrounding this archetypical example of a moral policy issue are quite different from those of the other two fetal policies. There is no consensus on the morally appropriate position on abortion. Although most of the public support the view that abortion should be legally protected, they also believe the state should regulate the practice.[7] The politics of abortion, however, are fueled by the actions of interest groups that hold more extreme pro-life and pro-choice positions and are closely linked to the two major political parties (Rozell and Wilcox 1996; Wilcox and Norrander unpublished 1997). The politics of fetal abuse and third-party fetal killings are dramatically different. In contrast to the division over abortion, both women who abuse drugs while pregnant and acts of violence that result in fetal deaths are universally condemned.

[5] The most relevant portion of the biblical story of Gideon's battle against idolatry is found in chapter 6 of Judges. According to the text, God spoke to Gideon and told him to destroy the temple where sacrifices were made to the heathen deity Ba-al. Gideon could not carry out the act during the day because Ba-al's temple was under the protection of the civil authorities, so he and ten servants destroyed it at night. When the authorities came to arrest him, Gideon convinced the Israelites that he had performed a righteous act and subsequently gathered them together to form an army that he led against their enemies.

[6] For more information about the Pensacola abortion clinic bombings and the moral reasoning of the bombers, see Condit 1990, 153–163; and Blanchard and Prewitt 1993.

[7] In his analysis of public opinion data, Wilcox (1995, 61–63) found that between 1972 and 1992 public attitudes toward abortion were remarkably stable. Roughly three-fourths of the public believe that a woman should be able to obtain an abortion when there are dangers to her health, chances of fetal deformity, or the pregnancy was caused by rape. But survey respondents are divided over whether a woman should have the legal right to terminate a pregnancy for social reasons (being poor, being unmarried, or wanting no more children). Nearly half believe that no such justification should be permitted, while 40 percent support legal abortion for any purpose. Since 1988 pollsters found that roughly 8 percent of the public favored banning abortions under virtually all circumstances, 39 percent favored legalizing abortions under virtually all circumstances, and the remainder supported keeping abortion as a legal option but limiting the reasons for obtaining one.

The Two Types of Morality Policies

According to Kenneth Meier (1994, 246–47), morality policies can be divided into two broad types: contested issues and one-sided issues. When morality policies pit organized citizen groups against one another, they are labeled contested issues. The struggle to end slavery in the nineteenth century is a classic example, and more recent contested morality policies include disputes over the prohibition of alcohol, school prayer, gun control, and sex education in the schools. Although still concerned with moral questions, one-sided morality issues do not divide the public because virtually everyone agrees on the "moral" position. In his description of these issues, Meier (1994, 247) writes, "Everyone is opposed to sin (especially if the costs of the associated policy are relatively small); as a result, there is universal opposition to drunk driving, to drug abuse (though not necessarily to drug access), to murder and so on. The only opposition to this type of morality policy is clearly the work of Satan." Meier (1994, 247) further argues that because these issues are uncontested, the policymaking process is dominated by political entrepreneurs who compete to be the strongest proponents of virtue.

> Morality policies pertaining to one-sided issues are rarely subjected to the expertise of bureaucrats; assessments of these morality policies are generally found only in academic journals, which no self-respecting politician would read. Even when the bureaucratic expertise is available, it is often swept aside in the rush to Armageddon. Such a policy process is much more likely to generate policies that will not work because the policy proposals have not been tempered by informed debate. (Meier 1994, 247)

Categorizing Fetal Policies

Although abortion is easily categorized as a contested morality policy issue, the placement of the other two fetal policies is a bit more problematic. On the surface, both issues (substance abuse by pregnant women and third-party fetal killings) appear to be examples of one-sided morality policies. Using drugs while pregnant and the killing of a fetus by beating, knifing, shooting, or otherwise physically harming a pregnant woman are "sinful" acts that are universally condemned. The politics generated by each are quite different, however. Furthermore, each challenges the assumptions of the morality policy typology in different ways.

At first glance, the politics of fetal abuse resembles those of a one-sided morality policy. The public, as well as policymakers, unanimously condemn pregnant women who abuse narcotics. The stated aim of fetal abuse policies is to save unborn children from physical and developmental problems caused by in utero exposure to drugs. Also as expected, political entrepreneurs have seized the issue, seeking political gain by pursuing punitive actions against these women. Yet the actual policies do not fit the expected pattern under Meier's scenario. Despite attempts by political entrepreneurs to exploit the issue, none of the hundreds of legislative proposals designed to single out pregnant addicts for criminal sanctions have been enacted.[8] Instead, fetal abuse policymaking has occurred in the less political judicial system, where some prosecutors have tried to expand interpretations of existing criminal statutes to include the fetus, and some judges and juries have agreed with them. This subject is discussed in more detail in Chapters 2 and 4.

The most notable differences between the politics of third-party killings and the two other fetal policies are the lack of both politics and political mobilization. Although it is a one-sided morality issue (e.g., no one defends individuals who kill fetuses), political interest has been minimal at best. From a policy standpoint, this apparent paradox generates interesting questions about policy formation. Does the morality policy typology apply only to some policies that deal with moral issues and not others? Is political salience a necessary component of morality policymaking, and if so, what determines the political salience of an issue? Finally, to what extent does the policymaking process simply replicate the existing status and gender biases of the society?

In this chapter and the next I examine the legal status of the fetus in current state criminal statutes, case law, and practices to ascertain any significant differences across policy areas in the treatment of actions that harm or potentially harm the fetus. The rest of this chapter focuses on contested politics associated with setting abortion policy in the states, while Chapter 4 examines the two one-sided morality policy issues, prenatal drug exposure and third-party fetal killings. The aim is to discover patterns under which the fetus is accorded value in some circumstances but not others. The morality policy framework will be used as a starting point, but I believe that its application must be extended to a broader range of political circumstances to account for status differences among the parties that harm the fetus and for the impact of cultural values.

Abortion Policymaking

Activists on both sides of the abortion struggle very consciously seek to impose their particular moral values on the rest of society, but few are as open about their aim as Joseph Scheidler of the Pro-Life Action League, who states, "For those who say I can't impose my morality on others, I say just watch me" (Scheidler reprinted in McKeegan 1992, 111). Like most disputes over morality policies, the conflicts are not amenable to compromises that split the differ-

---

[8] Such a result is also contrary to what would be expected under Schneider and Ingram's (1993) social construction typology. For another example of a politically weak and negatively constructed group receiving fewer policy burdens and a high level of policy benefits, see Schroedel and Jordan's (1998) test of the social construction model of AIDS policymaking.

ence between the two sides. Presumably, Scheidler (and other zealots on the abortion issue) would use the government, the only entity with a monopoly on the legal use of force, to enforce his moral vision.

The Supreme Court's 1973 decision that struck down all state laws restricting a woman's access to a first trimester abortion galvanized abortion opponents into action. Although several states had liberalized their abortion statutes during the preceding decade, pro-life groups did not expect the Supreme Court to issue a pro-choice decision as sweeping as *Roe v. Wade.* Some pro-life activists even characterized the Court's ruling as a coup d'etat (Cassidy 1996, 138) because the Court deviated from its traditional role in defining moral behavior for the country. As Charles Franklin and Liane Kosaki (1989, 751) write, "The United States Supreme Court has a historical role as a 'republican schoolmaster' inculcating virtues in the citizenry."

Responses to *Roe*

Roe's opponents responded by aggressively organizing at the state and national levels (Luker 1984).[9] Although there were important differences between the state and national groups, both used fetal imaging to shape political and cultural views about the meaning of fetal life. Television programs such as the Reverend Pat Robertson's *700 Club* brought fetal images to the mass public in a way not possible earlier. According to Rosalind Petchesky (1987, 57–58),

> Anti-abortionists . . . have long applied the principle that a picture of a dead foetus is worth a thousand words. Chaste silhouettes of the foetal form, or voyeuristic necrophilist photographs of its remains, litter the background of any abortion talk. These still images float like spirits through the courtrooms, where lawyers argue that foetuses can claim tort liability; through the hospitals and clinics, where physicians welcome them as "patients"; and in front of all abortion centers, legislative committees, bus terminals and other places that "right-to-lifers" haunt. The strategy of anti-abortionists is to make foetal personhood a self-fulfilling prophecy by making the foetus a *public presence* addresses a visually oriented culture.

Probably the most effective use of the mass media developed during this period to present the fetus as a "baby" was *Silent Scream*, a video that claims to show a twelve-week-old fetus being aborted. The narrator describes the fetus as a "living unborn child," "another human being indistinguishable from any of us," and tells us that it "senses pain." Petchesky (1987, 60) recounts the video's end: "The suction cannula is 'moving violently' toward 'the child'; it is the 'lethal weapon' that will 'dismember, crush, destroy,' 'tear the child apart' until only 'shards' are left. The foetus *'does sense aggression in its sanctuary,'* attempts to 'escape' (indicating more rapid movements on the screen), and fi-

[9] For a concise history of the development of different pro-life organizations, see Cassidy 1996.

nally 'rears back its head' in a 'silent scream.' " *Silent Scream*, was shown on television at least five times in one month (Petchesky 1987, 58).

Pro-life forces sought to elect pro-life state legislators. In the state legislatures, they tried to use *Roe*'s recognition of a compelling state interest in fetal life during the third trimester as a rationale for limiting a woman's right to obtain an abortion. Several state legislatures signaled their disapproval of *Roe* by passing nonbinding resolutions affirming that life begins at conception.[10] Americans United for Life, a pro-life legal organization, took the lead in developing model state legislation to restrict abortion (Center for Reproductive Law & Policy 1998b, 73). Pennsylvania became the first state to adopt an AUL-written law when it passed the 1982 Abortion Control Act, which included a mandatory twenty-four-hour waiting period, mandatory lectures by physicians, parental consent provisions for women under twenty-one years of age, and the requirement that all second trimester abortions be performed in hospitals. Although the law was subsequently overturned by the Supreme Court in *Thornburgh v. American College of Obstetricians & Gynecologists* (1986), the AUL continued to pursue the model law strategy.[11]

At the national level, most of the action involved the Supreme Court, and the appointment of conservative and generally antiabortion justices throughout the Reagan and Bush years whittled away at the *Roe v. Wade* majority. The implications of the changing composition of the Court were not apparent until 1989, when its decision in *Webster v. Reproductive Health Services* upheld a Missouri state law that imposed a series of restrictions on a woman's access to abortion. Although *Roe* was not overturned, the decision marked a sharp retreat from the trimester approach.

Pro-life politicians responded to *Webster* by increasing their efforts to enact new state laws that restricted abortion. Florida's Republican governor, Robert Martinez, immediately called the state legislature into a special session in an unsuccessful attempt to adopt a series of new restrictions on abortion. Pro-life politicians were successful in many other states, generally through the enactment of restrictions rather than outright bans, but some states went even fur-

---

[10] The Montana state legislature in 1974 became the first to pass a pro-life resolution: "The legislature reaffirms the tradition of the state of Montana to protect every human life, whether unborn or aged, healthy or sick. In keeping with this tradition and in the spirit of our constitution, we reaffirm the intent to extend the protection of the laws of Montana in favor of all human life." The legislatures in Illinois, Kentucky, Louisiana, Missouri, Nebraska, North Dakota, Pennsylvania, and Utah have adopted one or more resolutions affirming the sanctity of all human life. Arkansas in 1988 amended its state constitution to include the following: "The policy of Arkansas is to protect the life of every unborn child from conception until birth, to the extent permitted by the Federal Constitution" (Arkansas Constitution, Amendment 68).

[11] Eight years later, another AUL-written Pennsylvania law, containing many of the same restrictive provisions, was affirmed by the Supreme Court in *Casey* (Center for Reproductive Law & Policy 1998b, 73). In the intervening years, the composition of the Court had been dramatically altered by four additional appointments by antiabortion Presidents Reagan and Bush.

ther.[12] The Louisiana legislature voted to ban abortions except for pregnancies caused by rape or incest or when the life of the mother was threatened. Utah passed a similar law that added an exception for grossly deformed fetuses.[13]

Webster was a wake-up call to pro-choice groups that they needed to mobilize to preserve a woman's right to a safe and legal abortion. Membership in the most important national pro-choice organization, the National Abortion Rights Action League, surged between 1989 and 1990. Although the exact magnitude is disputed, all knowledgeable observers agree that the organization expanded dramatically after the *Webster* ruling.[14] The Maryland state affiliate of NARAL boosted its membership from seven hundred in 1986 to twelve thousand in 1992 (Carney 1995, 54), and the California Abortion Rights Action League (CARAL) doubled its membership (Russo 1995, 179).

Webster and subsequent abortion decisions, as well as the success of pro-life groups in passing state laws restricting access to abortion, invigorated pro-choice forces. After the Justice Department in 1989 announced its intention to seek the overruling of *Roe v. Wade*, pro-choice groups realized they could no longer count on the judiciary as a check on state governments committed to restricting abortion. A few days later, the executive directors of the National Organization for Women, NARAL, American Civil Liberties Union (ACLU), and Planned Parenthood met to plan and coordinate efforts to keep abortion legal (Rubin 1991, 243). According to Wilcox (1995, 59–60), pro-choice groups raised more money in 1989 than their pro-life counterparts, and their financial advantage has since widened. To some extent, the success of pro-life groups in eroding *Roe* undermined their ability to maintain the urgency of their rank and file in the early 1990s.

Throughout this period, lawyers working for the National Right to Life Committee have used the model law strategy, initially developed by the AUL, to keep up the pressure on state legislators (Rubin 1991, 251).[15] A model law, consisting of eight different restrictions on abortion, was disseminated at a September 1989 meeting of pro-life state legislators and lobbyists. The NRLC's model legislation included the following restrictions: ban abortion as a means of birth control, ban abortions for sex selection, require informed

[12] In 1990 state legislators introduced a total of 465 abortion-related bills, nearly all of which sought to restrict access to abortion. For more information about the increase in legislative activity in 1990, see "State Legislation on Reproductive Health in 1990: What Was Proposed and Enacted" 1991.

[13] The actions of the Louisiana and Utah state legislatures were primarily symbolic. Both states already had abortion bans that were rendered unenforceable by *Roe v. Wade*. Fifteen other states still have on the books pre-*Roe* laws that ban abortions. If *Roe* is ever overturned, these laws, as well as the new laws in Louisiana and Utah, would immediately become enforceable.

[14] Because the membership figures are used to indicate the relative strength or weakness of the organization, national leaders from NARAL refuse to disclose membership figures or verify the accuracy of others' estimates. According to Cassidy (1996, 150), the membership doubled between 1989 and 1990.

[15] For a detailed discussion of the model legislation, see Balch 1989.

consent, require spousal notification, require parental consent/notification, prohibit abortions in public facilities or by public employees, fund pregnancy counseling centers, and fund the provision of adoption information. Within the next year lawmakers in nearly every state had introduced bills incorporating parts of the model law (Rubin 1991, 251).

Even though it did not originate the model law strategy, the NRLC has taken the approach to a new level by making it both a legal device and a mechanism for mass mobilization. With more than three thousand local chapters, affiliates in every state and the District of Columbia, and more than $13 million in annual revenue,[16] the National Right to Life Committee is able to exert enormous pressure on legislators to support model bills. Moreover, the NRLC has focused much of its recent legislative efforts on getting states to pass bans on partial birth abortions—a particularly gruesome procedure—which makes it relatively easy to mobilize pro-life activists.

The adoption of a model law strategy by the NRLC has not resulted in a diminution of such efforts by the AUL, which in 1995 assisted pro-life forces in forty-two states and Puerto Rico to enact laws restricting access to abortion (*AUL Forum* figures reprinted by the Center for Reproductive Law & Policy 1998b, 72).

The Republican Party's success in the 1994 elections coupled with the NRLC and AUL model law strategy was responsible for the passage of twice as many antiabortion laws in 1995 and 1996 as in the preceding two years (NARAL 1997b, i).[17] The upward trend continued in 1997, when state legislatures considered 405 antiabortion measures, an increase of 84 percent over 1996, and enacted 55 of them (NARAL 1998, v). Some of the 1997 enactments, such as the Alabama law prohibiting postviability abortions except to save the woman's life or to prevent "substantial and irreversible impairment of a major bodily function," come very close to returning the states to the pre-*Roe* status quo. Pro-life forces in other states, such as the five that passed new prohibitions on the use of public funding to pay for abortions, have followed a more incrementalist approach of gradually whittling away at women's access to abortion services. The result, however, is the same—a dismantling of *Roe*.

State Laws Banning Abortion

In January 1998 the criminal codes of seventeen states contained statutory language criminalizing abortion at any stage of pregnancy if *Roe v. Wade* is ever repealed. The abortion bans are divisible into three categories according

---

[16] The National Right to Life Committee does not answer questions about its affiliates or about the size of the federation. These figures were compiled by the Center for Reproductive Law & Policy (1998b) from an undated fact sheet and other sources.

[17] In 1995 and 1996 state legislatures adopted thirty-two new antiabortion laws as opposed to the sixteen enacted in 1993 and 1994.

to the time of their enactment: bans that predated the reforms of the 1960s, bans that date from that reform era, and post-*Roe* bans. The older laws allow far fewer exceptions than do the later enactments.

The abortion laws in nine states have not been changed since their original passage (i.e., as part of the first wave of abortion regulations in the nineteenth and early twentieth centuries). These states resisted efforts in the 1960s and early 1970s to conform their abortion statutes with the American Law Institute guidelines described in Chapter 2. New Hampshire, which repealed its 1848 felony abortion statute in 1997, was the last to do so.

The states with the most stringent bans and the date of their enactments are as follows: Vermont (1846),[18] Michigan (1846),[19] Wisconsin (1849),[20] Oklahoma (1910),[21] Texas (1854),[22] West Virginia (1849),[23] and Arizona (1864).[24] Statutes in these states allow abortions to be performed only when the woman's life would be threatened by the pregnancy. The abortion bans in Massachusetts (1845) and Alabama (1841) are slightly more liberal; they also allow an exception when the woman's life or health is threatened by carrying the pregnancy to term.

The wording of the abortion statutes in eight other states with abortion bans made unconstitutional by *Roe* can generally be traced back to the model language proposed by the American Law Institute. Although the ALI guidelines were first promulgated in 1959, no state enacted new abortion laws using ALI language until 1966, when Mississippi adopted its fairly stringent reform measure. Mooney and Lee (1995, 609–10), in their study of pre-*Roe* abortion reforms, found a strong relationship between the timing of reforms and the statute's permissiveness. The later the adoption of reforms, the greater the loosening of the restrictions on abortion.

As expected, Mississippi law, which allows a woman to obtain an abortion

[18] The Vermont Supreme Court ruled that the provisions of this law that apply to physicians are unconstitutional, *Beecham v. Leahy*, 287 A.2d 836 (Vt. 1972); the rest of the statute has not been tested under the constitutional guidelines articulated in *Roe v. Wade* and subsequent Supreme Court decisions.

[19] The only provision of the Michigan abortion statute that has been challenged in court is the prohibition on nonphysicians performing abortions, upheld in 1973. See *People v. Bricker*, 208 N.W.2d 172 (Mich. 1973).

[20] Three years before the Supreme Court's *Roe v. Wade* decision, a federal court in Wisconsin held that the provisions of the state's abortion law were unconstitutional. See *Babbitz v. McCann*, 310 F.Supp. 293 (E.D. Wis. 1970).

[21] Both state and federal courts in Oklahoma found the provisions of the abortion ban unconstitutional in 1973. See *Jobe v. State*, 509 P.2d 481 (Okla. Crim. App. 1973) and *Henrie v. Derryberry*, 358 F. Supp. 719 (N.D. Okla. 1973).

[22] The Texas abortion statute was rendered unconstitutional by *Roe*.

[23] The West Virginia abortion ban was ruled unconstitutional in 1975. See *Doe v. Charleston Area Medical Center*, 529 F.2d 638 (4th Cir. 1975).

[24] Arizona's abortion ban was ruled unconstitutional in 1973. See *Nelson v. Planned Parenthood of Tucson, Inc.*, 505 P.2d 580 and 505 P.2d 590 (Ariz. 1973) and *State v. New Times, Inc.*, 511 P.2d 196 (Ariz. 1973).

if her life is threatened by the pregnancy or if she was the victim of a rape, is the most stringent of the ALI-inspired reform laws. California's pre-*Roe* abortion ban allows exceptions when the woman's life or health is threatened or if the pregnancy was the result of rape or incest. Five states (Arkansas, Colorado, Delaware, New Mexico, and Utah) ban abortion unless the woman's life or health is at risk, or the pregnancy is the result of rape or incest, or if the child would have serious physical deformities or defects. The Utah statute was enacted after *Webster*.[25]

Louisiana, which amended and reenacted its nineteenth-century abortion law in 1991, is an exception to the rule that late adopters are more liberal. The law, which was based on a model bill crafted by NRLC lawyers, prohibits abortion unless the pregnancy was the result of rape or incest or abortion is necessary to save the woman's life. One possible explanation for the stringency is that only 2 percent of the members of the Louisiana state legislature were women in 1991. To obtain a legal abortion for a pregnancy caused by rape, the woman must have reported the rape to police within seven days and received medical treatment within five days. The physician or other medical provider must certify that the woman was not already pregnant at the time of the rape, and the abortion must be performed within thirteen weeks of conception. An incest victim must report the crime to law enforcement officials and have the abortion performed within thirteen weeks. A federal appeals court in 1992 held that this law was unconstitutional and enjoined its enforcement (*Sojourner T. v. Edwards* 1992). The following year, the Supreme Court refused to hear the state's appeal.

Among the thirty-three states that do not have statutes banning abortion are four (Alaska, Hawaii, New York, and Washington) that repealed their abortion bans before *Roe* and twenty-nine that passed post-*Roe* repeals. Although all regions of the country contain states with and without bans, midwestern states are the least likely still to have statutory abortion bans.

The Shift toward Enacting Limited Abortion Bans

Because the pre-*Roe* abortion bans and the more recent bans enacted in Louisiana and Utah cannot be enforced, pro-life lobbyists and legislators have worked to secure the passage of partial abortion bans. Most of these efforts at the national level have involved attempts to prohibit intact dilation and extraction abortions, one of the procedures used after the twentieth week, when the pregnancy is too far advanced for the suction method to be used.[26] The fe-

---

[25] Although Utah amended and reenacted its pre-*Roe* ban in 1991, a federal court ruled in 1992 that the provisions of the law are unconstitutional. See *Jane L. v. Bangerter*, 809 F.Supp. 865 (D. Utah 1992), affirmed 61 F.3d 1493 (10th Cir. 1995).

[26] Even though a great deal of attention has been paid to the intact dilation and extraction procedure, it is neither the most common nor most gruesome method of terminating late pregnancies. The dilation and evacuation method is by far the most common procedure performed after twenty weeks. Physicians use serrated forceps to cut the fetus into pieces before removing it from the

tus is brought feet-first into the birth canal, where the physician punctures its skull and then sucks the brain tissue out through a catheter. Because the fetus is in the birth canal when the procedure is performed, it is much harder to draw a sharp line of demarcation between it and a newborn infant. For this reason, some pro-life groups have chosen to focus on enacting partial birth abortion bans rather than attempting to ban other specific late abortion procedures. Even strong supporters of abortion rights find the intact dilation and extraction procedure to be morally troubling. As Senator Daniel Patrick Moynihan noted, the procedure is "too close to infanticide" (Lavelle 1998, 31).

At the state level, pro-life legislators have succeeded in enacting two types of limited abortion bans: partial birth abortion bans and postviability abortion bans. The NRLC has been in the forefront of efforts to criminalize partial birth abortions while the AUL has primarily pushed for bans on virtually all postviability abortions. Although both types of bans would restrict a woman's ability to terminate a late-term pregnancy, the first proscribes a specific procedure[27] while the second is more general. As a practical matter, neither ban would affect many women. Roughly 89 percent of abortions are performed during the first trimester (Waldman, Ackerman, and Rubin 1998, 22).

Although the exact number of late-term abortions is under dispute, all knowledgeable observers consider it to be very low. According to the Alan Guttmacher Institute, only 1 percent of abortions occur after twenty weeks' gestation (Warren 1998, A3). Pro-life efforts to enact partial birth bans gained momentum, however, when Ron Fitzsimmons, the executive director of the National Coalition of Abortion Providers, estimated in 1997 that three to five thousand late-term abortions are performed annually (Carey 1998a, 128). Doubts were raised about these figures in 1998, when the Guttmacher Institute for the first time surveyed abortion providers to determine how often they performed dilation and extraction abortions. Only eight abortion facilities indicated that they did. Using this information, the Guttmacher Institute estimated that roughly 650 of these procedures are performed annually (Rubin 1998, A45). Pro-life groups immediately disputed the figures, charging that they were too low.

Partial Birth Abortion Bans

Pro-life forces affiliated with the NRLC coined the term "partial birth" abortion as part of their successful 1993 effort to defeat the Freedom of Choice bill, a congressional attempt to codify *Roe*. Following the 1994 elections, the NRLC worked with pro-life Republicans in Congress to craft model language for the Partial Birth Abortion Ban bill, which was passed in 1996 and 1997, only to be vetoed by President Bill Clinton.

---

uterus. The language used in many of the latest partial birth abortion laws is ambiguous with respect to which procedures are proscribed.

[27] The early partial birth bans proscribed only the intact dilation and extraction procedure. More recent partial birth abortion laws are less clear about which procedures are prohibited.

State pro-life groups also have mounted a major drive to pass laws banning the procedure. In 1995 Ohio passed the first state law making it a felony to perform intact dilation and extraction abortions; the statute also bans nearly all postviability abortions. Enforcement of the Ohio law has been enjoined.[28] The following year Michigan enacted a ban on partial birth abortions at any point in a pregnancy. The statutory language used in the Michigan partial birth abortion law and subsequent bans is broader than was used in the Ohio law, which applied only to intact dilation and extraction abortions. The Michigan law defined the banned procedure as "partially vaginally delivering a living fetus before killing the fetus and completing the delivery." Because it was unclear which specific procedures were banned, a court ruled the Michigan law unconstitutional and issued a permanent injunction to halt its enforcement.[29] Also in 1996 Utah made the performance of postviability "partial birth abortions" and "saline abortions" a felony offense.[30] In 1997 sixteen additional states banned the procedure, some not even allowing its use when the woman's health is at risk.[31]

By January 1998 a total of nineteen states had enacted some version of partial birth abortion bans. Courts in nine states had issued injunctions prohibiting enforcement of the laws and in another state (Illinois) the law is not being enforced because a lawsuit has been filed requesting a court order to halt enforcement.[32] In the remaining states the bans were being partially or fully enforced in January 1998.[33]

[28] A federal appeals court found the law unconstitutional, because it did not allow women to end pregnancies to avoid serious mental and physical health risks, and issued a permanent injunction against its enforcement. See *Women's Medical Professional Corp. v. Voinovich*, Nos. 96–3157/3159 (6th Cir. Nov. 18, 1997).

[29] See *Evans v. Kelley*, No. 97–CV–71246–DT (E.D. Mich. July 31, 1997).

[30] In Utah a fetus is considered to be viable at a gestational age of twenty weeks.

[31] In 1997 the following states adopted partial birth abortion bans: Alabama, Alaska, Arizona, Arkansas, Georgia, Illinois, Indiana, Louisiana, Mississippi, Montana, Nebraska, New Jersey, Rhode Island, South Carolina, South Dakota, and Tennessee. The Florida assembly and senate approved a partial birth ban that was vetoed by Governor Lawton Chiles. The veto was overturned by the assembly but the governor challenged their action on procedural grounds.

[32] The nine states that had court orders are Alaska, Arizona, Arkansas, Michigan, Montana, New Jersey, Nebraska, Ohio, and Rhode Island. See *Planned Parenthood of Alaska v. State*, No. 3AN-97–06019 (Alaska Super. Ct. July 30, 1997); *Planned Parenthood of Southern Arizona v. Woods*, No. CIV. 97-385-TUC-RMB (D. Ariz. Oct. 24, 1997); *Little Rock Family Planning Services v. Jegley*, No. LR-C-97-581 (E.D. Ark. July 31, 1997); *Evans v. Kelley*, No. 97-CV-71246-DT (E.D. Mich. July 31, 1997); *Intermountain Planned Parenthood v. State*, No. BDV 97-477 (Mont. Dist. Ct. Oct. 1, 1997); *Planned Parenthood of Central New Jersey v. Verniero*, No. 97-CV-6170 (D.N.J. Dec. 16, 1997); *Carhart v. Stenberg*, 972 F.Supp. 507 (D. Neb. 1997); *Women's Medical Professional Corp. v. Voinovich*, nos. 96-3157/3159 (6th Cir. Nov. 18, 1997); *Rhode Island Medical Society v. Pine*, C.A. No. 97-416L (D.R.I. July 11, 1997). All of the court orders except for those in Arizona, Michigan, and Ohio are temporary. In Illinois a lawsuit requesting a court order enjoining the enforcement of the law has been filed. See *Hope Clinic v. Ryan*, No. 97C8702 (N.D. Ill. filed Dec. 16, 1997).

[33] In 1997 a Nebraska court issued a preliminary injunction prohibiting the enforcement of a ban on dilation and extraction abortions performed on nonviable fetuses. See *Carhart v. Stenberg*, 972 F.Supp. 507 (D. Neb. 1997). In Alabama a lawsuit has been filed requesting an injunction, but

States in the Midwest and South were far more likely than those in the Northeast and West to enact partial birth abortion bans. Approximately half of the midwestern and southern states have such bans but less than a third of those in the other two regions. See Table 3.1 for a summary of state efforts to ban this procedure by region.

Postviability Abortion Bans in the States

Because the Supreme Court has recognized a compelling state interest in fetal well-being from the point of viability, many pro-life state legislators and lobbyists have focused on enacting laws outlawing postviability abortions. Lawyers from the AUL have attempted to develop model laws that redefine the point of "viability" to ever earlier stages and that narrowly restrict the range of health exceptions allowed women. For example, the AUL's model law, the Viable Unborn Child Protection Act, sets fetal viability at the gestational age of nineteen weeks and prohibits all postviability abortions except when necessary "to prevent either the death of the pregnant woman or the substantial and irreversible impairment of a major bodily function of the woman" (Americans United for Life 1996a).

By January 1998 forty-one states had passed laws proscribing postviability abortions. The restrictiveness of these bans can be assessed on two dimensions: what is defined as the point of viability and what exceptions are allowed.

The Supreme Court in *Webster v. Reproductive Health Services* (1989) defined viability as the point at which the fetus "has the capacity of meaningful life outside of the womb" but did not specify when this point occurs.[34] The definition of viability put forth in *Webster* raises the question, What is "meaningful life"? Most scholars believe that viability implies more than the possibility of simply surviving the birth process. Viability is the point at which the fetus has a good chance of surviving outside of the womb with technological support. Three years later, in *Planned Parenthood of Southeastern Pennsylvania v. Casey* (1992), the Court unambiguously reiterated that viability marked the point at which a state could intervene to prohibit nontherapeutic abortions but remained ambiguous as to when viability is reached.

Defining the point of viability is difficult because it is a function of both physiological development and medical technology. At the time of *Roe*, most medical experts placed viability at twenty-eight weeks, whereas today, it is

---

the law is still being enforced and on August 1, 1997, the attorney general issued a letter instructing prosecutors to apply the ban only to viable fetuses. See *Summit Medical Associates v. James*, No. 97-T-1149-N (M.D. Ala. filed July 25, 1997). In Georgia a court issued an interim order allowing the ban to be applied to viable fetuses. See *Midtown Hospital v. Miller*, No. 1:97-CV-1786-JOF (N.D. Ga. June 27, 1997). As of January 1998, the partial birth bans are being fully enforced in Indiana, Mississippi, South Carolina, South Dakota, Tennessee, and Utah.

[34] For a discussion of the relationship between medical technology and viability, see Zaitchik 1984.

Table 3.1. State laws on partial birth abortions by region (as of January 1998)

Northeast	Midwest	South	West
Ban			
New Jersey	Illinois	Alabama	Alaska
Rhode Island	Indiana	Arkansas	Arizona
	Michigan	Georgia	Montana
	Nebraska	Louisiana	Utah
	Ohio	Mississippi	
	South Dakota	South Carolina	
		Tennessee	
No Ban			
Connecticut	Iowa	Delaware	California
Maine	Kansas	Florida	Colorado
Massachusetts	Minnesota	Kentucky	Hawaii
New Hampshire	Missouri	Maryland	Idaho
New York	North Dakota	North Carolina	Nevada
Pennsylvania	Wisconsin	Oklahoma	New Mexico
Vermont		Texas	Oregon
		Virginia	Washington
		West Virginia	Wyoming

considered to be between twenty-four and twenty-six weeks. Before that point, critical organs, such as the lungs and kidneys, are unable to function even when the "baby" is attached to a respirator. A respirator can force air into the lungs, but if the air sacs are too immature to allow gas to pass from the lungs into the bloodstream, life cannot be sustained. More than 150 scientists and physicians filed an *amicus* brief in *Webster* stating, "There are no medical developments anticipated in the foreseeable future that would bring about adequate fetal lung development prior to 23 or 24 weeks of gestation" (Amicus Brief of 167 Distinguished Scientists and Physicians Including 11 Nobel laureates, for *Webster v. Reproductive Health Services* 1988).[35]

State Definitions of Viability

The Court's uncertainty over when a fetus reaches viability is reflected in state laws. In Michigan and New Hampshire quickening rather than viability determines when abortions may be legally performed. Because states are constitutionally prohibited from proscribing previability abortions,[36] Michigan

[35] A study by medical researchers at Case Western University Medical School found that infants born before a gestational age of twenty-five weeks continue to have extremely low survival rates (Hack and Fanaroff 1989). A British study of all babies born between 1983 and 1994 in northern England with a gestational age of 28 weeks or fewer showed that no babies of 22 or fewer weeks' gestation survived, and only 4 percent of those born at 23 weeks' gestation survived one year. Roughly one-fourth of all the surviving babies born at fewer than 28 weeks' gestation had severe disabilities (Tin, Warigar, and Hey 1997).

[36] See *Colautti v. Franklin*, 439 U.S. 379, 388–89 (1979).

and New Hampshire have not attempted to enforce the prohibition on previability, but postquickening, abortions. A Michigan court, however, has ruled that the law is constitutional when applied to viable fetuses.[37]

Twenty-four states prohibit postviability abortions but are statutorily silent as to gestational age.[38] Three of these states (Alabama, Louisiana, and Missouri) have statutory provisions requiring viability testing. In Alabama a physician must test for viability on a fetus estimated to be eighteen weeks of age or older, while in Missouri the testing age is twenty weeks. In Louisiana the statute requires viability testing before any abortion is performed, but the provisions have been ruled unconstitutional.[39]

Five states (Minnesota, Delaware, North Carolina, California, and Utah) define the point of viability as twenty weeks of age. The attorneys general of California and Delaware issued opinions stating that they believe these provisions are unconstitutional because medical opinion does not support the view that a twenty-week-old fetus is viable (65 Op. Attorney General of California 261, 1982; Attorney General of Delaware, Statement of Policy, March 24, 1977). In addition, two federal circuit courts have ruled that restricting abortion to gestational ages of twenty weeks or earlier is unconstitutional because the fetus is not viable at that point.[40]

Six states (Massachusetts, New York, Pennsylvania, Ohio, South Dakota, and Nevada) have bans that define viability as commencing at twenty-four weeks, and another four states (Iowa, Florida, Georgia, and Virginia) ban all third trimester abortions. Ohio is unique in that its law requires viability testing after the twenty-second week, a practice enjoined in 1995.[41]

No noticeable geographic pattern corresponds with earlier or later definitions of viability in the laws criminalizing postviability abortions. Although two of the three states with laws requiring viability testing are in the South, generalization on the basis of such a small number is impossible.

The Stringency of Postviability Bans

The statutes also vary in the number of exceptions allowed. California law, which has no exceptions to its postviability abortion ban, is the strictest. In

[37] See *Larkin v. Cahalan*, 208 N.W.2d 176 (Mich. 1973).

[38] The twenty-four states that ban postviability abortions but do not define the point at which the fetus is to be considered viable are Connecticut, Maine, Rhode Island, Illinois, Indiana, Kansas, Missouri, North Dakota, Nebraska, Wisconsin, Alabama, Arkansas, Kentucky, Louisiana, Maryland, Oklahoma, South Carolina, Tennessee, Texas, Arizona, Idaho, Montana, Washington, and Wyoming.

[39] See *Margaret S. v. Treen*, 597 F. Supp. 636 (E.D. La. 1984), affirmed at 794 F.2d 994 (5th Cir. 1986). Blanket viability testing may be constitutional under the reasoning of more recent Supreme Court decisions such as *Webster* and *Casey*.

[40] See *Hodgson v. Lawson*, 542 F.2d 1350 (8th Cir. 1976) and *Jane L. v. Bangerter*, 61 F.3d 1493 (10th Cir. 1995).

[41] See *Women's Medical Professional Corp. v. Voinovich*, No. C-3-95-414 (S.D. Ohio Dec. 13, 1995).

1982 the state attorney general opined that the law is unconstitutional because it lacks exceptions to save a woman's life or preserve her health as required by *Roe* (65 Op. Attorney General of California 261, 1982). Five states (New Hampshire, New York, Rhode Island, Michigan, and Delaware) allow only postviability abortions that are necessary to preserve the woman's life. Again, because *Roe* explicitly mandated exceptions to preserve a woman's life and health even in the last trimester, these laws are unconstitutional.[42] A Kansas statute, which allows abortions when necessary to protect the life of the woman or if the fetus has a severe deformity, also is presumptively unconstitutional on the basis of *Roe* because it does not allow abortions necessary to protect the woman's health (Opinion of the Kansas Attorney General, No. 91–130, Oct. 15, 1991).

The laws in twenty-nine states allow exceptions when the life or, in varying degrees, the health of the woman is threatened.[43] The laws in Pennsylvania, Ohio, and Indiana provide only minimal protection of the woman's health. The Pennsylvania law mandates "substantial and irreversible impairment of a major bodily function" of the woman for a postviability abortion to be permissible. The Ohio law has very similar language, requiring that the woman face a "serious risk of substantial and irreversible impairment of a major bodily function." Indiana's law allows a postviability abortion only to prevent "a substantial permanent impairment" of the woman's health. Because these laws provide only minimal protections to women's health, they are presumptively unconstitutional on the basis of *Roe*.

The other twenty-six states have constitutionally permissible language that safeguards the woman's life and health. Four states' statutes (Maryland, Texas, Idaho, and Utah) add an exception for severe fetal deformities. The postviability ban in Arkansas provides exceptions for abortions that are needed to protect a woman's life or health or when the pregnancy is the result of rape or incest. None of the other states provides exceptions for rape or incest.

Five of the nine states without statutes prohibiting postviability abortion are in the West, two are in the Northeast, and two are in the South.[44] Every state in the Midwest, in some manner, statutorily prohibits abortions after a fetus is viable.

[42] The Delaware state attorney general issued an opinion stating that the law banning postviability abortions is unconstitutional because it fails to include a provision allowing exceptions to be made to preserve the health of the woman (Statement of Policy, Attorney General of Delaware, March 24, 1977). See also *Delaware Women's Health Org: v. Wier*, 441 F.Supp. 497 n.9 (D. Del. 1977).

[43] The twenty-nine states that allow postviability abortions to be performed when the life or health of the woman is threatened are Connecticut, Massachusetts, Maine, Pennsylvania, Iowa, Illinois, Indiana, Minnesota, Missouri, North Dakota, Nebraska, Ohio, South Dakota, Wisconsin, Alabama, Florida, Georgia, Kentucky, Louisiana, North Carolina, Oklahoma, South Carolina, Tennessee, Virginia, Arizona, Montana, Nevada, Washington, and Wyoming.

[44] The nine states that do not ban postviability abortions are Alaska, Colorado, Hawaii, New Mexico, Oregon, New Jersey, Vermont, Mississippi, and West Virginia.

Measuring the Overall Restrictiveness of Postviability Bans

To compare the restrictiveness of each state's laws governing postviability abortions, I created a composite measure that included whether the state prohibited abortions after the fetus reaches viability, the gestational age that defines viability, and the extent of legal exceptions. For each state I calculated a score that assigned points for each of the following characteristics: existence of a statutory ban, viability defined as a gestational age of less than twenty-four weeks, no exception to protect the life of the mother, no exception to protect the health of the mother, no exception for fetal deformity, no exception for rape, and no exception for incest. The higher the score, the more restrictive a state's criminal laws dealing with postviability abortions. Possible scores range from zero for a state without a ban to seven for a state that has a ban with no exceptions. As shown in Table 3.2, there are nine states with zero scores and only one state with a score of seven. The modal score is four, for either states with a ban and a gestational age of twenty-four weeks or greater and three exceptions, *or* states with a ban, a gestational age of less that twenty-four weeks and only two exceptions.

Overall Restrictiveness of Abortion Bans

As of January 1998, only two states (Hawaii and Oregon) did not have some type of an abortion ban as part of their criminal laws. Of the twenty-five states with only one type of abortion ban, most were laws proscribing postviability abortions or bans on partial birth abortions; only four had old pre-*Roe* bans still on the books.[45] Of the seventeen states with two types of abortion bans, seven have an old pre-*Roe* ban as well as either a partial birth or postviability ban; the remaining ten have partial birth and postviability bans.[46] Finally, six states have total abortion bans, as well as partial birth and postviability bans. Louisiana and Utah enacted their total bans in the 1990s, but the other four states (Alabama, Arizona, Arkansas, and Michigan) had old pre-*Roe* bans. In general, the South and Midwest have a greater number of bans than do the Northeast and West. See Figure 3.1 for a visual depiction of the regional variations in the prevalence of abortion bans.

[45] Of the twenty-five states with only one abortion ban, Colorado, New Mexico, Vermont, and West Virginia have old pre-*Roe* bans. New Jersey and Alaska have partial birth bans, and the remaining states (Connecticut, Florida, Idaho, Iowa, Kansas, Kentucky, Maine, Maryland, Minnesota, Missouri, Nevada, New Hampshire, New York, North Carolina, North Dakota, Pennsylvania, Virginia, Washington, and Wyoming) have postviability bans.

[46] California, Delaware, Massachusetts, Oklahoma, Texas, and Wisconsin have old pre-*Roe* bans and postviability bans, and Mississippi has a pre-*Roe* ban and a partial birth ban. The ten states with partial birth and postviability bans are Georgia, Illinois, Indiana, Montana, Nebraska, Ohio, Rhode Island, South Carolina, South Dakota, and Tennessee.

Table 3.2. State laws on postviability abortions by region (as of January 1998)

No bans	Least strict bans	Average bans	Most strict bans
Northeast			
New Jersey		Connecticut	New Hampshire (6)
Vermont		Maine	New York (5)
		Massachusetts	Rhode Island (5)
		Pennsylvania	
Midwest			
		Illinois	Michigan (6)
		Indiana	Minnesota (5)
		Iowa	
		Kansas	
		Missouri	
		Nebraska	
		North Dakota	
		Ohio	
		South Dakota	
		Wisconsin	
South			
Mississippi	Arkansas (2)	Alabama	Delaware (6)
West Virginia	Maryland (3)	Florida	North Carolina (5)
	Texas (3)	Georgia	
		Kentucky	
		Louisiana	
		Oklahoma	
		South Carolina	
		Tennessee	
		Virginia	
West			
Alaska		Arizona	California (7)
Colorado		Idaho	
Hawaii		Montana	
New Mexico		Nevada	
Oregon		Utah	
		Washington	
		Wyoming	

Note: Of the states with postviability abortion bans, those with a composite score (shown in parentheses) of less than 4 constitute the least strict category. The average strictness category is composed of states with the modal score of 4. Those with scores greater than 4 constitute the most strict category.

Post-*Roe* Restrictions on Abortion

Because the Supreme Court in *Roe v. Wade* recognized that states may have a compelling interest in the health and well-being of fetuses, state legislatures throughout the post-*Roe* period have significantly influenced abortion regulation. Other than establishing the trimester framework, the *Roe* decision did

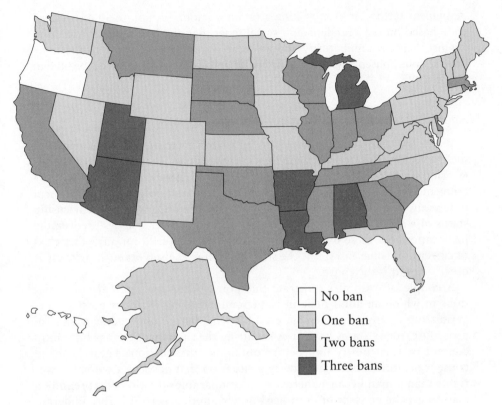

Figure 3.1. Number of abortion bans by state

not establish clear parameters of state authority, and pro-life state legislatures responded by enacting a variety of abortion restrictions. In 1989, *Webster* judicially approved several state regulations and limitations on the access to and availability of abortion services and opened the door to further judicial challenges.

In my analysis of state efforts to restrict abortion, I distinguish between state laws and regulations that apply to adult women and those that apply only to minors because minors (both male and female) are subject to many parental constraints whereas adults are considered to be legal persons responsible for their own actions. By definition, minors do not have the same legal status as adults. Most of the restrictions on a minor's access to abortion services are designed to involve either the parents, the parties typically considered by law and custom to be responsible for the actions of the minor, or the state acting in loco parentis. Stanley Mosk, one of the most liberal members of the California Supreme Court, explained that he supported the state's parental consent law for minors because it was no different from other state laws that require a minor to obtain parental permission before getting a driver's license, obtaining a permanent tattoo, or even visiting a tanning salon. To him, these restrictions were based on the "fundamental social tenet that children require protection against their own immaturity and vulnerability in making decisions that may have serious consequences for their health and well-being" (Mosk reprinted in Dolan 1997, A14).

Abortion Restrictions and Women's Personhood Status

When adult women's fundamental rights are constrained in ways unique to their sex and the exercise of these rights is made contingent on another, the citizenship status of women as a class is undermined. Although nearly every government law or regulation makes distinctions among people and treats them differently, many current fetal laws systematically undermine the citizenship status of women in ways that do not occur with male citizens. Moreover, the justifications for these infringements would not be upheld for any other class of citizens. In some cases, it is the state legislature that favors such policies; at other times, it is the courts.

A couple of examples illustrate this point. Although there are no situations in which an adult male in full command of his faculties must get the permission of any other person, even his wife, before undergoing a medical procedure, many states have laws requiring that a woman get her husband's consent or least notify him before obtaining an abortion. These husband consent or notification laws codify a situation that accords a woman fewer rights than a man because there are no comparable situations that require a man to get the consent of or at least notify another person before undergoing a medical procedure. Although the courts have ruled that the husband notification and consent laws are unconstitutional, they have held that pregnant women owe a higher standard of duty toward fetuses than any other group owes to another class. Only in pregnancy can a competent adult be forced by law to have her bodily integrity violated to provide for another "person." One of the ironies of these rulings is that, although there is no consensus on whether the fetus is legally a person and in most situations it is not accorded personhood status, a woman can be compelled to have her bodily integrity violated in a manner that courts have held cannot be done to provide for born human beings, whose personhood status is not under dispute. Moreover, there are no situations that require a man to violate his bodily integrity to provide for the needs of another person (born or unborn).

For more than thirty years the courts have ruled that mentally competent pregnant women can be forced to undergo medical treatments believed necessary to preserve fetal health and life (Condit 1995, 38). In 1964 courts for the first time approved a medical intervention (blood transfusion) on the grounds that it was needed to preserve the health of the fetus.[47] Subsequent courts have forced pregnant women to undergo a range of medical procedures, including but not limited to blood transfusions, cerclages,[48] and cesarean sections.[49] One of the most egregious examples was the case of Angela Carder, a twenty-seven-year-old woman with terminal lung cancer, who was admitted to the hospital when she was six months pregnant. With the support of her husband, other family members, and her physician, she decided not to have a cesarean section until her fetus reached a gestational age of twenty-eight weeks, when it had a reasonable chance of surviving without severe physical problems. When the fetus reached twenty-five weeks, hospital administrators convinced a panel of judges to issue an order mandating a cesarean section. Carder's physician argued that such an order would hasten her death and was unlikely to result in a viable fetus. After a court-ordered cesarean, the baby lived less than two hours and Carder died two days later (Daniels 1993, 31–32).

Under no other circumstance does a court allow the bodily integrity of one person to be violated to save the health or life of another person. In this regard, the fetus has greater rights than a born person. A born child does not have a right to force a parent to undergo any form of bodily invasion, even a blood test, without the person's consent. A parent has no legal duty to donate body parts or fluids or endure bodily intrusions to aid the child regardless of his or her need (McDonagh 1996, 102–3). Both common law and statutory law have long upheld the right of a person to refuse to allow others to invade his or her bodily integrity. This principle has been upheld even when the intrusion is minor and a relative's life is at stake. For example, the Illinois Supreme Court in *Curran v. Bosze* (1990) ruled that consent was required before two children could have blood drawn to determine whether their bone marrow might help save their half-brother, who was dying of leukemia.

In short, there is legal precedent for allowing violations of a woman's physical integrity and forcing her to use her body to sustain another person. Although the Supreme Court has been unwilling to give husbands the power to make these decisions, it has allowed states to grant such power to outside enti-

---

[47] See *Raleigh Fitkin–Paul Morgan Memorial Hospital v. Anderson*, 42, N.J. 421, 201 A.2d 537, 377 U.S. 985 (1964) and *Application of the President and Directors of Georgetown College Hospital*, 331 F.2d 1000 (1964).

[48] According to Condit (1995, 48), cerclage is a "procedure to suture the cervix to enable the pregnant woman to retain a pregnancy." In *Taft v. Taft*, 388 Mass. 331, 446 N.E. 2d 395 (1983) a man requested that the court order his wife to undergo this procedure. The trial judge ordered that the woman have a cerclage, but the Massachusetts Supreme Court overturned the lower court's decision. The woman did not have the procedure, carried the pregnancy to term, and had a normal delivery.

[49] For a summary of court-ordered medical interventions on pregnant women, see Kolder, Gallagher, and Parsons 1987.

ties such as hospital boards. But for the Court's intervention, a fair number of state governments would have ceded this power to husbands.

Restrictions on Adult Women

By January 1998 every state in the country had enacted laws that restricted access to abortion services for adult women.[50] Eight different restrictions apply to adult women: mandatory waiting periods, limits on public funding for abortions, conscience-based exemptions that allow medical providers or health facilities to refuse to perform abortions, counseling bans (or "gag orders") that prohibit public employees and groups receiving public funding from informing women about abortion or referring them to abortion providers, husband consent or notification laws, statutes requiring the payment of an extra premium to insurance companies for medical coverage of abortions, laws prohibiting insurance companies that provide medical coverage for public employees or are paid for by public funds from including abortion coverage as part of their plans, and informed consent laws.[51]

My method of analyzing abortion statutes is somewhat different than that of most previous researchers. Scholars (Halva-Neubauer 1990, 1993; Richard 1995) have typically either analyzed the passage of a single restrictive abortion law or counted up the number of restrictive laws that states have enacted after particular court decisions. The first approach is problematic because it fails to capture the overall character of abortion regulation in the particular state, while the second fails to take into account differences in the substantive content of the restrictions. Although the substantive content of a particular class of restrictions is often roughly comparable across states, there are important exceptions to that general rule. For example, among the thirty states that have enacted informed consent laws, the substantive content is radically different. Although a few simply require that women be told of the medical risks associated with abortion, others require attendance at one or more mandatory lectures on fetal development, the presentation of enlarged color photographs of fetuses at different gestational ages, and education about a wide range of pos-

---

[50] The state of Vermont places no limits on abortion because its one restriction on abortions for adult women has been ruled unconstitutional. In 1980 the state adopted a policy of not allowing public funds to pay for an abortion unless it was necessary to preserve the woman's life or the pregnancy was the result of rape or incest (Vermont Department of Social Welfare, Medicaid Policy M617, 1980). A Vermont court ruled that the policy violated the state constitution and issued a permanent injunction against the enforcement of the policy to the extent that it disallows payments for medically necessary abortions. See *Doe v. Celani*, No. S81-84CnC (Vt. Chittenden Cty. Super. Ct. May 23, 1986).

[51] Although the clear intent of the restrictions is to reduce the number of abortions performed, there is no consensus among scholars about whether this actually occurs. For an excellent summary of the research, see Haas-Wilson 1993.

sible alternatives to abortion. Some states actually mandate that health care providers counsel the women not to have abortions. The descriptive label "informed consent law" is deceptively simple, masking different degrees of state intrusion into the doctor-patient relationship.

For each of the eight different types of laws restricting access to abortion, measures were used to allow comparisons across states. The aim is to determine the extent to which laws in each state further the strategic agenda of pro-life forces (i.e., make it more difficult for a woman to obtain an abortion). Beyond counting the number of restrictions, I also consider other statutory attempts either to discourage women from obtaining abortions or to encourage them to continue pregnancies. According to two individuals associated with the AUL, a pro-life legal group that drafts model abortion statutes, the aim of these laws is to whittle away at *Roe* incrementally until a woman's right to an abortion is nonexistent: "It appears probable that repudiation of the abortion privacy right would come in a series of steps which would completely empty it of content, rather than from a law simply banning all abortions" (Rosenblum and Marzen 1987, 207).

Mandatory Waiting Periods

Laws in nineteen states require that women receive a state mandated lecture or written materials to read and then wait for a specified period of from one hour to three days before obtaining the abortion. Although the content of the lecture or reading material varies across states, they cover topics such as fetal development at the time of the proposed abortion and the risks associated with undergoing an abortion. As of January 1998 these laws were being enforced in twelve states (Idaho, Indiana, Kansas, Louisiana, Mississippi, Nebraska, North Dakota, Ohio, Pennsylvania, South Carolina, South Dakota, and Utah). In the other seven states (Delaware, Kentucky, Massachusetts, Michigan, Montana, Tennessee, and Wisconsin) the laws were not being enforced.[52]

Even though mandatory waiting period requirements do not legally prevent women from obtaining abortions, they do constitute a significant impediment for many women. A recent study of the impact of Mississippi's mandatory twenty-four-hour period found that it caused an increase from 19 to 25 percent in the number of residents traveling out of state for abortions and a 50

---

[52] Massachusetts, Michigan, Montana, and Tennessee are judicially enjoined from enforcing mandatory waiting periods. See *Planned Parenthood of Massachusetts v. Belotti*, 641 F.2d 1006 (1st Cir. 1981); *Mahaffey v. Attorney General*, No. 94-4067793-AZ (Mich. Cir. Ct. July 15, 1994); *Planned Parenthood of Missoula v. Montana*, No. BDV-95-722 (Mont. Dist. Ct. Nov. 28, 1995); and *Planned Parenthood Association of Nashville v. McWherter*, No. 92C-1672 (Tenn. Davidson Cty. Ct. Aug. 23, 1995). A Wisconsin court issued a temporary restraining order halting enforcement of that state's statute. See *Karlin v. Foust*, No. 975-F. Supp. 1177 (W.D. Wis. 1997). The state governments of Delaware and Kentucky have chosen not to enforce these laws until their compliance with the legal requirements specified in *Planned Parenthood of Southeastern Pennsylvania v. Casey* (1992) can be determined.

percent increase in the number of abortions performed after the twelfth week (Theodore, Henshaw, and DeClerque Skarrud 1997).

Limits on Public Funding of Abortions for Poor Women

Thirty-five states limit the use of public funds to pay for Medicaid abortions. Federal law requires that states receiving federal Medicaid funds include abortion coverage in cases when the woman's life is endangered by the pregnancy and in cases involving rape or incest. States that pass more stringent limits on the use of state funds to pay for Medicaid abortions than are spelled out in federal law are in violation of that law (FY 1995 Labor, Health and Human Services and Education Appropriations Act, Pub. L. 103–333, sect. 509). Because Alabama, Mississippi, and South Dakota allow state funds to pay for abortion only when the woman's life is threatened, they violate the latter provision. The remaining thirty-two states restrict the use of state money to pay for Medicaid abortion but do so within federal limits.[53] Finally, fifteen states provide state funding to cover virtually all Medicaid abortions.[54]

Conscience-Based Exemptions

All of the states, except for New Hampshire, Vermont, Alabama, and Mississippi, have laws, known as "conscience-based" exemptions, that allow some medical personnel or health facilities to refuse to perform abortions on moral grounds. This exemption has had an enormous effect on the availability of abortion services. In the late 1970s, roughly one-fifth of hospitals performed abortions throughout the first and second trimesters (Bond and Johnson 1982), but by 1996 only 16 percent of nonfederal hospitals performed abortions (Rubin 1998, A45). In 1996, 86 percent of counties in the United States did not have a single abortion provider and only 12 percent of obstetrical-gynecological residency programs included training in the performance of first trimester abortions and fewer still provided training in second trimester abortions (Rubin 1998, A45). In 1992 the American Medical Association's Council on Scientific Affairs cautioned that the shortage of trained abortion

---

[53] Twenty-seven states (Arizona, Arkansas, Colorado, Delaware, Florida, Georgia, Indiana, Kansas, Kentucky, Louisiana, Maine, Michigan, Missouri, Nebraska, Nevada, New Hampshire, North Carolina, North Dakota, Ohio, Oklahoma, Pennsylvania, Rhode Island, South Carolina, Tennessee, Texas, Utah, and Wyoming) use public funds to pay for Medicaid abortions when the woman's life is endangered or the pregnancy is the result of rape or incest. Three states (Iowa, Maryland, and New Mexico) provide funds for abortions in cases of life endangerment, rape, incest, and some conditions that threaten the woman's health. Virginia also provides funding when the fetus has a totally incapacitating physical deformity or mental deficiency. The Iowa law is similar to Virginia's but also funds abortions of fetuses with congenital illnesses.

[54] The fifteen states that use public money to help fund abortions for Medicaid recipients are Alaska, California, Connecticut, Hawaii, Idaho, Illinois, Massachusetts, Minnesota, Montana, New Jersey, New York, Oregon, Vermont, Washington, and West Virginia.

providers has "the potential to threaten the safety of induced abortion" (Council on Scientific Affairs, American Medical Association 1992, 3237). The shortage of abortion providers is most acute in North Dakota and South Dakota, each of which has only a single physician willing to perform the procedure (NARAL 1997, viii).

The medical implications for women of conscience-based exemptions is illustrated by a couple of examples. In 1989 Maralee Dinsdale, a Missouri woman, was carrying a twenty-two-week-old fetus that was severely deformed and lacked a brain. Her physicians urged her to abort the fetus as soon as possible, but no hospital in Missouri would perform the abortion. Dinsdale was forced to get the abortion at an out-of-state clinic unequipped to deal with high-risk patients.[55] When she began hemorrhaging in the middle of the abortion, Dinsdale had to be transported back to the hospital that had initially refused to perform the procedure (McKeegan 1992, 144).

In 1998 Michelle Lee, who had a life-threatening heart condition and was awaiting a transplant, discovered that she was ten weeks pregnant. Even though her cardiologist said that the pregnancy put Lee's life at risk, no hospital in Louisiana was willing to perform an abortion. The threats to Lee's life increased when organ donor networks discovered that she was pregnant and removed her name from the waiting list for a heart. Ultimately, Lee was able to obtain the abortion in Texas (Abortion Rights Activist 1998).

Even women in generally pro-choice states can find their lives put at risk by conscience-based exemptions. In 1998 a Manchester, New Hampshire, obstetrician was forced to send his patient by taxi to another hospital because the local hospital where he practiced refused to provide a medically necessary abortion for the woman, whose water had broken. Because it was unlikely that she could medically continue the pregnancy, and the fourteen-week-old fetus was clearly not viable, the appropriate medical response was for the physician to immediately perform an abortion. Failure to do so could result in the woman suffering a life-threatening infection. The local hospital, which had just merged with a Catholic one, refused to allow the doctor to perform the abortion (Meersman 1998, A4). Courts have ruled that conscience-based exemption laws in Alaska, Minnesota, and New Jersey are unconstitutional when invoked by public medical facilities.[56]

---

[55] Between 1982 and 1992 the number of abortion providers in Missouri dropped 59 percent, and 96 percent of the counties have no abortion providers (NARAL 1998, 72).

[56] The attorney general in Alaska issued an opinion that conscience-based exemptions violate the state constitution when applied to public nonsectarian medical facilities (Alaska Attorney General, Op. Attorney General No. 15, March 31, 1978). A court ruled the law was unconstitutional and issued a permanent injunction to prevent the use of the exemption by public medical facilities. See *Mat-Su Coalition for Choice v. Valley Hospital*, No. S-7417 (Alaska Nov. 21, 1997). The use of the conscience-based exemption by public facilities in Minnesota was ruled unconstitutional by a federal circuit court in 1976. See *Hodgson v. Lawson*, 542 F.2d 1350 (8th Cir. 1976). The New Jersey conscience-based exemption was held unconstitutional when applied to nonsectarian, nonprofit hospitals. See *Doe v. Bridgeton Hospital Association*, 366 A.2d 641 (N.J. 1976).

Counseling Bans

Six states (Louisiana, Missouri, North Dakota, Ohio, Pennsylvania, and Wisconsin) have enacted some version of a "gag rule" or counseling ban that prohibits health care providers from informing adult women about abortion services.[57] The Missouri statute prohibits only public employees from counseling a woman to have an abortion not necessary to save her life, but the Wisconsin law prohibits all entities receiving public funds from making abortion referrals unless the woman's life is at risk. The Ohio gag law prohibits agencies receiving state Department of Health funds from making abortion referrals unless there is a medical emergency. The Pennsylvania gag rule covers only those agencies receiving public funds whose primary purpose is to assist low-income pregnant women seeking abortion alternatives, but the Louisiana and North Dakota statutes are far more stringent. In Louisiana no state employee or person employed by a social service agency receiving governmental funds can "require or recommend" that a woman obtain an abortion. North Dakota law prohibits the use of state or federal funds to be used for family planning by a person, public agency, or private agency that recommends or makes referrals for abortions. The North Dakota law has been declared unconstitutional.[58]

Husband Consent or Notification Requirements

Four states (Kentucky, Pennsylvania, Rhode Island, and Utah) have laws requiring that under certain circumstances a husband be notified before his wife can obtain an abortion. Courts in all these states ruled that husband notification provisions are unconstitutional,[59] and Pennsylvania's notification requirement was ruled unconstitutional in *Casey* (1992). Five states (Colorado, Illinois, Louisiana, North Dakota, and South Carolina) passed laws requiring a husband's consent before a woman could obtain an abortion. The Louisiana law applied only to married women under the age of eighteen and is thus inapplicable to adult women. The specific provisions of the other husband consent laws vary but not on the basis of age. The Colorado law affected only married women who live with their husbands. In Illinois, a husband opposed to his wife's securing an abortion can seek an injunction prohibiting it. The law in North Dakota requires a husband's written consent before his wife aborts a potentially viable fetus, while in a similar vein, the South Carolina

[57] In 1996 Michigan enacted a ban against counseling applicable to adolescent health clinics and pregnancy prevention programs that receive funds from the state Department of Community Health. Because it is limited to minors, it was not included as a restriction on adult women.

[58] See *Valley Family Planning v. North Dakota*, 489 F.Supp. 238 (D.N.D. 1980), affirmed 661 F.2d 99 (8th Cir. 1981).

[59] See *Eubanks v. Brown*, 604 F.Supp. 141 (W.D. Ky. 1984); *Planned Parenthood of Rhode Island v. Board of Medical Review*, 598 F.Supp. 625 (D.R.I. 1984); and *Jane L. v. Bangerter*, 809 F.Supp. 865 (D. Utah 1992) and 61 F.3d 1493 (10th Cir. 1995).

statute requires the consent of the husband before a third trimester abortion. Louisiana and South Carolina's husband consent provisions were ruled unconstitutional before the Supreme Court ruled on the Pennsylvania notification requirement.[60]

Although the Supreme Court in *Casey* (1992) ruled that husband consent or notification laws were unconstitutional, the fact that nine states have such laws on their books indicates the extent to which state governments are willing to limit a woman's personhood status and her reproductive capacities.

Requiring the Payment of Extra Insurance Premiums

The legislatures in five states (Idaho, Kentucky, Missouri, North Dakota, and Rhode Island) have enacted laws that require insurance companies to offer abortion coverage only if an additional premium is paid. All but Rhode Island require insurance plans to exclude coverage of abortions that are not required to preserve the life of the woman unless the person pays an additional premium to purchase an optional rider. The Rhode Island law, which was declared unconstitutional in 1984, prohibited abortion coverage under basic insurance plans unless the life of the woman was threatened or the pregnancy was the result of rape or incest; broader abortion coverage required the purchase of an optional rider.[61]

Minnesota has a state-funded program that provides health insurance benefits for uninsured children and their families. Abortion coverage is not allowed under this plan unless the procedure is necessary to save the woman's life or if continuing the pregnancy would result in "substantial and irreversible impairment" of a major bodily function or if the pregnancy was caused by rape or incest.

Limits on Public Employees' Insurance Coverage

Eight states (Colorado, Illinois, Massachusetts, Michigan, Nebraska, Pennsylvania, Rhode Island, and Virginia) prohibit insurance companies that provide medical coverage for public employees or are paid for by public funds from including some forms of abortion coverage in their plans. The state constitution in Colorado proscribes the use of state funds to pay for abortions, and the state attorney general opined that group medical insurance plans covering state employees must exclude abortion coverage (Colorado Attorney General, Opinion of the Attorney General, February 6, 1985). In Illinois, Massachusetts, and Nebraska the insurance plans offered to state employees must exclude coverage of abortions not medically necessary to save the woman's

---

[60] See *Guste v. Jackson*, 429 U.S. 399 (1977) and *Floyd v. Anders*, 440 F.Supp. 535 (D.S.C. 1977).

[61] A federal court held that the exclusion of most abortions from medical insurance plans without an optional rider was unconstitutional. See *National Education Association v. Garraby*, 598 F.Supp. 1374 (D.R.I. 1984), affirmed 779 F.2d 790 (1st Cir. 1986).

life. In Michigan state employees or their dependents cannot be provided with abortion coverage unless the procedure is required to save the woman's life or if the coverage is mandated by civil service or as part of a union contract. The laws in Pennsylvania and Rhode Island are a bit more permissive, allowing state employee insurance plans to include abortion coverage for pregnancies resulting from rape or incest. The Rhode Island statute's inclusion of municipal employees was ruled unconstitutional.[62] The Virginia statute is the least restrictive because it allows state employee insurance providers to cover abortions if the woman's life is endangered by the pregnancy, if the pregnancy is the result of rape or incest, or if a physician certifies that the fetus has an incapacitating physical deformity or mental deficiency.

The Range of Informed Consent Provisions

Thirty states have informed consent laws that apply uniquely to abortion.[63] The provisions of the laws vary widely across the states. A few states have enacted general informed consent legislation, but most mandate very specific and detailed procedures. The informed consent laws differ with respect to the type of information provided to a pregnant woman interested in obtaining an abortion, the details covered, its mode of presentation, and the level of objectivity. Five general dimensions can be used to assess the relative stringency of the statutes: the form of communication, the amount and type of fetal development information, the type of medical information about abortion, medical information about childbirth, and the presentation of alternatives to abortion.

Some of the categories overlap significantly. For example, fetal development material can either be presented straightforwardly or in a manner that favors the pro-life position. The same applies to information that is presented about abortion. Although abortion is an extremely safe medical procedure when performed by a trained physician, some states attempting to scare women rather than inform them require the presentation of a litany of potential medical and psychological side effects, including the possibility of future infertility.

Forms of Communication

Some states use forms of communication that make it harder for a woman to choose an abortion. In general, the more pro-life states require verbal, face-to-face communication of at least some of the information rather than reliance

---

[62] See *National Education Association v. Garraby*, 598 F.Supp. 1374 (D.R.I. 1984).

[63] Although many states have laws requiring that physicians inform patients in advance of the risks associated with medical procedures, these states have separate laws that list specific informed consent requirements that apply only to patients seeking an abortion: Alabama, Alaska, California, Connecticut, Delaware, Florida, Idaho, Indiana, Kansas, Kentucky, Louisiana, Maine, Massachusetts, Michigan, Minnesota, Mississippi, Missouri, Montana, Nebraska, Nevada, North Dakota, Ohio, Pennsylvania, Rhode Island, South Carolina, South Dakota, Tennessee, Utah, Virginia, and Wisconsin.

on information packets, tape-recorded messages, or other nonpersonal means. Fifteen states specify that at least some information be communicated verbally,[64] while the rest either require the use of written material or do not specify a particular method.[65] Some of the more stringent states (Indiana, Louisiana, Montana, Nebraska, and Utah) require that women receive more than one verbal presentation. Several states require oral communication plus delivery of written material to the woman,[66] and a few states (Connecticut, Florida, Indiana, Massachusetts, and Rhode Island) require her to sign a statement confirming that she understands the implications of abortion.

Another way that a state can further the aims of the pro-life position is by directly communicating its opposition to abortion when a woman tries to obtain one. A strong pro-life bias is evident in the requirement that a woman seeking an abortion in Kentucky, Louisiana, or Utah be read or given a printed statement explicitly urging her to seek out public and private agencies that will assist her in carrying the pregnancy to term.

Fetal Development Information

Generally, the more information about fetal development the greater chance that the woman will begin to think about the fetus as a "person" and decide not to abort it. All but nine of the states with informed consent laws require that women be informed of the probable gestational age of their fetuses.[67] Pregnant women in Kansas,[68] Louisiana, Michigan, and Ohio must receive a packet of state-prepared materials about fetal development. The Michigan

[64] The fifteen states requiring oral communication are Connecticut, Delaware, Indiana, Louisiana, Michigan, Mississippi, Montana, Nebraska, North Dakota, Ohio, Pennsylvania, South Dakota, Tennessee, Utah, and Wisconsin. Michigan and Ohio require that every woman seeking an abortion receive both verbal and written information. The Ohio law specifies that a physician describe verbally or through some other nonwritten means the nature of the procedure, risks, and probable medical age of the fetus and give the patient a packet of state-prepared written materials. Montana requires two lectures, but a tape recording can be substituted for one face-to-face meeting.

[65] Massachusetts, Kansas, and Alabama specify that written materials constitute the primary means of information dissemination. The statutes in Maine, Rhode Island, Minnesota, Missouri, Florida, Kentucky, South Carolina, Virginia, Alaska, California, Idaho, and Nevada do not specify a means of communication.

[66] In addition to requiring some oral communication, the following states also mandate that a woman receive an informational packet: Alabama, Louisiana, Michigan, Ohio, and South Carolina. Kentucky, Maine, Mississippi, Montana, Nebraska, North Dakota, Pennsylvania, South Dakota, Utah, and Wisconsin offer additional written material, but the woman is not required to accept it. In most of these states the woman is offered the "right to review" additional material.

[67] The nine informed consent states that do not require disclosure of the gestational age are Alabama, Alaska, California, Connecticut, Florida, Idaho, Minnesota, Missouri, and Virginia.

[68] The Kansas publication *If You Are Pregnant* is an average informed consent document. Although the choice of pictures and text have a pro-life slant, the booklet presents the medical risks of both abortion and childbirth.

pamphlet describes the anatomical and physiological characteristics of the fetus at four-week gestational increments, and the Ohio and Louisiana packets include the chances of viability at two-week gestational increments. Another nine states mandate that women be offered specific materials about fetal development, and all but Kentucky require that depictions of physiological and anatomical developments in two-week gestational increments be included.[69]

A prime strategy of pro-life groups for a long time has been to use informed consent requirements as a means of forcing pregnant women to view fetal images (Petchesky 1987, 195). Louisiana and Ohio require that all women considering abortion receive color photographs of fetuses at various developmental stages. The Louisiana statute also mandates that the color photographs be enlarged. Michigan law requires depictions of fetuses at various stages but does not specify whether that means photographs or drawings. Another five states (Indiana, Mississippi, Pennsylvania, South Dakota, and Utah) include photographs of fetuses in their optional materials and the latter three require that the photos be in color and enlarged. Utah also requires that a woman be offered a chance to view a video showing ultrasound images of fetal heartbeats at monthly increments, beginning at a gestational age of three weeks, until the fetus reaches viability. If the woman refuses, she must receive a copy of the video. Finally, the laws in Tennessee and Wisconsin require that a woman be informed that physicians have a legal duty to care for potentially viable fetuses, and those in Kansas and Louisiana mandate that she be told of a duty to care for any child "born alive."

The Provision of Abortion Information

The states differ in the volume and types of abortion information that must be disseminated, and some are heavily weighted toward a pro-life position. Several states require that women be provided with factually inaccurate or misleading information. For example, the AUL's model informed consent law, which has served as a template for antiabortion activists across the country, includes the requirement that women be informed of the purported link between abortion and breast cancer (Americans United for Life 1996b). Based on its review of more than thirty studies, however, the National Cancer Institute (1996) charges that attempts to associate abortion with increased risk of breast cancer or deadlier forms of it "misrepresent the information in the scientific literature."

Only a basic, factual description of the procedure is required in seventeen states,[70] and twenty-seven (all but Minnesota, Florida, and South Carolina) require disclosure of possible risks associated with abortion. In South Carolina a

[69] The nine states that offer optional state-prepared packets about fetal development are Kentucky, Mississippi, Montana, Nebraska, North Dakota, Pennsylvania, South Carolina, South Dakota, and Utah.

[70] The seventeen states that require a woman be given a description of the abortion procedure are Alabama, California, Connecticut, Delaware, Idaho, Kansas, Louisiana, Maine, Michigan, Minnesota, Nevada, Ohio, Pennsylvania, Rhode Island, South Carolina, Utah, and Virginia.

discussion of abortion risks is included in an optional informational packet. The informed consent laws in ten states (Delaware, Idaho, Kansas, Mississippi, Montana, Nebraska, North Dakota, South Dakota, Utah, and Wisconsin) mandate disclosure of a specific list of risks. For example, North Dakota, Nebraska, and South Dakota require that women receive medically accurate warnings of the risks of infection, hemorrhaging, danger to subsequent pregnancies, and infertility. Mississippi and Montana add breast cancer to the list, and Delaware, Idaho, Kansas, and Utah require disclosure of the impact on future childbearing. Five states (Alaska, Indiana, Michigan, Utah, and Wisconsin) require that women receive information about the emotional and psychological impact of abortion, and it is part of an optional package in Montana and Nebraska.

Of course, informed consent should be expected before any surgical procedure, so a law requiring that abortion providers follow this procedure does not necessarily further the pro-life position. But states that require detailed disclosures of specific and extremely rare complications or possible emotional and psychological effects deviate from standard medical practice to frighten women away from having abortions.[71] Tennessee law provides another example of the ways that informed consent laws can be used to frighten women. The law requires that as part of a state-mandated lecture a physician tell a woman "that in a considerable number of cases abortion constitutes a major surgical procedure," but it does not require that similar language be used in discussing childbirth.[72]

The Provision of Childbirth Information

Because the alternative to abortion is childbirth, any comprehensive informed consent law would require a discussion of childbirth and its associated risks. Only seventeen states mandate disclosure of the risks associated with giving birth, but none specifies such risks;[73] in South Carolina it is optional.

As we have seen, the presentation of information about the risks associated with the two procedures is not comparable. Even though a 1982 study found that the mortality rate for pregnancy-related causes is roughly twelve times greater than the comparable rate from abortion-related causes (Scales with Chavkin 1996, 220), more states require a discussion of abortion risks, including some that mandate disclosure of extremely remote risks. Although none treats childbirth comparably, eleven states (Connecticut, Massachusetts, Rhode Island, Missouri, Wisconsin, Delaware, Kentucky, Alaska, California,

---

[71] Medical studies have found no evidence of women suffering from abortion-induced psychological trauma. See, for example, Stotland 1992.

[72] A court has ruled that the "major surgical procedure" language in the state-mandated lecture is unconstitutional. See *Planned Parenthood Association of Nashville, Inc. v. McWherter*, No. 92C-1672 (Tenn. Davidson Cty. Ct. Aug. 23, 1995).

[73] The seventeen states that require a general discussion of unenumerated risks associated with childbirth are Alabama, Indiana, Kansas, Louisiana, Maine, Michigan, Mississippi, Montana, Nebraska, North Dakota, Ohio, Pennsylvania, South Dakota, Tennessee, Utah, Virginia, and Wisconsin.

Idaho, and Nevada) are especially biased in their presentation of information, requiring the dissemination of specific and wide-ranging risks from abortion but not from childbirth.

The Presentation of Alternatives to Abortion

Finally, informed consent laws vary with respect to requirements about the presentation of alternatives to abortion. The laws in five states (Minnesota, Nevada, South Dakota, Tennessee, and Virginia) lack even general requirements that such alternatives be presented. Eighteen states mandate the dissemination of general information covering alternatives, and another seven states grant women the option to receive it.[74]

The laws in some states specify the types of information about alternatives to be given or made available to women. The disclosure of adoption as an alternative is mandatory in only eleven states and part of an optional package in another seven states.[75] Seventeen states mandate that women be informed that public aid for indigent pregnant women exists,[76] and two states (Florida and Maine) include such information as part of optional packages. Finally, eleven states direct that women be told that fathers are responsible for providing support for children.[77]

Measuring the Pro-Life Content of State Abortion Laws

As we have seen, there are enormous differences in abortion laws in the fifty states. To estimate the relative pro-life content of the statutes in each state, a composite measure that assigned points for each aspect of a state's abortion laws that either constrained the abortion choice or facilitated the choice to continue a pregnancy was created. Potential scores range from 0 to 24, with higher scores indicating that the laws reflect the pro-life position.

---

[74] The eighteen states that require that a woman be informed of alternatives to abortion are Alabama, California, Connecticut, Delaware, Idaho, Indiana, Kansas, Kentucky, Louisiana, Massachusetts, Michigan, Missouri, Nebraska, Ohio, Rhode Island, South Carolina, Utah, and Wisconsin. In addition, Alaska, Florida, Maine, Mississippi, Montana, North Dakota, and Pennsylvania require that a woman be given the opportunity to receive additional information about abortion alternatives.

[75] In Alabama, Idaho, Indiana, Kansas, Kentucky, Louisiana, Michigan, Ohio, Rhode Island, Utah, and Wisconsin a woman must be specifically informed about adoption as an alternative to abortion, but in Maine, Pennsylvania, North Dakota, Nebraska, Mississippi, South Carolina, and Montana it is part of an optional informational packet.

[76] The seventeen states that require disclosure of sources of public assistance for pregnant women are Idaho, Indiana, Kansas, Kentucky, Louisiana, Michigan, Mississippi, Montana, Nebraska, North Dakota, Ohio, Pennsylvania, South Carolina, South Dakota, Tennessee, Utah, and Wisconsin.

[77] The eleven states that require that a woman be informed of the father's legal responsibility for providing support for a child are Indiana, Kansas, Louisiana, Mississippi, Montana, Nebraska, North Dakota, Ohio, Pennsylvania, South Dakota, and Utah.

States with lower scores place fewer restrictions on access to abortion and tend to treat abortion and pregnancy as medical procedures, reflecting a pro-choice position.

For each state a score was calculated that assigned points for laws with each of the following characteristics: mandatory waiting periods, limits on the use of public funds for Medicaid abortions, conscience-based exemptions for medical professionals or facilities, bans on counseling about abortion, husband consent or notification, payment of an extra insurance premium for coverage of abortions, limits on public employees' insurance coverage of abortions, informed consent, encouragement to continue the pregnancy, mandated verbal communication, at least two mandatory lectures, written materials in addition to oral communication, required signature on consent forms, mandated disclosure of fetal gestational age, mandatory state-prepared materials on fetal development, mandatory provision of fetal photographs at different gestational ages, required disclosure of the physician's duty to care for viable fetus or a child born alive, mandatory provision of detailed information about specified risks of abortion, required disclosure of possible psychological and emotional complications of abortion, required disclosure of the risks of abortion but not childbirth, mandated dissemination of options to abortion, provision of adoption information, disclosure of possible sources of public assistance, and required mention of father's responsibility to provide for a child.

The composite scores ranged from a low of 1 to a high of 17. Despite the passage of laws restricting abortion in every state, most had relatively low scores. Roughly half of the states have composite scores of less than five points. Table 3.3 lists the states that fall into each of four quartiles reflecting the degree to which their abortion laws attempt to discourage the practice: pro–abortion rights, minimal restrictions on abortion, moderately pro-life, and strongly pro-life.

The pro-life content of state laws restricting access to abortion and postviability abortion bans are highly congruent. States with laws on access to abortion that are generally supportive of abortion rights are less likely to have enacted postviability abortion bans. Nearly all of the states classified as strongly pro-life on the basis of their laws governing abortion access also had enacted laws banning postviability abortions. Kansas and Wisconsin are the only states with strongly pro-life scores that do not have bans on postviability abortions. In contrast, of the nine states without postviability abortion bans, five (New Jersey, Vermont, West Virginia, Hawaii, and Oregon) were classified as pro–abortion rights, three (Alaska, Colorado, and New Mexico) were classified as minimally restrictive, and one (Mississippi) was classified as moderately pro-life.

There is less congruence between states' positions on partial birth abortions and their level of restrictiveness on abortion access. Five of the strongly pro-life states (Kansas, Kentucky, North Dakota, Pennsylvania, and Wisconsin) have not enacted bans on partial birth abortions, but only one state that is classified as pro–abortion rights adopted a partial birth abortion ban.

Table 3.3. Strictness of state abortion limitations by region (as of January 1998)

Pro-abortion rights	Minimal restrictions	Moderately pro-life	Strongly pro-life
Northeast			
New Hampshire	Maine (4)	Connecticut (6)	Pennsylvania (10)
New Jersey		Massachusetts (8)	Rhode Island (11)
New York			
Vermont			
Midwest			
	Illinois (2)	Missouri (7)	Indiana (14)
	Iowa (2)		Kansas (11)
	Minnesota (2)		Michigan (14)
			Nebraska (12)
			North Dakota (12)
			Ohio (14)
			South Dakota (10)
			Wisconsin (13)
South			
Maryland	Arkansas (2)	Alabama (5)	Kentucky (12)
West Virginia	Georgia (2)	Delaware (9)	Louisiana (17)
	North Carolina (2)	Florida (5)	
	Oklahoma (2)	Mississippi (9)	
	Texas (2)	South Carolina (9)	
	Virginia (4)	Tennessee (8)	
West			
Hawaii	Arizona (2)	Alaska (5)	Utah (14)
Oregon	California (4)	Idaho (9)	
Washington	Colorado (4)	Montana (8)	
	New Mexico (2)	Nevada (6)	
	Wyoming (2)		

Note: States with a composite score (shown in parentheses) of 1 point were classified as pro-abortion rights. Those with composite scores from 2 to 4 were classified as favoring minimal restrictions. States with scores from 5 to 9 were classified as moderately pro-life while states with scores greater than 9 were classified as strongly pro-life.

Restrictions on Minors

More than three-quarters of all states have enacted laws restricting an un-emancipated minor's access to abortion services. The major statutory distinction is between states that require parental consent and those that have mandatory parental notification, although a few require counseling. An additional distinction is whether the consent or notification laws allow judicial bypass (allow a judge to issue a court order allowing the minor to obtain an abortion without satisfying the parental consent or notification requirements). The ostensible intent of parental consent/notification laws is to ensure parental involvement in this very important health-related decision. Researchers (Clary

1982; Cartoof and Klerman 1986; Blum, Resnick, and Stark 1987, 1990) have found that minors usually consult with their parents before seeking abortions; this is particularly true of younger women.

Although judicial bypass procedures appear to provide an opportunity for young women in troubled homes to obtain abortions without putting additional strains on their family relationships, judges vary widely in their willingness to approve such measures. Christine Sensibaugh and Elizabeth Allegeir (1996) conducted the first study of the decision-making criteria used by judges in deciding whether to issue a court order allowing a minor to obtain an abortion. They found there were large differences in the criteria used by judges and in their weighing of the criteria. The authors also found that judges varied enormously in their willingness to grant judicial bypasses. Some judges never did so, while others granted nearly all requests. This finding is consistent with earlier research (Koff 1993) showing that judges differed in the likelihood of granting a judicial bypass to minors seeking abortions. In some cases, minors are advised to "shop" for a judge with a history of leniency or to travel to another state to avoid parental consent/notification requirements entirely (Koff 1993).

Parental Consent Laws

The twenty-two states with laws that require parental consent before a minor girl can have an abortion differ with respect to whether one or both parents must consent; procedures, if any, to bypass the consent requirements; and additional conditions to obtaining an abortion.

Only three states (Massachusetts, Mississippi, and North Dakota) have laws requiring the consent of two parents, and all allow a minor to petition for a court order stating that she is mature enough to make the decision on her own. A court found the Massachusetts law unconstitutional, and the Supreme Court has found a two-parent notification law unconstitutional because it does not protect the right of a minor to obtain an abortion if it is in her best interest.[78]

The nineteen states with one-parent consent requirements provide various means for the minor to obtain an abortion without such consent. The laws are not being enforced in three states (Alaska, Colorado, and New Mexico) that lack judicial bypass procedures or any other way for the minor to obtain an abortion without the consent of a parent.[79] The remaining sixteen states

[78] A court held that the Massachusetts two-parent consent requirement was an unconstitutional violation of the *Declaration of Rights* that provides greater protection of reproductive choice than the national Constitution. See *Planned Parenthood League of Massachusetts v. Attorney General*, 677 N.E.2d 101 (Mass. 1977). Also in *Hodgson v. Minnesota*, 497 U.S. 417 (1990), the Supreme Court ruled that a minor has the right to have an abortion without notifying both parents.

[79] The Alaska attorney general issued an opinion that the state's one-parent consent law was unconstitutional in 1981 (Alaska Attorney General, Opinion J-66-81681, October 7, 1981), and the attorney general of New Mexico issued a similar opinion in 1990 (New Mexico Attorney General,

have one-parent consent laws that allow judicial bypass.[80] Two of these (North Carolina and South Carolina) allow a grandparent to consent under some conditions, and Wisconsin allows a grandparent, aunt, uncle, or sibling over the age of twenty-five to give permission. Wyoming law allows a minor to get an abortion without parental consent if she gets a court order and waits forty-eight hours following written notice to a parent of her intent to have an abortion.

Although supporters of these laws point out the need for parents to be involved in decisions affecting the physical health and well-being of their children, one effect of such laws is to delay the point at which an abortion is performed, resulting in later and more risky abortion procedures. Minors who become pregnant unexpectedly typically find it more difficult than adult women to decide on whether to have abortions or continue the pregnancy and are, therefore, more likely to end up having abortions later than are adult women. Government-mandated delays such as parental consent/notification laws and judicial bypass requirements exacerbate the problem (Melton 1987; Melton and Russo 1987).

A second effect of these requirements is an increase in the number of young women getting black market abortions. Karen Bell testified before the Senate Judiciary Committee that her daughter was afraid to tell her that she was pregnant and tried to avoid Indiana's parental consent law by obtaining an illegal abortion. She died as a result of medical complications resulting from a botched abortion (Carey 1998b, 1394).

Parental Notification Laws

Two states (Arkansas and Minnesota) that have two-parent notification laws allow for judicial bypass, but two other states (Idaho and Utah) do not have judicial bypass provisions in their two-parent notification laws. These states do not make the two-parent notification requirement mandatory; instead it should be followed "if possible."[81] Arkansas and Minnesota also require the minor to wait forty-eight hours after her parents have been notified before getting an abortion.

Opinion No. 90-19, October 3, 1990). Colorado's one-parent consent law was ruled unconstitutional in *Foe v. Vanderhoof*, 389 F.supp. 947 (D. Colo. 1975).

[80] The sixteen states with single-parent consent laws that allow judicial bypass are Alabama, Arizona, California, Indiana, Kentucky, Louisiana, Maine, Michigan, Missouri, North Carolina, Pennsylvania, Rhode Island, South Carolina, Tennessee, Wisconsin, and Wyoming. These laws are not being enforced in Arizona and California. In Arizona a court issued an injunction to halt enforcement. See *Planned Parenthood of Southern Arizona, Inc. v. Neeley*, 804 F.Supp. 1210 (D. Ariz. 1992). A California court ruled that the provision was unconstitutional and issued a permanent injunction against enforcement. See *American Academy of Pediatrics v. Lungren*, 32 Cal. Rptr. 2d 546 (Cal. App. 1994) and 882 P.2d 247 (Cal. 1994).

[81] It is unclear whether the language in the Idaho and Utah two-parent notification laws will withstand judicial challenge. In *Hodgson v. Minnesota*, 497 U.S. 417 (1990), the Supreme Court ruled that a minor's access to abortion without two-parent notification must be protected if it is in her best interest.

The single-parent notification laws, existing in thirteen states,[82] have different requirements regarding judicial bypass, mandatory waiting periods, and nonparental notification. Only Maryland does not have a judicial bypass provision in its single parent notification statutes, but a court found the Nevada judicial bypass procedures to be inadequate.[83] Four states (Kansas, Maryland, Nevada, and Virginia) do not have mandatory waiting periods following parental notification. A twenty-four-hour wait is required in Delaware, Georgia, Ohio, and West Virginia, while a forty-eight-hour wait is mandatory in Illinois, Iowa, Montana, Nebraska, and South Dakota. Most of the states have provisions allowing someone other than a parent to be notified of the minor's decision to have an abortion. Five (Delaware, Kansas, Maryland, Virginia, and West Virginia) allow the parental notification requirement to be waived by health professionals under certain circumstances.[84] Illinois and Iowa allow for the notification of a grandparent instead of a parent, and Ohio allows for a grandparent, stepparent, or adult sibling to substitute for a parent. The Kansas statute also requires mandatory counseling from a medical professional or qualified counselor. At the end of 1997, single-parent notification laws were being enforced in all of these states except Illinois, Iowa, and Montana.[85]

Two states (Connecticut and Maine) restrict a minor's access to abortion in ways that fit neither parental consent nor notification laws. The Connecticut law more closely resembles the informed consent laws for adult women than the typical parental consent or notification laws for minors. A minor under sixteen cannot obtain an abortion until she has received counseling from a physician, nurse, physician's assistant, or qualified counselor who will discuss alternative choices, including abortion as well as adoption; offer to provide a list of public and private agencies to help her; and discuss the possibility of consulting her parents or relatives about the decision. The Maine law combines features of a typical parental consent law with aspects of the Connecticut law. A minor under eighteen must obtain the consent of a parent or an adult family member unless she gets counseling from a physician, nurse, physician's

[82] The thirteen states with one parent notification laws are Delaware, Georgia, Illinois, Iowa, Kansas, Maryland, Montana, Nebraska, Nevada, Ohio, South Dakota, Virginia, and West Virginia.

[83] A court held that the Nevada law's judicial bypass provisions were constitutionally inadequate and issued a permanent injunction to prevent them from being enforced. See *Glick v. McKay*, 937 F.2d 434 (9th Cir. 1991).

[84] In Delaware a grandparent or mental health professional can certify that an abortion is in the best interest of the minor.

[85] A court issued a permanent injunction prohibiting the enforcement of the Illinois statute. See *Zbaraz v. Ryan*, No. 84 C 771 (N.D. Ill. Feb. 9, 1996). A temporary restraining order has stopped enforcement of the law in Montana. See *Wicklund v. State*, No. ADV-97-671 (Mont. Dist. Ct. Nov. 3, 1997). A court ruled the judicial bypass provisions inadequate in the Nevada law, and a permanent injunction was issued. See *Glick v. McKay*, 937 F.2d 434 (9th Cir. 1991). Although the Iowa law is still being enforced, a lawsuit was filed requesting a court order enjoining its enforcement. See *Planned Parenthood of Greater Iowa v. Miller*, No. 496CV10877 (S.D. Iowa filed Aug. 1, 1997).

assistant, or counselor regarding alternative choices for managing the pregnancy; information on prenatal care, alternatives to abortion, and agencies that could assist her; and the possibility of involving her parents or family members in the process. The minor may ask the court to grant her majority rights for the purpose of making the abortion decision without her parents.

Measuring the Restrictiveness of Laws Governing Minors

Although the state laws governing minors' access to abortion are usually characterized as parental consent or notification statutes, their actual content varied significantly across states. A composite measure of the relative restrictiveness (i.e., pro-life content) of the provisions was developed. For each state a score was calculated that assigned points according to whether the law restricted minors' access to abortion, had mandatory parental consent or notification provisions, required the consent or notification of both parents, did not allow for judicial bypass, did not provide a means for another adult relative or a professional to substitute for the parent(s), required a mandatory waiting period, and required mandatory counseling before an abortion. Higher scores are associated with more restrictive state laws governing a minor's access to abortion services and indicate the adoption of relatively pro-life policies. Possible scores range from zero to seven, but the highest actual composite score is five. The distribution of scores across the states conforms to the normal bell-shaped curve. Twenty-one states have the modal score of three, with fourteen lower and sixteen higher scores.

The geographic pattern is generally similar to that found for adult women's access, with some important differences. The Midwest is the most restrictive region for both adult women and minors, while the Northeast and West are the least restrictive. With regard to minors, however, far more states, especially in the South and the West, are in the two most restrictive categories. The difference in the South is most pronounced in Maryland and West Virginia, which shift from the least restrictive category (first quartile) for adult women to the second most restrictive category (third quartile) for minors. In the West the biggest shifts occur in New Mexico and Wyoming, which move from the minimal restrictions category (second quartile) for adult women to the stringent restrictions category (fourth quartile) for minors. The greater restrictiveness is probably owing to increased concern about the preservation of general parental authority over minors, as well as the efforts of pro-life forces. Table 3.4 summarizes the restrictiveness of state laws governing minors' access to abortion services.

Measuring the Overall Restrictiveness of Abortion Laws

To assess the overall stringency of state abortion laws, I measured the restrictiveness of the abortion bans, partial birth and postviability bans, other limitations on adult women's access to abortion, and finally, restrictions ap-

Table 3.4. State restrictions on minors' access to abortions by region (as of January 1998)

No restrictions	Minor restrictions	Average restrictions	Stringent restrictions
Northeast			
New Hampshire	Connecticut	Maine	Massachusetts (4)
New Jersey		Pennsylvania	
New York		Rhode Island	
Vermont			
Midwest			
	Wisconsin	Illinois	Minnesota (5)
		Indiana	Nebraska (4)
		Iowa	North Dakota (4)
		Kansas	South Dakota (4)
		Michigan	
		Missouri	
		Ohio	
South			
Florida	North Carolina	Alabama	Arkansas (5)
Oklahoma	South Carolina	Delaware	Georgia (4)
Texas		Kentucky	Mississippi (4)
		Louisiana	
		Maryland	
		Tennessee	
		Virginia	
		West Virginia	
West			
Hawaii		Arizona	Alaska (4)
Oregon		California	Idaho (5)
Washington		Colorado	Montana (4)
		Utah	Nevada (4)
			New Mexico (4)
			Wyoming (4)

Note: The minor restrictions category consists of states with a composite score (shown in parentheses) of 2, and the average restrictions category consists of states with a composite score of 3. The states in the stringent restrictions category have composite scores greater than 3.

plicable only to minors. The scores reflect a continuum of the different types of abortion laws that states have enacted. Possible scores range from zero to thirty-four. Higher scores indicate that pro-life positions are reflected in the abortion laws while lower scores reflect pro-choice orientations. Scores ranged from a low of one point, which was awarded to Hawaii and Oregon, to a high of twenty-three points in Louisiana. States were then divided into quartiles based on the overall restrictiveness of their abortion laws.

This approach differs from previous scholarship in several important ways. First, this study included abortion bans (both those enacted before and after *Roe*) as part of the measure of restrictiveness. Previous researchers, most notably Glen Halva-Neubauer (1990, 1993), have not included the pre-*Roe* abortion bans

Table 3.5. Overall restrictiveness of abortion laws by region (as of January 1998)

Pro-abortion rights	Minimal restrictions	Moderately pro-life	Strongly pro-life
Northeast			
New Hampshire (2)	Connecticut (9)	Massachusetts (14)	Rhode Island (16)
New Jersey (2)	Maine (8)	Pennsylvania (14)	
New York (2)			
Vermont (2)			
Midwest			
	Illinois (7)	Missouri (11)	Indiana (19)
	Iowa (6)	South Dakota (14)	Kansas (15)
	Minnesota (8)		Michigan (20)
			Nebraska (18)
			North Dakota (17)
			Ohio (19)
			Wisconsin (17)
South			
Maryland (5)	Florida (6)	Alabama (11)	Delaware (15)
North Carolina (5)	Georgia (8)	Arkansas (10)	Kentucky (16)
Oklahoma (4)	Virginia (8)	South Carolina (13)	Louisiana (23)
Texas (4)		Tennessee (13)	Mississippi (15)
West Virginia (5)			
West			
Hawaii (1)	Arizona (8)	Alaska (10)	Idaho (15)
Oregon (1)	California (9)	Montana (14)	Utah (20)
Washington (2)	Colorado (8)	Nevada (11)	
	New Mexico (7)		
	Wyoming (7)		

Note: States with a composite score of less than 6 were classified as pro-abortion rights. Those with composite scores from 6 to 9 were classified as favoring minimal restrictions. States with scores from 10 to 14 were classified as moderately pro-life while states with scores greater than 14 were classified as strongly pro-life.

when measuring the restrictiveness of state laws. I chose to include them to obtain a comprehensive measure of abortion laws on the books in each state, because we cannot discount the possibility that *Roe* will be overturned. Moreover, most states chose to repeal these bans so I consider the failure to do so a signal of opposition to abortion. Second, I examined the substantive content of abortion laws and regulations and did not simply count the number of enactments. Because individual regulations in a particular category of abortion law can vary widely in the number of restrictions on the abortion choice, this approach better assesses the restrictiveness of state laws. The findings are summarized in Table 3.5.

States differ significantly in the numbers and types of abortion regulations. Some of the differences reflect distinctions between minors and women in general, but some relate to geography. Although every geographic region except the Midwest is represented in each of the four quartiles, there are important regional differences. When all types of abortion laws and regulations are considered, statutes in the midwestern states are far more likely than those in other portions of the country to reflect the pro-life position. No midwestern state falls in the least restrictive quartile. Somewhat surprisingly, the southern states are fairly evenly represented in each of the four quartiles, while the Northeast and West tilt toward the pro-choice end of the continuum.

Distinctions based on the type of law are more dramatic. The strong pro-life positions in the Midwest are not the result of the old pre-*Roe* abortion bans because all but two midwestern states (Wisconsin and Michigan) repealed them after *Roe*. But every state in the region has banned postviability abortions, and most also have prohibited partial birth abortions as well. Also, several states, particularly in the South and West, have enacted more restrictions on minors than on adult women, as the normal coalition of pro-life forces have successfully framed the issue as a question of parental rights and child welfare rather than one of abortion.

Summary

Regardless of geographic region, abortion continues to be a hotly contested issue, and deeply committed individuals and organizations are active in all states. Because it is rooted in strongly held and disparate views of morality, there is little room for compromise and scant chance that it will disappear from the political arena in the near future. Although public opinion polls consistently indicate heavy support for abortion as a legal option, a majority of respondents are willing to accept some limitations. Throughout the 1980s and early 1990s pro-life groups tried to capitalize on this by enacting a range of restrictions on access to abortion. The effectiveness of this incrementalist approach varied, depending on whether the woman seeking an abortion was an adult or a minor, the gestational age of the fetus, the type of abortion procedure, and the region of the country.

More recently, pro-life efforts have focused on building support for limited abortion bans, either based on gestational age of the fetus or on the type of procedure. These efforts have been extremely successful; by January 1998 postviability bans had been adopted in forty-one states and partial birth abortion bans had been enacted in nineteen states. There is no indication that these efforts will slow in future years. Because pro-life groups have been effective in building support for bans on late-term abortions, they are continually attempting to find new ways to reinforce the view that late-term fetuses and newborn infants are essentially the same. For example, in early 1998 a California assembly member, George Runner Jr. (R-Lancaster), introduced legislation requiring that anesthesia be given to fetuses aborted during the third trimester. The politics of the proposal were summed up by assembly member Scott Baugh (R-Huntington Beach). "If someone admits that a fetus is being tormented by the abortion, then they're a step closer to saying the procedure shouldn't be permitted" (Warren 1998, A24).

CHAPTER 4

Prenatal Drug Exposure and Third-Party Fetal Killings

One-Sided Morality Policymaking and Fetal Status

Although both prenatal drug exposure and acts of violence against pregnant women can severely harm the fetus, the two engender very different politics. The term "fetal abuse" is applied only to physical and developmental harms caused by prenatal drug exposure and not to cases when a third party knifes, shoots, kicks, or hits a pregnant woman and harms the fetus. Politicians and the media have devoted a great deal of attention to the former but comparatively little to the latter.

Individuals and groups that have mobilized to protect fetal life threatened by abortionists and substance-abusing pregnant women have not exhibited the same outrage against third parties who kill fetuses. Despite research indicating that pregnant women are at least 35 percent more likely to be physically abused by their partners than are nonpregnant women (Gelles 1988, 844–45),[1] political entrepreneurs have not exploited the issue for electoral gain. Even the surgeon general's denunciation of third-party fetal killings failed to increase the political salience of the issue.[2] Few seem to care about the injuries and loss of fetal life caused by acts of violence against pregnant women and their fetuses.

The politics and policy dichotomies arising from these two fetal issues raise fundamental questions about the validity of the arguments by pro-life groups

[1] Most researchers believe that roughly 4 to 8 percent of all pregnant women are battered during their pregnancies and that up to 15 percent of other pregnant women must be considered at risk because of previous physical abuse (Hillard 1985, 186; Helton 1987, 5; Amaro, Fried, Cabral, Zuckerman, and Levenson 1988, 1).

[2] In 1992 the surgeon general reported that between two and four million women are battered annually, making battering the leading cause of injury among women of childbearing age (Novello, Rosenberg, Saltzman, and Shosky 1992, 3132). See also Goldberg and Tomlanovich 1984; McLeer and Anwar 1989; Abbott, Johnson, Koziol-McLain, and Lowenstein 1995; and Dearwater, Coben, Campbell, Nah, Glass, McLoughlin, Bekemeier 1998.

about the sanctity of all innocent human life (born and unborn) and about the generalizability of the morality policy framework developed by Meier (1994) and other scholars. Most notably, why do some one-sided morality issues emerge as potent political mobilizers while others fail to generate attention? In this chapter I consider the very different politics regarding these two fetal issues.

Policy Responses to Substance Abuse by Pregnant Women

Unlike abortion, which has been debated continuously since and sporadically before the *Roe v. Wade* decision in 1973, fetal abuse has been part of the policy agenda for only a relatively short time. Despite an actual decline in drug use during the 1980s, the public in 1990 ranked drugs just behind poverty and homelessness as the country's worst noneconomic problem (Gallup and Newport 1990), largely in reaction to media stories about crack cocaine and crack babies.

The Role of the Media in Defining the Problem

Even though the biggest actual increase in cocaine usage occurred in the 1970s, when many middle-class individuals began taking cocaine, the media did not focus attention on drug use until the "crack" epidemic of the mid-1980s (Reinarman and Levine 1997, 18). The word "crack" was first used to refer to a type of cocaine in a 1985 newspaper article.[3] By the end of 1986 more than a thousand articles about crack had appeared in major newspapers and magazines and *CBS News* had aired a prime-time report on the crack epidemic viewed by fifteen million people (Feldman, Espada, Penn, and Byrd 1993, 133; Inciardi 1993, 37). In 1986, *Time* and *Newsweek* each devoted five cover stories to the crack epidemic in America (Reinarman and Levine 1997, 20). According to James Inciardi (1993, 37), *Newsweek* devoted more coverage to crack than it had to any national issue since Vietnam and President Richard Nixon's resignation. Much of the coverage was highly sensational (Bourgeois and Dunlop 1993, 97–98), and some media outlets compared the devastation wrought by crack use in the cities to that of the plague in medieval times (Inciardi 1993, 37).

The use of the drug by pregnant women and the resulting crack babies figured prominently in nearly all the media accounts. Media portrayals of crack-addicted women often focused on their willingness to do anything, no matter how degrading, to obtain the drug, and the destruction of women's natural "maternal instincts" (Gomez 1997, 15–16). For example, in a six-month period, the *Los Angeles Times* ran three long articles, two with pictures, about a group offering to pay two hundred dollars to women addicted to crack if they would undergo sterilization (Ourlian 1997; Morrison 1997; Smith 1998).

---

[3] This article appeared in the *New York Times* on November 17, 1985 (Feldman, Espada, Penn, and Byrd 1993, 133).

Much of the concern about fetal abuse arose from the dramatic increase in the number of drug-exposed infants, but studies (Glink 1991; Gomez 1997) have shown that these portrayals of crack babies and the crack epidemic were extremely one-sided. To some degree, this is a function of the journalistic need to attract readers by "hooking" them by beginning articles with human inter-est anecdotes (Bertin and Beck 1996, 41).[4] If such anecdotal portrayals are typ-ical of common experience, they are instructive. If apocryphal, like the stories of crack-addicted women, they tend to distort public perception. For example, one newspaper story described a "typical" inner city crack addict as an African American woman who let her five children go hungry because she traded the family's food stamps for drugs (Stern 1990).

Not only did the human interest stories about drug-exposed infants emphasize the worst cases but reporting of scientific research on prenatal exposure was also highly biased. Joan Bertin and Laurie Beck (1996, 43–44) found that scientific studies, even in the most prestigious medical journals, which concluded that the effects of drug exposure were massively overstated, were not picked up by the popular press, whereas studies showing problems were extensively reported.[5]

Public opinion polling data reflected the media's focus on the drug problem. The percentage of survey respondents ranking drugs as "America's most seri-ous problem" increased from 2 to 13 percent during the six-month period in 1986 when the media's coverage was the greatest (Jensen, Gerber, and Bab-cock 1991, 656). According to Shona Glink (1991, 538–539), the public's strong support for the use of criminal sanctions against pregnant addicts is traceable to the media's vilification of them.[6] Moreover, researchers have found that state and local politicians respond rapidly to local media coverage of policy problems under their purview (Schroeder 1995, 105–6).

The Politics of Fetal Abuse

According to Meier (1994, 247), one-sided morality issues generate a "poli-tics of sin" featuring universal opprobrium of those engaging in the activity and a discourse dominated by political entrepreneurs who "compete to be the

[4] By the late 1990s most of the hysteria generated by the crack scare of the previous decade had abated. Media stories about a new drug scare, a crank epidemic in the nation's heartland, have not resulted in a new wave of public concern. Even human interest stories featuring suffering babies exposed to crank in utero have gained the attention of neither the public nor policymakers. It is still too early to tell whether the lack of a response is owing to public weariness over "drug ba-bies" and their problems or the fact that a majority of the women using crank while pregnant are white rather than minority women. For examples of recent media articles on crank, see Pasternak 1998a and Kirn 1998.

[5] See also Koran, Grahm, Shear, and Einarson 1989.

[6] For more on biases in the media coverage of the crack epidemic, see Williams 1990 and Bower 1995. For a more general analysis of racial and gender biases in the media coverage of drug abuse and government public service announcements warning against the dangers of narcotics use, see Ellwood 1994.

most aggressive morality advocates." I examine whether the issue of substance abuse by pregnant women fits Meier's "politics of sin" characterization and whether the policy debate is dominated by "morality advocates."

To some degree, politics of sin is an accurate characterization. Pregnant women who use drugs violate our fundamental cultural beliefs about motherhood. According to psychologists, "the predominant image of the mother in white Western society is the ever-bountiful, ever-giving, self-sacrificing mother" (Bassin, Honey, and Kaplan 1994, 2). Rather than placing the needs of her child above all else, a pregnant woman who uses drugs is viewed as self-indulgent, placing her desire to get "high" ahead of the need of her offspring to be born healthy. Instead of a happy, plump, gurgling Gerber baby, the addict gives birth to a crack baby, whose suffering has been captured by print journalists and television commentators. Crack babies have figured prominently in a dozen movies, and at least two different pop music songs claim the title "Crack Babies" (Gomez 1997, 3).

The media depiction of drug-using pregnant women is not accurate. The typical female addict was physically and sexually abused as a child and often started using drugs out of a desire to self-medicate (i.e., temporarily escape the pain caused by physical abuse, rape, or incest) (Leff 1990, E1; Roberts 1991; Paltrow 1992, iv). But the media rarely tell this story, perhaps because it is more complicated than the simplistic moral tale of the bad woman harming her innocent unborn child. Jean Schroedel and Paul Peretz (1994) found that the *New York Times* in 1989, 1990, and 1991 printed thirty-four articles about fetal abuse. Of the 853.5 column inches devoted to the problems of infants exposed prenatally to drugs or alcohol, nearly 200 column inches were taken up by pictures, mostly of the infants and children harmed by their mothers' substance abuse. Less than half of the articles discussed mitigating circumstances that might have led to the substance abuse or the lack of treatment programs that make it difficult for pregnant addicts to end their drug use.

Public opinion polls report virtually universal condemnation of women who expose their infants to illegal drugs in utero. In one survey, fifteen hundred people were asked what should be done with women whose drug use while pregnant hurt their unborn children, and 71 percent favored sending the women to jail (Hoffman 1990, 33). In a 1989 *ABC News* poll, 82 percent agreed with the following statement: "A pregnant woman, who uses crack cocaine and addicts her unborn child should be put in jail for child abuse" (Roth 1997 cited in Gomez 1997, 26). Another poll, using somewhat different wording, also uncovered strong support for criminal prosecutions of such women ("Courts" 1991). Many take a stronger position: punishing women for legal behaviors, such as drinking, that have the potential to inflict harm on the fetus (Kantrowitz, Quade, Fisher, Hill, and Beachy 1991, 52).

Much of the public debate has been dominated by political entrepreneurs, but their impact on actual policymaking has been less than Meier (1994, 247) predicts. He writes:

> Morality policies pertaining to one-sided issues are rarely subjected to the expertise of bureaucrats; assessments of these morality policies are generally found only in academic journals, which no self-respecting politicians would read. Even when bureaucratic expertise is available, it is often swept aside in the rush to Armageddon. Such a policy process is much more likely to generate policies that will not work because policy proposals have not been tempered by informed debate. (Meier 1994, 247)

At both the national and state levels, politicians have attempted to exploit the issue to curry favor with voters. In the 1992 and 1996 presidential debates, crack babies were invoked by Ross Perot and Robert Dole as "a vivid shorthand for broader American anxieties about drugs, crime, and 'family values'" (Gomez 1997, 3). Between 1987 and 1991 eight different congressional committees held fourteen hearings on prenatal drug exposure (Gomez 1997, 4), and hundreds of bills dealing with the problem were introduced into state legislatures. For example, between 1986 and 1996, fifty-seven bills specifically targeting prenatal drug exposure were introduced in the California legislature (Gomez 1997, 28).

Despite the efforts of political entrepreneurs to enact harsh measures to punish drug-abusing pregnant women, most of the actual enactments have been surprisingly mild. Although in the late 1980s and early 1990s bills to criminalize such conduct were introduced in many state legislatures, none was actually passed. In California, none of the punitively oriented bills was even reported out of committee and considered on the floor (Gomez 1997, 41). By 1994 the number of such proposals had dropped so dramatically that only two state legislatures (Indiana and Mississippi) considered bills and neither was enacted.[7] The Florida Senate considered and subsequently dropped two less punitive measures in 1994.[8] As of January 1998, no state had enacted a criminal statute specifically classifying pregnant women distinct from other drug users.

The efforts to transform the public anger against these women into a campaign for new criminal sanctions has largely failed. Most lawmakers have not been "aggressive morality advocates," preferring instead to follow the empirical research, which shows that incarceration is unlikely to improve fetal well-

---

[7] Under Indiana House Bill 1184 (1994) a woman who gave birth to a drug-affected child would have been guilty of a Class D felony. Mississippi House Bill 670 (1994) also would have made it a felony for a woman to use a controlled substance during the last trimester of a pregnancy if it resulted in the birth of an addicted child. The Indiana bill died, and the Mississippi bill was killed by committee.

[8] Florida Senate Bill 2662 (1994) would have allowed a newborn's positive toxicology test for cocaine to be used as evidence in criminal actions against the mother, and Florida Senate Bill 2666 (1994) would have required that women charged with cocaine possession on the basis of either a blood test performed as part of a prenatal exam or a positive test of their newborn babies have the contraceptive implant Norplant embedded in their bodies, as well as any other penalties imposed by the law. Both bills died.

being.[9] Numerous studies have found that pregnant addicts in prisons have higher miscarriage rates and higher levels of birth abnormalities than addicts on the street (Barry 1985, 1989, 1996; McCall, Casteel, and Shaw 1985; Shelton and Gill 1989).[10] Because of the poor prenatal care given to incarcerated addicts, all of the relevant medical and professional associations have opposed the use of criminal sanctions to combat substance abuse by pregnant women.[11] In subsequent sections I examine the policies that have been enacted and the response of "street level" bureaucrats in the criminal justice system to the problem of pregnant addicts.

Legislative Responses to the Problem of Prenatal Drug Exposure

Even though no state has enacted criminal statutes that specifically designate pregnant substance-abusing women for additional criminal penalties,[12] many have passed a variety of new laws and adopted a range of regulations to address the problem. Punitively oriented approaches maintain that pregnant ad-

[9] While many people favor the incarceration of pregnant addicts because they believe it cuts off access to illegal narcotics, drugs are widely available in prisons and jails (Wilson and Leasure 1991, 36). One study of prison drug use found that 36 percent of pregnant inmates admitted using illegal narcotics while incarcerated (Egley, Miller, Granados, and Ingram-Fogel 1992: 132).

[10] The Supreme Court in *Estelle v. Gamble*, 429 U.S. 97 (1976), ruled that "a prisoner must allege acts or omissions sufficiently harmful to evidence deliberate indifference to serious medical needs" to show a violation of the Eighth Amendment's prohibition on cruel and unusual punishment. In the past fifteen years women prisoners have filed numerous lawsuits charging that their medical care violated this standard. Nearly all of these cases have resulted in settlements or court rulings that support the charges. In one case, guards refused to remove shackles that held a woman's legs together even though she was in labor, causing the deaths of twin babies. See *West v. Manson*, No. N83–366 (D. Conn. Filed May 9, 1983, and settled June 14, 1984). Although the state of California already had lost a series of lawsuits over poor medical conditions in its prisons, in 1995 another suit was filed, charging that the fifty-four hundred women incarcerated in the Central California Women's Facility and the California Institution for Women have been denied adequate medical care. One of the litigants has alleged that prison staff did not take seriously her complaints of bleeding during her fifth month of pregnancy and subsequent pain, resulting in a stillbirth (Sward and Wallace 1995, A16). See *Shumate v. Wilson*, No. CIV-S-95–619 WBS PAN (U.S.D. Ct., E.D. Cal. Filed April 4, 1995). On July 25, 1997—four days before trial was scheduled to begin—the California attorney general's office reached a settlement in *Shumate*; the state agreed to pay $1.2 million in legal fees, place its medical staff under court-ordered scrutiny for eight months, and reform many of its standard practices for dealing with medical problems of inmates (McKee 1997a, 1; McKee 1997b, 1).

[11] The American Medical Association, American Academy of Pediatrics, American Nurses Association, American Public Health Association, American Society of Addiction Medicine, Center for the Future of Children, National Association of Maternal and Child Health Programs, National Association of Public Child Welfare Administrators, and the March of Dimes have adopted policies that advocate the expansion of drug-treatment programs for pregnant women and oppose the use of criminal sanctions to reduce prenatal exposure to illegal narcotics.

[12] Although no state has passed statutes singling out pregnant women for additional criminal sanctions for abusing narcotics, New Jersey has passed a law doubling the criminal penalties against persons who distribute a controlled substance to a pregnant woman (N.J. Stat. Section 2C:35–8 1996).

dicts must be coerced into behaving responsibly, while public health approaches emphasize education, medical treatment, and the provision of social services to pregnant addicts.

Some states have used the child welfare system to punish women without directly criminalizing their actions as pregnant drug users. For example, several states consider a newborn's positive toxicology screen for narcotics to be prima facie evidence of child abuse that could lead to the loss of custody. In contrast, the public health approach is based on the premise that pregnant addicts want to do what is best for their children but lack the means to do so. State laws that require drug-treatment programs to give priority to pregnant women reflect the latter approach.

By January 1998 thirty-five states had laws that dealt specifically and often distinctively with prenatal narcotics exposure.[13] Some have enacted primarily punitive laws, others have chosen to emphasize treatment and education, and some have combined aspects of each. One characteristic common to nearly all the states is an unwillingness to commit new revenues to combating the problem.[14] For example, the two recent California governors (George Deukmejian and Pete Wilson) blamed the high cost of social services to drug-affected infants and their families for their vetoes of bills passed by the state legislature (Gomez 1997, 41).

Punitive Legislative Enactments

Although no two states have enacted identical measures, sixteen require that social service agencies (usually child welfare departments) become involved when there is evidence of prenatal drug exposure.[15] For example, Ohio has adopted an unusual punitive statute that requires all pregnant women who are recipients of state medical assistance to undergo drug-screening tests at their

---

[13] The fifteen states without such laws are Alabama, Alaska, Hawaii, Idaho, Maine, Michigan, Mississippi, Montana, New Mexico, New York, South Carolina, Texas, Vermont, West Virginia, and Wyoming. Some of these states had repealed earlier enactments and others had allowed the funding for earlier initiatives to expire. Also in some states, the relevant social service agencies have regulations and policies (both written and unwritten) designed to address the problem.

[14] The concern with controlling costs is evident in the relevant Oregon statute, which begins: "Because the growing numbers of pregnant substance users and drug- and alcohol-affected infants place a heavy financial burden on Oregon's taxpayers and those who pay for health care, it is the policy of this state to take effective action that will minimize these costs" (Oregon Revised Statutes Section 430.905). A few paragraphs later, the same statute states that "the Department of Human Resources shall study, within the resources of the department, problems of substance-abusing pregnant and postpartum women and their infants" (Oregon Revised Statutes Section 430.910).

[15] The laws of the following states contain at least some punitive component: California, Illinois, Indiana, Iowa, Kansas, Kentucky, Massachusetts, Minnesota, Missouri, Nevada, Ohio, Oklahoma, Oregon, Virginia, Wisconsin, and Utah. Social service agencies in some of the other states have adopted regulations that are punitively oriented. From the standpoint of the target population, the effect of these regulations may be substantially the same as statutes, but trying to encompass all of the regulatory changes, as well as case and statutory laws, would be a massive undertaking so I leave that to future researchers.

first prenatal visit. Women found to have substance abuse problems must participate in a drug-treatment program or face reduction and eventual termination of welfare benefits for aid to dependent children (Ohio Stat. Section 5111.017 1997). The state legislature did not, however, make any provisions to assure that appropriate treatment facilities exist.

The general laws of fifteen states require that medical providers and other professionals report to the appropriate state agencies positive toxicology tests in pregnant women and newborns, as well as any other evidence of possible drug use by pregnant women. Eight of these states have laws that mandate the reporting of prenatal drug exposure to the child welfare department (or an equivalent social service agency). The other seven require that suspected cases of prenatal substance abuse be treated the same as cases of suspected child abuse or neglect, following the normal reporting requirements.[16]

Because social service agencies in some of the remaining states have promulgated regulatory policies that require mandatory reporting of prenatal drug use, the practice extends beyond the eight states. For example, in 1988 the Department of Health and Rehabilitative Services in Florida promulgated a policy requiring that anyone who has cause to suspect that a newborn is drug dependent must report it to the Florida Abuse Registry. Child Protective Services investigators are then sent to determine the existence of abuse or neglect. But a single positive toxicology screen is not prima facie evidence of abuse or neglect (Pearson and Thoennes 1995, 58–60).

The harshest use of the child welfare system occurs in states that treat a positive toxicology screen or other evidence of prenatal drug exposure as prima facie evidence of child abuse or neglect or its equivalent. For example, Minnesota defines "neglect" as follows:

Neglect includes prenatal exposure to a controlled substance, as defined in Section 253B.02, subdivision 2, used by the mother for nonmedical purposes, as evidenced by withdrawal symptoms in the child at birth, results of a toxicology test performed on the mother at delivery of the child at birth, or medical effects or developmental delays during the child's first year of life that medically indicate prenatal exposure to a controlled substance. (Minn. Stat. Section 626.556 1996)[17]

[16] The eight states that require the reporting of suspected cases of prenatal drug exposure to child welfare agencies or their equivalent are California, Illinois, Kansas, Massachusetts, Minnesota, Missouri, Utah, and Virginia. In Kentucky a positive toxicology test in a newborn must be evaluated by responsible parties at the hospital to determine whether abuse or neglect has occurred and whether an investigation is necessary. The remaining six states (Indiana, Iowa, Nevada, Oklahoma, Oregon, and Wisconsin) do not specifically require that cases involving suspected prenatal drug exposure be reported to the appropriate social service agencies, although their child abuse statutes categorize such infants as being in "need," "subject of protective services," or "abused," triggering normal reporting requirements for suspected cases of child abuse and neglect.

[17] According to Pearson and Thoennes (1995, 49–50), the prenatal drug laws in Minnesota are "perhaps the strongest in the nation," but the punitive intent of the laws is undercut by the state's traditional approach to treating substance abuse as a public health problem rather than a criminal matter.

Minnesota's adoption of mandatory reporting requirements prompted a monthly increase from eighteen to forty in the number of reported cases of prenatal and postpartum substance abuse (Pearson and Thoennes 1995, 53). In most cases, legal custody of the infant is given to the Department of Social Services, but the woman retains physical custody, contingent on her treatment and maintenance of a suitable home environment (Pearson and Thoennes 1995, 54).

In seven additional states, prenatal drug exposure constitutes prima facie evidence of abuse, neglect, or its equivalent. Missouri classifies exposed children as "being at risk for abuse or neglect," Nevada defines them as "in need of protection," and in Oklahoma they are "in need of special care and treatment" (R.S. Mo. Section 191.737 1996; Nev. Rev. Stat. Ann. Section 432B.330 1997; O.S.L. Sect. 15 Chap. 353 10 1996). Indiana describes children with fetal alcohol syndrome and those born with even a trace amount of a controlled substance as "in need of services" while Iowa considers the presence of an illegal drug in a newborn's system to be evidence of "child abuse" (Indiana Statutes Section 34–1–10 1997; Iowa Code Section 232.68 1996). Oregon does not specify that prenatal exposure to narcotics is prima facie evidence of child abuse or neglect, stating only that "it is the policy of this state that the provider encourage and facilitate having the child when born, become subject to protective services" (ORS Section 430.915 1996). Wisconsin specifically includes prenatal drug exposure within its definition of abuse and also requires that, "because of that compelling interest [in the potential life of the fetus], the court may order protective custody of that child even though such custody requires custody of the mother as well and the court may not have jurisdiction over the mother" (Wis. Stat. Section 48.02 1995–1996).[18]

California law states that "a positive toxicology screen at the time of the delivery of an infant is not in and of itself a sufficient basis for reporting child abuse or neglect," but it does trigger an assessment of whether the child is at risk (California Civil Code Section 11165.13 1996). The language in laws of the other six states (Illinois, Kansas, Kentucky, Massachusetts, Utah, and Virginia) with regard to reporting requirements is ambiguous about the evidentiary significance of prenatal drug exposure to child abuse or neglect, but it has been interpreted as prima facie evidence in Illinois.

According to child welfare administrators, the Illinois law has not significantly affected the processing of child abuse and neglect cases. Hospitals are required to report positive drug screens to the Illinois Department of Children and Family Services, which must send an investigator to assess the situation within twenty-four hours. If the positive drug test is the only indication of problems, the case is usually closed and the infant sent home with the mother (Pearson and Thoennes 1995, 67–68).

[18] Because most of these states handle child welfare issues through civil rather than criminal process, they have generated far less attention than similar criminal cases involving prenatal drug exposure. Hundreds of women, however, have lost custody of their babies on the basis of a single positive drug screen at birth (Siegel 1997, 251).

Most of the states that have reporting requirements do not specifically state whether evidence of drug use, such as positive toxicology screens, can be used in a criminal case against the woman. Four (California, Kansas, Kentucky, and Virginia) expressly prohibit the use of this information in a criminal prosecution of the mother. The Iowa statute specifically prohibits the use of a positive test result obtained before the birth of the child in a criminal prosecution of the woman for exposing the child prenatally to illegal narcotics but is silent about the admissibility of a drug screen obtained after the birth (Iowa Code Section 232.71).

Public Health–Oriented Legislative Enactments

Despite strong public support for policies emphasizing punishment, a majority of state legislatures have enacted laws that treat substance abuse by pregnant women as a public health rather than a criminal issue. Except for Utah and Indiana, the states that require medical providers to report pregnant women whom they suspect of using drugs to child welfare agencies also have laws that treat it as a public health concern.

Thirty-one states have adopted laws that take a public health approach to the problem of perinatal drug exposure.[19] Their policy enactments can be divided into three broad categories: those that require research on the problem, initiate preventive public education campaigns, and provide drug treatment for pregnant addicts. None of the actual policies adopted in the different states entails large public expenditures.

Although the specific mandates vary, twelve states require additional research into the problems caused by substance abuse during pregnancy.[20] In some cases, a new task force or commission is given the responsibility for studying the problem, while in others an existing public agency is instructed to undertake a new study. The specific research mandate varies from state to state; the most noticeable difference is over whether analyses of mothers are included in studies of drug-exposed infants. Arkansas, California, Louisiana, Minnesota, North Carolina, and North Dakota limit the scope of such research programs to the needs of infants and children prenatally exposed to narcotics. In contrast, Connecticut, Illinois, Nevada, New Hampshire, Oklahoma, and Oregon take a more holistic approach, requiring the study of both children and their mothers. No state limited the scope of research to the moth-

[19] The thirty-one states with at least some public health–oriented laws are Arizona, Arkansas, California, Colorado, Connecticut, Delaware, Georgia, Florida, Illinois, Iowa, Kansas, Kentucky, Louisiana, Massachusetts, Maryland, Minnesota, Missouri, Nevada, New Hampshire, New Jersey, North Carolina, North Dakota, Ohio, Oklahoma, Oregon, Pennsylvania, Rhode Island, South Dakota, Virginia, Washington, and Wisconsin.

[20] The twelve states that require studies on both to the problem of substance-abusing pregnant women and the needs of drug-exposed infants are Arkansas, California, Connecticut, Illinois, Louisiana, Minnesota, Nevada, New Hampshire, North Carolina, North Dakota, Oklahoma, and Oregon. North Dakota limits the research to the problem of fetal alcohol syndrome.

ers only, reflecting the stigmatization and secondary status of drug-abusing women even in states that emphasize the public health approach.

Sixteen states have passed laws designed to educate women about the harmful effects of using drugs when pregnant.[21] The content of the campaigns and their target audience varies from state to state. Some states require preventive education campaigns directed at the general public while others have more specific target audiences. Among the former group, in Arizona and Connecticut, high schools must provide preventive drug education that covers the adverse effects of drug use by pregnant women; North Carolina distributes pamphlets describing the harms caused by fetal alcohol syndrome and perinatal cocaine exposure with marriage licenses; and Delaware mandates that all professional counselors and medical practitioners post and give written and verbal warning to pregnant patients about the possible problems, complications, and harms caused by narcotics use.

Among the states that target specific groups, most focus on pregnant women. Colorado, Kansas, Louisiana, Massachusetts, and South Dakota have laws requiring that health care providers inform all pregnant women of the adverse consequences of prenatal drug exposure. Minnesota simply requires that health care professionals be trained in effective drug-prevention methods designed to reduce the number of drug-exposed infants. Iowa law requires that birth center clients receive drug education, and Maryland has a similar requirement for pregnant women receiving medical assistance. Oregon, North Dakota, and Wisconsin target "high-risk" women patients in their education campaigns, although North Dakota's program is limited to prevention of fetal alcohol syndrome. New Jersey also focuses on the dangers of alcohol.

None of these initiatives directly meets the needs of pregnant women already addicted to narcotics. Researchers (Tracy, Talbert, and Steinschneider 1990, 13; DeLeon and Jainchill 1991, 279; Brown 1992, 18; Farkas and Parran 1993, 39) unanimously agree that residential drug-treatment programs that address the broader social context of women's addiction are the most effective means of combating the problem of prenatal drug exposure. According to Xylina Bean, chief neonatologist at Martin Luther King Jr./Drew Medical Center and founder of Shields for Families, a treatment program in Los Angeles, pregnant women in treatment have a success rate of 75 percent, but there is a severe shortage of openings in these programs (Smith 1998, E3). The problem is that most drug-treatment programs were established in the 1950s and 1960s to treat heroin addicts. Because men were nearly five times more likely

---

[21] The sixteen states with preventive public education initiatives designed to warn women of the dangers of using drugs while pregnant are Arizona, Colorado, Connecticut, Delaware, Iowa, Louisiana, Kansas, Maryland, Massachusetts, Minnesota, New Jersey, North Carolina, North Dakota, Oregon, South Dakota, and Wisconsin. Again, the focus in North Dakota is on the prevention of fetal alcohol syndrome. New Jersey also limits its education campaign to warning against the use of alcohol during pregnancy.

to abuse heroin than women, few programs considered the needs of female addicts, much less pregnant addicts.

The current situation is quite different. Women are more likely than men to became addicted to crack cocaine. Roughly 60 percent of crack addicts are women (Walker, Eric, Pivnick, and Drucker 1991, 7). Yet a National Institute on Drug Abuse study found that only one-fourth of addicts receiving treatment in 1990 were women and only a minuscule proportion of these were pregnant (NIDA 1992, 35). The same survey found that only 0.1 percent of all addicts in treatment had access to child care at their treatment centers (NIDA 1992, 45). Fears of insurance liability for drug-affected children is an important reason why many treatment providers refuse to accept pregnant women in their programs.

Despite the well-documented shortage of drug-treatment programs willing to accept them (Feig 1990, 16; Moss 1990, 288; Paltrow 1991, 85; Romney 1991, 341), the federal government has done very little to expand the number of treatment slots for pregnant addicts. States receiving federal drug-treatment block grants were not required to allocate any funds for treatment of female addicts—much less pregnant addicts—until fiscal year 1985, when block grant recipients had to spend 3 percent of the funds for alcohol- and drug-abusing women. That figure was later increased to 5 percent (Public Law 99–117, October 7, 1985).

State governments have not chosen to pick up the slack left by the federal government. No state legislature responded to the problem of prenatal drug exposure by significantly increasing public funding for drug treatment targeted at pregnant addicts. Even in states with the best ratio of treatment slots to pregnant addicts, facilities are often geographically concentrated in a single area (Pearson and Thoennes 1995, 57). For example, Minnesota is a leader in drug-treatment services for pregnant women, but nearly all the facilities are in the Minneapolis area (Pearson and Thoennes 1995, 57). Even when funding is available, community opposition can often derail attempts to locate treatment facilities in a neighborhood. For example, in Minot, North Dakota, a planning commission turned down a proposed treatment center for pregnant addicts in 1998 after neighbors objected (Zent 1998).

The failure to expand treatment slots is even more paradoxical when one considers recent research (Rydell and Everingham, 1994), which shows that drug treatment is a far more cost-effective means of combating narcotics addiction than is incarceration. This finding was corroborated by a study performed by the California Department of Alcohol and Drug Programs (1994), which found that for every dollar spent on drug treatment taxpayers saved seven dollars that would otherwise be spent on crime and health care.

Illinois is the only state that statutorily has earmarked part of a special fund for the provision of drug-treatment services for pregnant addicts. Money from the Illinois Substance Abuse Services Fund is used to pay for the hospitalization of pregnant women with substance abuse problems. The fund also pays for services to drug-affected newborns and supplements existing county funding for more generalized substance abuse treatment. Three other states (Florida, Pennsylvania, and Rhode Island) have passed laws that pledge the state to providing additional substance abuse treatment to pregnant women.[22]

In addition, seven states have passed laws authorizing the creation of pilot projects providing drug treatment to pregnant addicts.[23] Their limited scope and often uncertain funding render the chances of success dubious. Two other states (Nebraska and Tennessee) have tried to improve access to existing services. Nebraska has implemented a case management program to ensure that high-risk pregnant women not covered by medical insurance gain access to needed services, and Tennessee employs older women from the community to act as "resource mothers" for high-risk pregnant teenagers. Neither of these programs expands the number of treatment slots available for pregnant addicts.

Some states have chosen a different strategy to address the availability of treatment for pregnant addicts. Instead of new programs, six states acted to prohibit drug-treatment facilities from discriminating against pregnant women. Kansas, Louisiana, and Missouri have passed laws with specific antidiscrimination clauses, and the latter two are also part of a group of five states that make treatment services for pregnant women a priority. Arizona, Georgia, and Maryland are the other states that prioritize the treatment of pregnant addicts.

Assessing the Legislative Response

Overall, of the thirty-five states with prenatal drug laws, only two (Indiana and Utah) have adopted purely punitive measures, while nineteen states have followed a completely public health–oriented approach. The remainder have combined both approaches. Moving beyond simple categorization, I developed two composite quantitative measures to assess the overall character of each state's statutes: one that confers points for each punitive provision and a second that assigns points for each public health–oriented provision. For the

[22] In 1996 the Rhode Island state legislature instructed the Department of Human Services to "provide enhanced services" to a wide range of pregnant women eligible for state-funded medical assistance. Although outpatient drug treatment was among the enumerated services, the exact level of commitment is yet to be determined (R.I. Gen. Laws Section 42–12.3–3 1996). The Florida state legislature in 1996 created the Pregnancy Outcomes Program, committing each county health program to provide services to indigent pregnant women at risk of medical complications because of drug or alcohol abuse (Fla. Stat. 154.011 1996). In 1997 Pennsylvania enacted a law mandating that the state Department of Health has a "duty" to provide residential drug and alcohol treatment and related services to pregnant women with substance abuse problems (Penn. Admin. Code Section 2123 1997).

[23] The seven states that passed laws enabling pilot projects to be developed are California, Colorado, Kentucky, Minnesota, Ohio, Virginia, and Washington. The Ohio and Virginia laws specifically require that only available funds will be used by these programs. Washington State also has been the site of two federally funded demonstration projects that provide drug treatment and other services to pregnant women and mothers with substance abuse problems. For a description of the federal projects, see Pearson and Thoennes 1995, 39–40.

punitive composite measure, I assigned a maximum of four points, one for each of the following provisions: mandatory drug testing of pregnant women receiving public assistance, mandatory reporting of positive toxicology screens, the use of positive drug screens as prima facie evidence of child abuse or neglect, and no general prohibition on the use of positive drug tests as evidence in criminal trials. For the public health composite measure, I assigned points for the presence of each of six public health provisions: research on problems associated with prenatal drug exposure, research on problems of substance-abusing pregnant women, preventive drug-education campaigns, commitment to expanding drug treatment for pregnant addicts, requirement that public treatment facilities and publicly funded facilities not discriminate against pregnant addicts, and priority treatment of pregnant addicts. State-by-state totals are summarized in Table 4.1.

Policies differ substantially by region. The northeastern states are least likely to have enacted laws that punish pregnant women for using illegal drugs. Only two had not passed any legislation, and Massachusetts has enacted two punitive provisions (as well as one public health–oriented measure). Other than Michigan, every state in the Midwest had passed measures dealing with the problem of prenatal drug exposure. The Midwest is also the harshest in approach, although most states combined both punitive- and public health–oriented responses. Despite stereotypes depicting southern lawmakers as rigid, law-and-order zealots, the region's legislative responses were not particularly punitive. Each of the three southern states that had adopted punitive measures also had passed some public health–oriented initiatives. In fact, the policies of eight southern states were exclusively public health oriented, and five states had not enacted any laws. The West is the most difficult region to characterize because nearly half the states were silent on the issue, one had exclusively punitive enactments, three had taken a completely public health–oriented response, and three combined both punitive and public health–oriented initiatives.

Criminal Prosecution of Pregnant Addicts

Before the advent of crack, only a handful of women were prosecuted for exposing their children prenatally to narcotics. Using 1985 as the beginning of the crack epidemic (or, more accurately, as the point when policymakers and the public first became aware of the problem), I was able to find records of only nine court cases that at least partially involved prenatal substance abuse before the "crisis," all in either California, Michigan, New York, or Wyoming. In contrast, since 1985 more than 240 women have been prosecuted for prenatal substance abuse in at least thirty-four states.[24]

---

[24] Criminal prosecutions of pregnant women for substance-abuse offenses related to the well-being of their fetuses have taken place in the following states: Alabama, Alaska, Arizona, California, Connecticut, Florida, Georgia, Idaho, Illinois, Indiana, Kentucky, Maryland, Massachusetts, Michigan, Mississippi, Missouri, Nebraska, Nevada, New York, North Carolina, North Dakota,

Table 4.1. State laws on fetal drug exposure (as of January 1998)

No enactments	Punitive-oriented	Public health–oriented
Northeast		
Maine	Massachusetts (2)	Connecticut (3)
New York		Massachusetts (1)
Vermont		New Hampshire (2)
		New Jersey (1)
		Pennsylvania (1)
		Rhode Island (1)
Midwest		
Michigan	Illinois (2)	Illinois (3)
	Indiana (3)	Iowa (1)
	Iowa (3)	Kansas (3)
	Kansas (1)	Minnesota (3)
	Minnesota (3)	Missouri (2)
	Missouri (3)	Nebraska (1)
	Ohio (1)	North Dakota (2)
	Wisconsin (3)	Ohio (1)
		South Dakota (1)
		Wisconsin (1)
South		
Alabama	Kentucky (1)	Arkansas (1)
Mississippi	Oklahoma (3)	Delaware (1)
South Carolina	Virginia (1)	Georgia (1)
Texas		Florida (1)
West Virginia		Kentucky (1)
		Louisiana (3)
		Maryland (2)
		North Carolina (2)
		Oklahoma (2)
		Tennessee (1)
		Virginia (1)
West		
Alaska	California (1)	Arizona (2)
Hawaii	Nevada (3)	California (2)
Idaho	Oregon (3)	Colorado (2)
Montana	Utah (1)	Nevada (2)
New Mexico		Oregon (3)
Wyoming		Washington (1)

Note: The number of punitive- and public health–oriented provisions are in parentheses.

Ohio, Oklahoma, Oregon, Pennsylvania, South Carolina, South Dakota, Tennessee, Texas, Utah, Virginia, Washington, Wisconsin, and Wyoming. Because criminal prosecutions are local, there is no reliable clearinghouse that collects these data or even county-by-county information on prosecutions. In compiling the figures, I used data collected by groups involved in the litigation of such cases, records of cases that have been appealed to higher courts, and secondary sources such as newspaper articles chronicling prosecutions. But I may have missed some nonpublicized prosecutions in some states.

The Criminal Justice System and the "Politics of Sin"

The idea that the criminal justice system is supposed to be free of political biases and pressure is something of a myth (Jacob 1996, 253). As Michael Lipsky (1980) pointed out, "street level bureaucrats" such as police officers and social service workers exercise tremendous discretionary power.[25] Sometimes the individual prejudices and biases of bureaucrats lead to poor decision making; other times, ignorance is the culprit. These decisions can have an enormous impact for the affected parties. For example, a police officer who decides to arrest a pregnant woman because she appears to be under the influence of drugs exposes her to the entire apparatus of the criminal justice system. A public health clinic nurse who decides that a pregnant patient on public assistance fits the "profile" of a narcotics addict and orders a toxicology screen has set in motion a process that may bring her into the criminal justice system or to the attention of child welfare authorities (Pearson and Thoennes 1995, 41–42).

Local district attorneys also have a significant amount of discretion over whether to dismiss or formally charge a person with a crime, the number of charges to be filed, and their severity (Freidman 1977; Jacoby 1980, 29; Jacob 1984, 190; Gersham 1992; Jacob 1996, 256; Berman 1997, 193). Political considerations can affect these decisions. Because the media focus extensively on violent crime, prosecutors are probably the most visible local officials other than the mayor (Eisenstein 1973, 20). A district attorney's choice to court these opportunities for media attention often turns on two general political considerations: whether the district attorney holds an appointive or elective office and the individual prosecutor's level of political ambition. Obviously, elected prosecutors have incentives to seek favorable publicity from the media, and for politically ambitious individuals, this is amplified.

Politics also can affect judges, who are elected in some states and appointed in others (Jacob 1996). Some studies have indicated that the distinction affects judicial decision making.[26] Although judicial elections traditionally have been political nonevents, in recent years they have become far more visible and closely fought. According to Thad Beyle (1995, 160), observers of state judicial politics were shocked by the tenor of the 1986 elections for chief justices in California, North Carolina, and Ohio—"all had well-publicized, negative, and very expensive races." In California, Chief Justice Rose Elizabeth Bird and two

[25] According to Jacob, individual police departments and individual officers exercise a great deal of discretion over whether a suspect is arrested. Priorities vary among police departments with respect to items as basic as law and order, emphasis on vice and narcotics arrests, and choice of neighborhoods to patrol. Examples of the offenses that individual officers often choose to ignore include minor traffic violations and family assaults (Jacob 1984, 184).

[26] For example, one study found that elected judges try to avoid making politically unpopular decisions that would alienate voters (Hall 1992). Other studies found that elected judges are more liberal than appointed judges in cases dealing with consumer issues but more conservative in cases dealing with the rights of criminal defendants (Nagel 1973; Hall 1987).

other justices lost their bids for reelection, primarily because they opposed the death penalty. The conflict in North Carolina involved the governor's choice of a new chief justice, while in Ohio it concerned the highly partisan style of the chief justice. This trend toward a more politicized judiciary has continued. The reasons are simple—state court judges do a significant amount of policymaking (Berman 1997, 178). Although their interpretation of the law may be quite different from that of state legislators, the governor, and the public, unless overruled by higher court decisions, constitutional amendments, or, in the case of statutory interpretation, by new laws, it is the law of the state (Beyle 1995, 159–60).[27] Although most of the publicized, closely contested judicial races have involved state supreme courts, some local judicial contests have also become politically volatile. For example, in Chicago the 1988 reelection bid of the chief judge of the Cook County Circuit Court turned into a heated race when activists in the African American community started a "Just Vote No" campaign to protest the lack of black judges on the court (Jacob 1996, 272).

Judicial decisions concerning abortion and fetal rights have also become more politically salient. In early 1998 pro-life groups in California launched a campaign to unseat Chief Justice Ronald George and Justice Ming Chin because they were part of a 5–4 majority that overturned a state law requiring minors to obtain parental consent as a condition to obtaining an abortion. Because both are Republicans and were appointed by Republican governor Pete Wilson, the conflict polarized the party into pro-choice and pro-life factions (Morain 1998, A3).

A Case Study of Prosecutorial Policymaking

Although sometimes ill-conceived, policymaking often occurs virtually by default, the result of seemingly small and unrelated decisions by individuals with discretionary authority. Charleston, South Carolina, provides such an example.[28] In 1988 Shirley Brown, a nurse at the Medical University of South Carolina (MUSC), began noticing an increasing number of women suffering from a relatively rare condition, *abruptio placentae*,[29] resulting in stillbirths. Brown relayed her concerns to Dr. Edgar O. Horger III, the head of fetal-maternal medicine at the hospital. After studying the medical literature, they concluded that the most likely cause was prenatal exposure to cocaine and then ran toxicology screens on pregnant women fitting a drug-use profile.[30]

---

[27] Although judges have significant discretionary power, the public and political officials will act if their decisions are too far removed from public sentiments. For example, after their supreme courts invalidated death penalty laws, voters in California and Massachusetts passed constitutional initiatives to reinstate them (Berman 1997, 180).

[28] For more detailed accounts see Siegel 1994 and Jos, Marshall, and Perlmutter 1995. This summary is drawn primarily from these two sources. Other sources are cited in the text.

[29] *Abruptio placentae* is an abrupt separation of the placenta before labor begins, typically caused by high blood pressure or physical trauma such as auto accidents or prenatal battering. More recently, it has been associated with prenatal exposure to cocaine.

[30] Initially, physicians simply ordered drug screens anytime they suspected drug use, but in April 1989 the hospital adopted a formal protocol. Drug screens were ordered when patients met any of

Three of the first four women screened tested positive, as did another 116 in the first year.

Concerned about the hospital's moral and legal responsibility to prevent child abuse, Brown and Horger reported their findings to the local prosecutor, Charles Condon, a rising star in the Republican Party, thereby initiating a change in the problem's definition from public health to punitive. Although no South Carolina criminal statutes covered prenatal drug exposure, Condon decided it was a criminal matter. His office, in conjunction with the local police, developed an interagency plan for handling the problem.[31] Prenatal patients who tested positive were told they must successfully undergo drug treatment or be arrested. At the start, drug-using women who first visited the hospital when they went into labor were simply arrested after giving birth. This policy was abolished after three months. Instead, the women were given the option of deferred prosecution if they successfully completed drug treatment. Most pregnant addicts heard of the policy from television public service announcements in which Condon warned them to avoid drugs or face arrest.

Because MUSC was the only public hospital within a fifty-mile radius that accepted Medicaid patients, indigent pregnant women had no alternatives for prenatal care and deliveries. Nearly all of the patients screened for drug use were African American, as were those testing positive. Some were "taken from their hospital room hours or days after delivering and led to jail in handcuffs and shackles. Others sat in jail cells waiting to give birth, then, when in labor, were brought by ambulance, in handcuffs and shackles, to the hospital. One tells of being seized in a chokehold, near full-term, and escorted forcibly into treatment" (Siegel 1994, 16).

At this time, the Charleston area lacked any drug-treatment programs designed to meet the unique needs of pregnant addicts. MUSC's own inpatient drug-treatment program refused to accept pregnant women (Center for Reproductive Law & Policy 1997, 1). In fact, no residential treatment program in the Charleston vicinity accepted substance-abusing women, and not a single outpatient program provided child care or transportation so women with children could participate.[32] Despite the obvious need, city leaders opposed constructing a federally funded downtown drug-treatment center targeting pregnant addicts. After a protracted battle, a more modest outpatient facility was built in a less desirable location.

During the five years of collaboration between MUSC and the prosecutor's

---

the six following criteria: no prenatal care, *abruptio placentae*, intrauterine fetal death, preterm labor, intrauterine growth retardation, and a history of drug or alcohol abuse (Siegel 1994, 15).

[31] The lack of statutory authority for the interagency plan for criminalizing prenatal substance abuse in South Carolina led one Charleston judge to make the following joke: "They call us the great state of Charleston. We don't need law. Remember, we plunged the U.S. into the Civil War" (Pearson and Thoennes 1995, 82).

[32] Horst (1991, 35), in his study of pregnant addicts, found that the availability of child care was the most important factor in determining whether they would enter a drug-treatment program.

office, nearly 280 women, the vast majority African American, were arrested or threatened with prosecution (Center for Reproductive Law & Policy 1997, 1). In 1993 a multimillion-dollar lawsuit was filed against MUSC contesting the constitutionality of its program. The plaintiffs charged that the policy violated their rights to privacy, liberty, and equal protection as "an unconstitutional experiment on African-American women." The following year, pursuant to a settlement on related charges with the Civil Rights Division of the Department of Health and Human Services, MUSC ended the program. In a separate action, the federal Office of Protection from Research Risk determined that the program constituted human experimentation without the required review and approval process. In 1997, however, a federal jury rejected the plaintiffs' claims that their constitutional rights had been violated (Center for Reproductive Law & Policy 1997, 1).

Probably no politician has been more effective in using the fetal abuse issue to further his political career than Charles Condon. Shortly after the public service announcements began airing on local television, Condon decided to seek higher elective office—that of state attorney general. Much of his ultimately successful campaign touted his record of incarcerating pregnant substance-abusing women who failed to get treatment. As state attorney general, he has continued to advocate the incarceration of pregnant addicts to save fetuses from exposure to narcotics.[33] In 1996 a case involving a MUSC patient convicted of child abuse on the basis of a positive toxicology screen reached the South Carolina Supreme Court, which held that the term "child" in the state's child neglect law applied to viable fetuses (*Whitner v. State* 1996). Attorney General Condon hailed the decision as a vindication of his policy and instructed local prosecutors throughout the state to begin prosecuting substance-abusing pregnant women ("Abuse" 1996).[34]

Legislative versus Judicial Fetal Abuse Policymaking

In this one-sided morality policy domain, the dearth of legislative enactments punishing the socially ostracized pregnant drug user is surprising. The failure of state legislatures to enact punitive laws cannot be attributed to a lack of effort by individual legislators. Although hundreds of bills to criminalize drug use by pregnant women have been introduced, only a handful have been seriously considered.

[33] For an example of Condon's arguments and political rhetoric, see Condon 1995.

[34] Law enforcement officials from around the country began to reexamine their policies regarding pregnant substance abusers after the *Whitner* decision. For example, Los Angeles County sheriff Sherman Block stated that he would like to find a California state legislator willing to sponsor legislation that would allow him to incarcerate pregnant addicts (Nazario 1998, A18). The seventy-three-year-old sheriff was in the midst of a very tough reelection campaign when he made these comments. See Daunt and Meyer 1998 for a summary of the difficulties faced by Sheriff Block in his campaign. In the end, Block's stance on the prosecution of pregnant addicts did not affect the electoral outcome because he died just before the election.

The reason for this failure is a combination of politics and institutional design. Many of the bills are "legislative chaff"—bills with no realistic chance of passage that are introduced by legislators to impress their constituents of their activity on a "hot" topic. Because prenatal substance abuse in the late 1980s and early 1990s was just such an issue, bill sponsorship was a means to showcase legislators' concern. An important distinction between legislative chaff and serious legislation is whether sponsors serve on a committee that has jurisdiction over the topic.[35] Once introduced, bills are referred to standing committees, which usually must report them out before consideration by the entire legislature on the floor.[36] Committee workloads vary. Standing committees with heavy schedules consider only a small portion of bills; most are never even discussed in a committee meeting. According to Beyle (1995, 87), the growth in individual legislators' workloads has forced many to consult experts in a policy area when considering votes on bills. This practice of taking cues from colleagues and lobbyists with substantive expertise is becoming increasingly common. Not surprisingly, bills supported by party leaders and committee members are more likely to be considered than are others.[37] The usual committee procedure for bills under consideration is to hold hearings to which experts are invited to give prepared testimony about the proposal and to answer questions from committee members. Usually committee votes occur only after the legislation has been thoroughly debated. Proponents and opponents are given many opportunities to persuade the members.

By design, legislatures are deliberative bodies in which gatekeepers have a myriad of opportunities to halt the progress of legislation. Legislatures also are permeable institutions, susceptible to outside influences. Every state except Nebraska has a bicameral legislature, and each chamber has its own set of leaders and committees. This structure provides many occasions for drug-treatment professionals and medical experts to interject themselves into the debate and derail efforts to criminalize fetal abuse.

In contrast, the criminal justice system provides fewer chances for outside professionals to become involved in the process. Moreover, the purpose of criminal justice is to determine whether the law has been transgressed and, if so, to punish guilty parties—not to determine the most effective policy for dealing with a particular social problem. Many important policy decisions that emanate from the criminal justice system are made on an ad hoc basis, without input from experts. Police officers and district attorneys do not normally con-

[35] Committees often attract members whose areas of expertise and experience match that of their substantive jurisdiction. Although these appointments bring substantial knowledge to committee deliberations, they also raise conflict of interest concerns (Berman 1997, 134–35).

[36] Approximately one-third of the states require that committees report all bills to the floor, regardless of whether they favor or oppose the initiatives. In the other states, only legislation that is favorably voted on in committees is typically reported out (Berman 1997, 137).

[37] For a summary of the strategies used by party leaders to influence committee decision making on legislation, see Jewell and Whicker, 1994.

sult with policy wonks before making an arrest or deciding whether to press charges. Although expert testimony has become an accepted part of the modern courtroom, judges exercise broad discretion over the type of testimony that is permitted. In short, there are far fewer checks on Meier's "rush to [policy] Armageddon" in the criminal justice system than in the legislative one.

For this reason, individual biases, prejudices, and misperceptions are more likely to shape the responses to fetal abuse from the judicial system than the legislative one.[38] For example, in 1989 a New York family court judge removed a newborn from her mother's custody because the woman had tested positive for marijuana, despite evidence that she had no history of drug use and that she followed the advice of a nurse to smoke marijuana during labor as a means to reduce the pain (Siegel 1997, 251).[39]

Barry Becker and Peggy Hora's (1993) survey of California trial judges found that most could not name a single drug-treatment program for pregnant women and nearly half would consider sentencing a pregnant woman to jail to protect the fetus. To prevent the birth of children with fetal alcohol syndrome, a tribal court judge on the Pineridge, South Dakota, reservation has adopted the policy of incarcerating women for drinking while pregnant (Paltrow 1992, 29).

In a similar vein, all but one judge attending a seminar on alcohol and narcotics abuse at the National Judicial College said they would immediately remand to jail a pregnant woman on probation for a drug offense if she tested positive for heroin. The judges were shocked to learn that their action would probably result in a miscarriage caused by abrupt heroin withdrawal (Kandall and Chavkin 1992).

Policy Responses to Third-Party Fetal Assaults and Killings

Unlike fetal abuse, the problem of third-party acts of violence toward fetuses (and pregnant women) has not generated widespread public outrage. Although no one defends individuals who beat, kick, stab, and shoot pregnant women, most consider it a minor problem (i.e., one not meriting government attention). The media are far less intrigued by fetal harms caused by deliberate acts of violence against pregnant women than by problem of fetal abuse. Only extraordinarily violent or salacious accounts garner any coverage, and even that is usually minimal. For example, when a fourteen-year-old girl who became pregnant following rape and sexual abuse by an adult cousin was later attacked and punched in the abdomen by the man, who told her that he was trying to kill the fetus, the story received only a couple of column inches of text and no pictures in the middle of an inner section of the newspaper (*Los Ange-*

[38] According to Berman (1997, 180), individual judges often use their legal opinions to encourage legislatures to consider preferred policy alternatives. Sometimes their opinions are sent directly to legislators.

[39] See *Nassau County Department of Social Services v. Leavy*, Family Court, Nassau Co. (1989).

les Times, January 15, 1998, B4). In contrast, the same Los Angeles newspaper ran a several-part front-page series titled "Orphans of Addiction" on the impact of parental substance abuse on children, focusing on both prenatal and postnatal effects and featuring multiple color photographs of addicted women and their children living in squalor (Nazario 1997a, 1997b).

The "Orphans of Addiction" story led to the creation of a county-wide Task Force on Alcohol and Other Drug Affected Parents, consisting of twenty government agencies and other groups working with substance abuse and child welfare issues, to develop a comprehensive plan to deal with the problem (Nazario and Krikorian 1998, B1 and B8). The photographer was awarded a Pulitzer Prize for the heartrending photographs that accompanied the story. Although the actual physical harm was significantly greater in the first instance than the second, the fetal battering story received very little media coverage and certainly did not lead to policy changes.

Cultural Biases and Problem Definition

To understand the reasons for this difference in popular perception requires an examination of the general process of problem definition. According to Stone (1988, 1989, 1997), causal stories play a central role in transforming an act of nature into a policy problem:

> Problem definition is a process of image making, where the images have to do fundamentally with attributing cause, blame, and responsibility. Conditions, difficulties, or issues thus do not have inherent properties that make them more or less likely to be seen as problems. . . . [Political actors] compose stories that describe harms and difficulties, attribute them to actions of other individuals or organizations, and thereby claim the right to invoke governmental power to stop the harm. (Stone 1989, 282)

Although these stories may not describe much about the magnitude and "true" causes of a particular harm, they do tell us a great deal about the power differential of groups in society. Causal stories congruent with dominant cultural values resonate more than those that challenge deeply held beliefs. A physician can blame a stillbirth on many different causes. In the past, most stillbirths and other adverse birth outcomes were considered to be an act of nature or God's will (i.e., not attributable to human behavior and therefore not a problem amenable to government action). Recent medical advances, particularly those that encourage physicians to view the fetus as a second patient, have focused their attention on the ways that human actions can either improve or impair fetal health. Nevertheless, physicians' assignment of blame for adverse birth outcomes is still affected by their value system. The view that mothers are primarily responsible for children is deeply embedded in our culture. It is hardly surprising, then, that society first looks to mothers when there are fetal mishaps. Despite evidence that males are at least as likely to inflict fetal harms, causal stories that assign blame to men face enormous cultural barriers. After delivering an infant with bruises on its arms, neck, and shoulder, a swollen eye, and intraventricular hemorrhaging caused by prenatal battering, doctors at the hospital urged other physicians to pay closer attention to the problem of third-party acts of violence against pregnant women and their fetuses. Following the baby's death, the physicians plaintively wrote to *Lancet*: "We consider it a delusion to think that the fetus is exempt from the hazards of an environment in which child abuse and spouse abuse are commonplace. Are there others with similar concerns who can help elaborate the battered fetus prototype?" (Morey, Begleiter, and Harris 1981, 1294). Despite growing evidence that physical trauma adversely affects fetal development and that it may be the single largest cause of birth defects, there still is no battered fetus prototype.

The medical evidence shows that complications from physical trauma occur in roughly 6 to 7 percent of all pregnancies; only half of these are accidental (Stauffer 1986, 91; Campbell, Oliver, and Bullock 1992, 5). Presumably a high proportion of the remaining cases originated in violence against pregnant women, because domestic violence is a leading factor in women's treatment in emergency rooms. The increased interest in fetal well-being and the continued resistance to consideration of prenatal battering in cases where the fetus shows signs of prebirth physical trauma is paradoxical, if not troubling.

Cultural Reasons for Discounting Prenatal Battering

The rejection of domestic abuse (and, by extension, prenatal battering) as a public problem is rooted in society's past acceptance of the practice, at least to the Middle Ages, when church doctrine held that wives were to submit themselves to beatings and kiss the rods used against them. Early but sporadic opposition to the practice was discovered by Mary Van Stolk in a fifteenth-century priest's sermon admonishing male parishioners to have more patience with their wives. "You men have more patience with the hen that befoutleth thy table but layeth a fresh egg daily, than with thy wife when she bringeth forth a little girl. . . . Consider the fruit of the woman, and have patience: not for every cause is it right to beat her" (Van Stolk 1976, 12).

Under English common law a wife's legal personhood was subsumed in her husband's, who was solely responsible for controlling her actions. William Blackstone was writing seminal canons of English law in the latter half of the eighteenth century, when the prescribed degree of violence that a man might justifiably use against his wife was changing. Under the old common law a man was allowed to wound his wife severely with whips and fists; by Blackstone's time that amount of "chastisement" was beginning to be viewed as unreasonable (Lindgren and Taub 1993, 3). In 1782 one judge held that it was acceptable for a man to beat his wife with a rod as thick as his thumb but no larger (May 1978, 139).

This explicit legal acceptance of men's right to beat their wives was also part of the American legal tradition. In 1824 North Carolina passed a law allowing a man to beat his wife if he used a switch no thicker than his thumb. Not until half a century later did a court rule that men had no inherent right to beat their wives, but it added that it should be treated as a private matter unless the woman was permanently injured (Hilberman 1980, 1338). State laws explicitly allowing wife beating survived until the Progressive Era (Bohn 1990, 86).

Even today the criminal justice system tends to treat spousal abuse as an exception to the typical situation in which the intentional infliction of physical harm to another person is treated as a crime and prosecution is automatic. Only in cases of spousal battering is criminal prosecution often dependent on the victim vigorously pressing charges against the perpetrator (Eisenberg and Micklow 1979, 146–47; Hilberman 1980, 1338). Until the 1980s district attorneys would generally not file charges against a batterer unless the victim pressed charges. Widespread protest by women activists changed this situation; today, some district attorneys will act even when the victim refuses to cooperate. Practices still vary enormously across jurisdictions because police and prosecutors have wide discretion. Even when women victims are willing to press charges, they still sometimes find it difficult to do so. Police respond slowly if at all to domestic violence reports and often convince the woman not to press charges (Dobash and Dobash 1979, 207–17; Bohn 1990, 94).

The medical system, as the only other social institution that regularly encounters victims of battering, also has an opportunity to intervene and stop the violence. Studies have found that battered women will go to hospital emergency rooms when seriously injured but will seldom truthfully disclose the reason for their injuries (Dobash and Dobash 1979, 181; Novello, Rosenberg, Saltzman, and Shosky 1992, 3132; Sugg and Inui 1992, 3158). Even highly implausible explanations, however, are rarely questioned by hospital staff (Eisenberg and Micklow 1979, 155–156; Hilberman 1980, 1342; Bohn 1990, 95). One physician explained: "I think that some physicians, and I do the same thing, if you are very busy and have a lot of patients waiting, you just don't ask a question that you know is going to open a Pandora's box. Even if it crossed your mind, you don't ask" (Sugg and Inui 1992, 3158). Another study of a large metropolitan hospital found that emergency room physicians identified only one female patient out of thirty-five as battered; subsequent research revealed that approximately one of four had probably been physically assaulted (Stark, Flitcraft, and Frazier 1979, 466). This underreporting was corroborated by subsequent research that found that emergency room staff identify domestic violence in as few as 5 percent of the cases (Goldberg and Tomlanovich 1984).

In the past, medical personnel neither asked pregnant patients about possible incidents of domestic violence nor considered it as a cause of miscarriage and stillbirth. Until 1992, the American Medical Association had no guidelines on consideration of domestic violence as a cause of injuries to female patients.

Recent attempts by the AMA, the March of Dimes, and the U.S. surgeon general to raise awareness of the problem have had little effect. In 1986 the March of Dimes launched a major campaign about the adverse impact of battering on fetal health. The foundation funded a pilot education program, literature for health care professionals, a video on battered pregnant teenagers, curriculum materials for high school classes, and a film titled *Crime against the Future* featuring then U.S. surgeon general C. Everett Koop (McFarlane 1989, 73–83), but these efforts failed to generate concern about the problem.

Research (Carmody and Williams 1987) on the self-perceptions of batterers has shown that most abusive men have never experienced any form of negative public sanctions because of their violence against women, nor did they expect to experience any as a result of future battering incidents. The absence of social sanctions cannot simply be explained away as continuing evidence of society's deeply ingrained sexism. While clearly part of the story, it is not the totality. A study by Klein, Campbell, Soler, and Ghez (1997), using both public opinion survey data and analyses of focus group discussions, found that public perceptions of domestic violence contain contradictory elements. The researchers found that in the 1990s there was a sharp increase in the percentage of survey respondents, who believe that "outside intervention is necessary if a husband hits his wife—even if she is not physically injured." Even though 82 percent of respondents in late 1995 supported outside intervention, nearly half (46 percent) of the respondents to the same survey also indicated that stress or drinking rather than the desire to hurt their wives is the reason for abuse. According to the researchers, "This widely held excuse for battering helps explain how friends, family, and institutions can continue to resist holding men accountable for their behavior" (1997, 89). They also found that 38 percent of respondents "wouldn't know what to say to an abused woman" (1997, 100). In other words, there are indications that public education campaigns designed to inform people about community resources and ways to discuss the issue could alter the social climate that appears to condone domestic violence, especially within marriages.

By minimizing the prevalence and severity of battering against women (pregnant and nonpregnant), the criminal justice system, the medical profession, and the public have reinforced the social definition of battering as a private issue rather than one to be addressed through government action. In some of the most highly publicized fetal abuse cases women have been blamed while men have escaped scrutiny. In one Wyoming case, a pregnant woman went to the hospital because she had been beaten by her husband and was arrested and charged with child abuse because she also had been drinking (Pollitt 1990, 416; Paltrow 1991, 88). In another case, a Georgia woman who delivered a stillborn child two days after a severe beating by her boyfriend was arrested because a fetal blood specimen tested positive for cocaine (Reproductive Freedom Project 1994, 24).

A cursory reading of case files shows that a high percentage of the more than 240 women charged with fetal abuse crimes had also been physically assaulted while pregnant. Notwithstanding sometimes clear evidence of third-party physical assaults, the prosecutors charged only the women. Because drug-addicted women violate our cultural norms about appropriate maternal behavior, the tendency is to blame the woman.

Jessica Pearson and Nancy Thoennes (1995, 108) found that in cities whose social service agencies have a public health orientation toward prenatal drug use, officials were far more likely to identify prenatal battering as a significant problem. Those from agencies with a punitive orientation, however, focused solely on the women's drug use and did not consider prenatal battering to be a problem. Pearson and Thoennes (1995, 20–32) studied the records of nearly a thousand women reported for drug use during pregnancy from Seattle, Minneapolis, Miami, and Charleston. These cities were picked because they had diverse policy responses to prenatal drug use. Seattle and Minneapolis follow the public health approach, while Charleston is the preeminent example of a city that uses a punitive and prosecutorial approach, and Miami is a hybrid. The researchers (1997, 108) found that in Seattle and Minneapolis, officials reported that 22 and 28 percent of the women were identified as victims of domestic violence. In contrast, officials in Miami identified only 1 percent of the women as battered, and Charleston officials did not identify a single woman as battered.

A case from Indiana, a state that has only punitive enactments, illustrates how a punitive approach to prenatal drug use can lead to prosecutors focusing solely on the actions of the woman and ignoring violent actions of men who are at least as culpable. In 1993 Catherine Barnett was arrested and charged with homicide, criminal neglect of a dependent, possession of cocaine, and failure to pay substance excise tax for the delivery of cocaine. Shortly before giving birth, Barnett had been held against her will by two men and forced to engage in acts of prostitution. When she began to experience abdominal pain, and even after her water broke, the men prevented Barnett from going to the hospital. Instead, they gave her cocaine and demanded that she raise an additional $200 (presumably through prostitution) before they would let her get medical attention. After finding her hemorrhaging in a car, the police took her to a hospital, where she delivered a one-pound baby who died five days later. In a plea bargain agreement, Barnett pleaded guilty to reduced charges and served a one-year prison sentence. The men were not charged (Reproductive Freedom Project 1994, 21).

Legislative Responses to Third-Party Fetal Assaults and Killings

State legislatures' most noticeable response to the problem of prenatal battering is its nonexistence. Although the prevalence and severity of third-party acts of violence against women increase during pregnancy, it has not been considered a serious social problem warranting a governmental response. As of

January 1998, only half of the states criminalized third-party killing of a fetus, and only Illinois, Ohio, and Pennsylvania considered third-party assaults that did not result in fetal deaths a crime.[40] Moreover, unlike what has happened with in utero drug exposure, no states have attempted to revise child abuse statutes to apply to cases of fetal battering. The problem has not reached the legislative policy agenda in most, if not all, of the fifty states, an alarming phenomenon in light of the tremendous attention devoted to the other two fetal policy areas (abortion and substance abuse by pregnant women).

According to Laura Gomez (1997, 38–39), lobbyists and legislators in California viewed the issue of prenatal drug exposure through an abortion lens. Those with pro-choice views about abortion strongly opposed criminalizing prenatal drug exposure because it would be used as a wedge issue, allowing further government restrictions over a woman's right to control her reproductive capabilities. Pro-choice lawmakers and lobbyists made up the vast majority of those supporting public health–oriented measures. Although pro-life legislators favored criminalization, some pro-life groups feared that it would encourage pregnant addicts to choose abortion rather than risk prosecution for fetal abuse. The pro-life groups—the Committee on Moral Concerns, the Traditional Values Coalition, and the California Pro-Life Council—unanimously opposed bills with a public health orientation.

The pro-life movement's relative silence about third-party acts of violence is even more surprising given its deep involvement in the crusade against prenatal drug exposure. At the national level, pro-life groups have been in the forefront of the movement to protect the fetus from harms caused by substance abuse during pregnancy. For example, the National Right to Life Committee has endorsed the prosecution of pregnant addicts for child abuse because "just as born children can be subject to abuse and neglect, so can unborn children" (Schacter 1986). Apparently, the movement is so obsessed with the behavior of pregnant women that far more grievous actions by men are ignored.

Third-Party Fetal Killing Statutes

In January 1998 twenty-three states had statutes making it a crime for a third party (not while performing an abortion) to kill a fetus. Although fifteen of these laws were enacted after *Roe*, the pro-life movement has not mobilized

[40] In late 1996 Ohio and Minnesota passed laws mandating that a person who physically assaults a fetus but does not cause its death is criminally liable and can be charged with assault (Ohio Revised Code Annotated 2903.13A; Minn. Stat. Section 609.2671). In 1997 Illinois created the criminal offense of "Battery of an Unborn Child." A person can be charged with this offense if he "intentionally or knowingly without legal justification and by any means causes bodily harm to an unborn child"; the latter is defined as "any individual of the human species from fertilization until birth" (720 ILCS 5/12–3.1). Pennsylvania also created a new felony offense "Aggravated Assault of Unborn Child" in late 1997 (18 Pa.C.S. 2606).

a campaign against third-party fetal killings.[41] In early 1998 Pamela Fiber, my research assistant, contacted thirty-two national pro-life organizations to determine whether they considered prenatal battering and third-party fetal killings to be a problem.[42] Only one of the groups, Americans United for Life, considered third-party acts of violence against fetuses an issue worth pursuing. The AUL through its Legal Defense Fund holds legal seminars on pro-life issues and publishes a quarterly newsletter on legal and legislative issues. It has provided pro-life legislators with model fetal homicide legislation, which was pursued by the Ohio state legislature, passing on a nearly unanimous vote by both chambers.[43]

After an eight-month-old fetus was killed in an auto accident, the pregnant woman's family was outraged because the driver of the other car could not be prosecuted under Pennsylvania law for the death of the fetus. They initiated a campaign to extend the state's criminal homicide statutes to cover embryos and fetuses. The Pennsylvania Pro-Life Federation and the Catholic Family Institute worked with pro-life state legislators in developing H.B. 1299/S.B. 45, which closely resembled the AUL model fetal homicide statute that Ohio passed in 1996 ("State Bill" 1997; interview with Pennsylvania Pro-Life Federation spokesperson, November 17, 1999). The legislation defines the killing of an "unborn child" at any stage of prenatal development as murder or manslaughter. In House floor debates, the primary sponsor of H.B. 1299, Dennis O'Brien (R–Philadelphia), was asked if a person who intentionally knocked

[41] The fifteen states that enacted laws criminalizing third-party fetal killings after 1973 are Arizona, Arkansas, Georgia, Illinois, Indiana, Louisiana, Minnesota, New Hampshire, New Mexico, North Dakota, Ohio, Pennsylvania, Rhode Island, South Dakota, and Utah. Two (New Mexico and Minnesota) had feticide statutes in the nineteenth century but repealed them before *Roe* and enacted new laws in 1985 and 1986.

[42] The thirty-two organizations were identified through the Pro-Life Network Index of Prolife Resources on the Web, Prolife.Org, the Ultimate Pro-Life Resource List, and *The Encyclopedia of Associations* (1997). Though obviously not a complete listing of all pro-life organizations in the country, it does provide a good cross section of the groups. The groups were American Association of Pro-Life Obstetricians and Gynecologists; American Association of Pro-Life Pediatricians; American Life League; Americans United for Life; Catholics United for Life; Christian Americans for Life; Collegians Activated to Liberate Life; Daughters of St. Paul; Eternal Life; Feminists for Life; Heartbeat International; Human Life Foundation; Human Life International; International Life Services; Jewish Anti-Abortion League; Libertarians for Life; Liberty Godparent Home; Life Issues Institute; March for Life Fund; National Committee for a Human Life Amendment; National Life Center; National Organization of Episcopalians for Life; National Right to Life Committee; Operation Rescue; Orthodox Christians for Life; Pharmacists for Life; Presbyterians Pro-Life; Pro-Life News; Pro-Life Action League; Pro-Life Alliance of Gays and Lesbians; Pro-Life Organization/Life Action Advocates; and Seamless Garment Network.

[43] Despite their unwillingness to criminalize third-party fetal battering and killing, at least some antiabortion activists favor prosecuting women who have abortions under murder statutes. In 1995 the American Coalition for Life Activists circulated a "Contract with the American Abortion Industry," which calls for prosecuting women, even victims of rape or incest, who have abortions "under the same laws that apply to the killing of any other human being" (Reprinted in Smith 1995).

over a petri dish of fertilized eggs could be charged with "multiple homicide." O'Brien responded, "If you knew, and it was your intent, then yes" (*Lancaster New Era* 1997, A1). The bill easily passed the House and Senate with strong bipartisan majorities and was signed into law by the state's pro-life Republican governor, Tom Ridge.

Evidence of pro-life groups' involvement in a campaign to pass a third-party fetal killing law was found only in Ohio and Pennsylvania, but I believe that some other enactments are part of a more general trend according greater value to fetal life. Others are simply statutory revisions that retain fetal killing as a crime but change its category of offense.[44] Of the other eight states with statutory prohibitions on third-party fetal killings, five still had the nineteenth-century laws on their books.[45] In examining all twenty-three of these criminal statutes, I categorized them according to severity of the criminal charge, stringency of the sentencing provisions, and gestational age of the fetus.

Severity of the Charge

The twenty-three states vary widely in the charges that can be made against an individual accused of killing a fetus. Fifteen have expanded existing criminal laws to apply to fetuses, but others have created new categories of criminal charges unique to fetal killings. Only in states whose statutes treat third-party fetal killings identically to the killing of a born person can the fetus be legally considered a full person; implicitly or explicitly the other states have accorded it lesser value. As of January 1998, only four states (California, Minnesota, Ohio, and Utah) included fetuses in their murder statutes.[46] All of the others consider third-party fetal killings separately from the killing of a born person and usually as a less serious offense. Eight states include fetuses in their manslaughter statutes but not murder statutes.[47] Arkansas treats fetal killings as first-degree battery. New Hampshire includes the following language in its

---

[44] For example, Illinois in 1986 eliminated its feticide statute and replaced it with the crime of "intentional homicide of an unborn child," which as a Class C felony has a maximum sentence of fifteen years, shorter than under the old feticide statute. Under the old feticide statute (Ill. Rev. Stat. 1981, ch. 38 par. 1005-8-2[a]), Keith Shum received a sentence of sixty years in prison for his 1981 killing of a viable fetus. For a discussion of the feticide statute in place at the time of his offense, see *People of the State of Illinois v. Keith Shum*, 117 Ill. 2d 317; 512 N.E.2d 1183; 111 Ill. (1987).

[45] The five states with nineteenth-century fetal killing laws are Florida, Iowa, Michigan, Mississippi, and Oklahoma. California added fetuses to its murder statutes in 1970. Nevada passed its law in 1911, and Washington did so in 1934 but revised it in 1975. Two states (Alabama and Tennessee) that enacted fetal killing statutes in the nineteenth century subsequently repealed them.

[46] When the California legislature amended the state's murder statute in 1970 to include the fetus, it failed to revise the manslaughter statute, which means that a person can be convicted of murder but not manslaughter for killing a fetus.

[47] The eight states in which a person can be charged with manslaughter are Arizona, Florida, Michigan, Mississippi, Nevada, Oklahoma, Rhode Island, and Washington. In Florida the law specifies that the maximum charge for fetal killing is second-degree manslaughter.

first-degree assault provisions: "A person is guilty of a class A felony if he. . . . purposely or knowingly causes injury to another resulting in miscarriage or stillbirth" (New Hampshire Revised Statutes Annotated 631:1, 1996).[48]

The remaining states have created new categories of crimes that apply only to fetal killings. Four (Georgia, Indiana, Iowa, and Louisiana) classify third-party fetal killings as feticide,[49] and another four (Illinois, North Dakota, Pennsylvania, and South Dakota) define it in functionally equivalent terms— "intentional homicide of an unborn child," "murder of an unborn child," and "fetal homicide." The final state (New Mexico) has created an ambiguous category that seeks to avoid entirely the question of fetal personhood; a third party who kills a fetus can be charged with the crime of "injury to a pregnant woman."

Stringency of the Sentencing Provisions

The stringency of the maximum punishment also varies, from a three-year prison sentence to the death penalty. The least severe penalties are in New Mexico, Indiana, and Arizona, which have maximum sentences of three, four, and five years, respectively. The maximum sentence in three states (Iowa, Nevada, and New Hampshire) is ten years, four (Florida, Louisiana, Michigan, and Illinois) allow individuals to be sentenced to up to fifteen years in prison, Arkansas and Mississippi permit a maximum of twenty years, and Rhode Island and South Dakota sanction up to thirty years. Seven states have life in prison as the maximum punishment for fetal killing: Georgia, Minnesota, North Dakota, Oklahoma, Pennsylvania, Utah, and Washington. Among the four "murder" states, California and Ohio categorize it as a capital crime, and Utah and Minnesota provide life in prison as their maximum sentence.

Gestational Age of the Fetus

The states differ over the gestational age covered by their statutes, ranging from those that criminalize the killing of a fetus of any gestational age to those that treat the killing as a crime only if the fetus has reached specific developmental points. All of the nine states that criminalize the killing of an embryo or fetus from fertilization or conception onward enacted their laws

[48] New Hampshire's homicide statute makes the distinction between fetal killings and the killing of a born person even sharper by specifically excluding the fetus: "As used in this section and RSA 630: 1–a, 1–b, 2, 3, and 4, the meaning of 'another' does not include a foetus" (New Hampshire Revised Statutes Annotated 630:1 IV, 1996).

[49] In Louisiana, the charge can be reduced to second-degree feticide if the pregnant woman provoked the violence: "The killing of an unborn child which would be first-degree feticide, but the offense is committed in sudden passion or heat of blood immediately caused by provocation of the mother of the unborn child sufficient to deprive an average person of his self control and cool reflection" (Louisiana Revised Statute Section 14:32.7, 1995).

after *Roe*.[50] The statutes in four other states (California, Indiana, Louisiana, and Utah) do not specify gestational ages, but the California Supreme Court in 1994 ruled that a fetus did not have to be viable and it was covered by the state's murder statute beginning at a gestational age of seven or eight weeks (*People v. Davis* 1994). Iowa's feticide statute is unique in that it is applicable only when the woman's pregnancy has reached the third trimester. Finally, nine states have criminal statutes that apply only to "quick" fetuses.[51] A "quick" fetus is one whose movement within the womb can be felt—a point that typically occurs at a gestational age of sixteen to twenty weeks.

Assessing the Legislative Response

Although this section focuses on differences among states with criminal statutes that apply to third-party fetal killings, it is important to remember that a majority of states do not have such enactments. Figure 4.1 shows the states with statutes that criminalize third-party fetal killing and those that do not. Moreover, even states with strongly pro-fetal-rights statutes generally do not criminalize acts of violence that do not result in fetal deaths—an important distinction between how fetal life and born life are viewed. The minority of states that criminalize third-party fetal killings vary widely in the value they confer on fetal life.

In assessing that value, points were assigned based on the severity of the criminal charges, the stringency of the sentencing provisions, and the gestational age of the fetus covered by the statutes. For the first criterion, three points were assigned to states whose murder statutes apply to fetuses, two points to states in which manslaughter is the maximum charge, and one point to those that define it otherwise. In assessing the stringency of the sentencing provisions, four points were given to states that made it a capital crime, three for life in prison, two for prison sentences of fifteen to thirty years, and one point for shorter periods of incarceration. Finally, three points were given to states that criminalized the killing of fetuses of any gestational age, two points for those that used "quickening" as the line of demarcation, and one point for those that used the third trimester or did not specify an age.

The scores ranged from three to nine out of ten possible points. Both the highest and the lowest point totals were garnered by midwestern states; Indiana and Iowa had three points each, and Minnesota and Ohio had nine apiece. Such discrepancies are owing, at least in part, to the greater random variation among states in the Midwest, the region with the highest number of criminal

---

[50] The nine states that criminalize third-party fetal killings from the point of fertilization or conception onward are Arizona, Arkansas, Illinois, Minnesota, New Mexico, North Dakota, Ohio, Pennsylvania, and South Dakota.

[51] The nine states that use "quickening" as a demarcation point are Florida, Georgia, Michigan, Mississippi, Nevada, New Hampshire, Oklahoma, Rhode Island, and Washington.

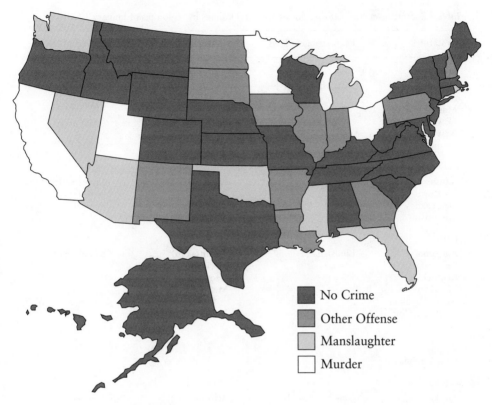

Figure 4.1. Third-party fetal killing statutes by state

laws that apply to fetal killing. Only four midwestern states (Kansas, Missouri, Nebraska, and Wisconsin) lack statutory proscriptions on third-party fetal killings, while only three northeastern states (New Hampshire, Pennsylvania, and Rhode Island) and slightly more than a third of the states in the South and the West have criminalized third-party fetal killings. See Table 4.2 for a comparison of the stringency of criminal statutes governing third-party acts of violence that result in the death of a fetus.

Judicial Responses to Third-Party Fetal Killings

In marked contrast to prenatal drug cases, in which women are prosecuted and often incarcerated even when their offspring are born alive with no signs of adverse consequences, I failed to find a single prosecution of a third party's act of violence that did not result in the death of the fetus. Because the criminal justice system has ignored nonlethal third-party acts of violence against fetuses, the interstate comparisons will only deal with fetal killings. I first briefly

Table 4.2. State laws criminalizing third-party fetal killings by region (as of January 1998)

No statutes	Least stringent laws	Average laws	Stringent laws
Northeast			
Connecticut	New Hampshire (4)	Rhode Island (6)	Pennsylvania (7)
Maine			
Massachusetts			
New Jersey			
New York			
Vermont			
Midwest			
Kansas	Indiana (3)	Illinois (6)	Minnesota (9)
Missouri	Iowa (3)	Michigan (6)	North Dakota (7)
Nebraska		South Dakota (6)	Ohio (9)
Wisconsin			
South			
Alabama	Louisiana (4)	Arkansas (6)	Oklahoma (7)
Delaware		Florida (6)	
Kentucky		Georgia (6)	
Maryland		Mississippi (6)	
North Carolina			
South Carolina			
Tennessee			
Texas			
Virginia			
West Virginia			
West			
Alaska	New Mexico (4)	Arizona (6)	California (7)
Colorado		Nevada (5)	Utah (7)
Hawaii			Washington (7)
Idaho			
Montana			
Oregon			
Wyoming			

Note: States with composite scores of 3 or 4 points are classified as having laws that are in the less stringent category. Those with composite scores of 5 or 6 are classified as having average laws, and those with scores greater than 6 are classified as having stringent laws.

consider states with statutory laws that cover fetal killings but then focus on judicial actions in states without such statutory language. Obviously, the potential for judicial activism is far greater in states where the legislatures have not spoken, making them more suited to compare with the role of courts in fetal abuse cases.

Prosecutions in Statutory Law States

Even in the twenty-three states that make killing a fetus a criminal offense, prosecutors are reluctant to charge individuals with these crimes. For example, Louisiana has a feticide statute with a maximum sentence of fifteen years, but the killing of a seven-month-old fetus was not prosecuted. The facts in the 1996 case are quite straightforward. In the course of robbing a crack house, the defendant killed a pregnant woman and a fetus by repeatedly shooting them with a shotgun, but he was tried only for the murder of the woman.[52]

Judicial Activism in Three States without Specific Code Law

In the absence of specific code law, states use common law precepts and case law to determine whether an action is a criminal offense. The common law born alive rule held that no crime was committed absent proof of a live birth and evidence showing that the subject's acts caused the subsequent death. As of January 1998, the courts in only three of the twenty-seven states without statutory provisions criminalizing third-party fetal killings[53] had modified the traditional common law born alive rule to make third-party killings a crime under some circumstances.

In Massachusetts and South Carolina, court rulings replaced the born alive rule with fetal viability to determine whether a crime has been committed against the fetus.[54] In both states, individuals who kill viable fetuses can be charged with murder, a capital offense. Despite the Massachusetts Supreme Court's decision in *Commonwealth v. Lawrence* (1989),[55] very few individuals have been prosecuted for the offense. For example, a Massachusetts man stabbed a pregnant co-worker in the abdomen, resulting in the death of a five-month-old fetus, but was not charged with killing the fetus (*Commonwealth v. Somnuk Viriyahiranpaiboon* 1992). Similarly, South Carolina prosecutors have not aggressively pursued criminal charges against individuals whose violent acts have caused the deaths of viable fetuses.

Although Missouri's murder statutes do not include specific language applicable to the fetus and its courts have followed the born alive rule, a Missouri appeals court recently held that the state's murder statutes apply to a fetus.[56] The court based its ruling on language in the preamble to the state's abortion statute, which states: "The general assembly of this state finds that:

---

[52] See *State of Louisiana v. Ronnie C. Davis*, 685 So. 2d 276 La App. (1996).

[53] The twenty-seven states without statutes criminalizing third-party fetal killing are Alabama, Alaska, Colorado, Connecticut, Delaware, Hawaii, Idaho, Kansas, Kentucky, Maine, Maryland, Massachusetts, Missouri, Montana, Nebraska, New Jersey, New York, North Carolina, Oregon, South Carolina, Tennessee, Texas, Vermont, Virginia, West Virginia, Wisconsin, and Wyoming.

[54] See *Commonwealth v. Lawrence*, 404 Mass. 378; 536 N.E.2d. 571 (1989) and *State v. Horne*, 282 S.C. 444, 319 S.E.2d. 703 (1984).

[55] Five years earlier in *Commonwealth v. Cass*, 392 Mass. 799 (1984), the Supreme Judicial Court of Massachusetts had indicated that it was moving toward considering a viable fetus to be a "person" when it ruled that the state's vehicular homicide statute covered viable fetuses.

[56] Even though the fetus had a gestational age of twenty-six to twenty-eight weeks at the time of its death, the question of viability was not an issue in the case. The defendant attempted to argue that the born alive rule meant that he could not be prosecuted for murder, but the state contended that the legislature's intent in Section 1.205 was that all state laws were to treat the fetus as a "person" from the point of conception onward. See *State of Missouri v. Barry J. Holcomb*, 956 S.W.2d 286 Mo. (1997).

1.) The life of each human being begins at conception; 2.) Unborn children have protectable interests in life, health, and well-being" (Missouri Revised Statute 1.205 1994).[57]

Judicial Responses in Traditional Common Law States

The remaining twenty-four common law states have not aggressively sought to criminalize third-party fetal killings.[58] District attorneys have been reluctant to prosecute individuals for fetal killings, and the courts have been unwilling to extend the definition of "person" in murder and manslaughter statutes to include fetuses.[59] Records of such prosecutions exist in roughly half of the traditional common law states.[60]

Prosecutorial reluctance extends even to cases in which the fetus is close to term. For example, in 1981 Larry Heath arranged for his wife, who was then nine months pregnant, to be kidnapped and murdered. At least one of his many motives was directly related to the fetus. Suspecting his wife of infidelity, Heath believed that he was not the father. Yet neither Heath nor the two assailants that he hired were prosecuted for the killing of the obviously viable fetus.[61] In another case, a Virginia man used a .45 caliber handgun to shoot a fourteen-year-old girl who was carrying his baby three times in the abdomen. Even though the girl survived and the seven-month-old fetus died, the defendant was charged with malicious wounding of the girl but not for the fetal killing.[62]

When forced to rule on the personhood status of the fetus in applying murder statutes, courts in the traditional common law states generally have cited the born alive rule and the failure of state legislatures to revise murder statutes for not judicially extending them to cover fetuses.[63] The North Carolina Supreme

[57] Section 1.205 of the Missouri Revised Statutes is the preamble to the state's abortion law that was the subject of the Supreme Court's *Webster* (1986) decision.

[58] There have been only a handful of law journal articles about third-party fetal killings and the continuing applicability of the born alive rule. See Bentley 1983; Perko 1990.

[59] Because states do not keep separate records of fetal killing prosecutions, only cases that involved appeals to higher state courts were considered. These seem to provide a generally good record because a person convicted of killing a fetus would probably appeal on the ground that the common law born alive rule precludes a fetus from being considered a person in these states.

[60] No records of prosecutions for fetal killing in twelve states were found: Alabama, Alaska, Colorado, Delaware, Hawaii, Maine, Maryland, Montana, Nebraska, Texas, Virginia, and Wyoming. The twelve traditional common law states that have attempted to prosecute individuals for the killing of a fetus are Connecticut, Idaho, Kansas, Kentucky, New Jersey, New York, North Carolina, Oregon, Tennessee, Vermont, West Virginia, and Wisconsin. The Tennessee case was from 1923, however, so it can hardly be considered a recent effort to enhance the legal status of the fetus.

[61] See *Larry Gene Heath v. Charlie Jones*, 941 F.2d 1126 (1991 U.S. App.).

[62] See *Christopher C. Goins v. Commonwealth of Virginia*, 251 Va. 442 (1996).

[63] See *State v. Anonymous*, 40 Conn. Supp. 498; 516 A.2d 156 (1986); *Volk v. Baldazo*, 103 Idaho 570, 651 P.2d 11 (1982); *State of Kansas v. Willard Green*, 245 Kan. 398; 781 P.2d 678 (1989); *Hollis v. Commonwealth*, 652 S.W.2d 61 Ky (1983); *Giardina v. Bennett*, 111 N.J. 412, 545 A.2d 139 (1988); *People v. Vercelletto*, Family Court of New York, Ulster County, 135 Misc. 2d 40; 514 N.Y.S.2d 177 (1987); *State v. Beale*, 324 N.C. 87, 376 S.E.2d 1 (1989); *State v. Smith*,

Court refused to consider a fetus that was in the process of being born a person. In late 1986, Donald Rae Beale fired a shotgun at the head of his pregnant wife, who was twelve days past her due date and had been having labor contractions. Both Mrs. Beale and the fetus died as a result of the shotgun blast. Even though the North Carolina Supreme Court had ruled two years previously that a viable fetus was a person under the state's Wrongful Death Act,[64] the same court held that any extension of the murder statute is "best left to the discretion and the wisdom of the legislature" (*State v. Beale* 1989).

The Kansas Supreme Court ruled that even evidence of a live birth is not always enough to warrant legal personhood status. In 1986, Willard Green shot his estranged girlfriend in the arm, chest, and head. Physicians failed in their attempts to resuscitate the woman but did manage to deliver a thirty-four- to thirty-five-week-old fetus, which died shortly thereafter. Even though physicians detected heartbeats about ten minutes after birth, they classified the death as a stillbirth. Although a jury found Green guilty on two counts of first-degree murder (for the mother and child), the Kansas Supreme Court reversed one of the convictions and held that "a viable fetus is not a human being as that term is used in the first-degree murder statute." Construing "viable fetus" to be within the term "human being" exceeds judicial power and denies a defendant due process. Imposing criminal liability for the killing of a fetus is a legislative function" (*State of Kansas v. Willard Green* 1989).

Court rulings denying the applicability of murder statutes to viable fetuses have provided impetus for some of the revisions in state criminal codes making fetal killings a chargeable offense. The California Supreme Court's decision in *Keeler v. Superior Court of Amador County* (1970)[65] that an unborn viable fetus was not a "human being" within the meaning of the state's murder statute prompted the legislature to revise the definition of murder to read, "the unlawful killing of a human being, or a fetus, with malice aforethought" (California Penal Code Sect. 187.a, 1997).[66] Similarly, the Louisiana Supreme Court

---

310 Ore. 1, 791 P.2d 836 (1990); *Morgan v. State*, 148 Tenn. 417, 256 S.W. 433 (1923); *State v. Oliver*, 151 Vt. 626, 563 A.2d 1002 (1989); *State ex rel. Atkinson v. Wilson*, 175 W. Va. 352, 332 S.E.2d 807 (1985); *State v. Black*, 188 Wis.2d 639, 641, 526 N.W.2d 132, 133 (1994).

[64] See *DiDonat v. Wortman*, 320 N.C. 423, 427–28, 358 S.E.2d 489, 491–92 (1987).

[65] The facts in the case were never in dispute, only whether a crime had been committed. The defendant became enraged after learning that his former wife had become pregnant by another man. He looked at her abdomen and said, "I'm going to stomp it out of you." He then pushed her, shoved his knee against her abdomen, and hit her several times in the face. Mrs. Keeler fainted. When she regained consciousness, the defendant had left and she was able to drive herself to the hospital, where a cesarean section was performed. The stillborn fetus's head was severely fractured and the pathologist ruled that death was caused by the fracture, which led to cerebral hemorrhaging. He further found that this type of injury could have been caused by a blow to Mrs. Keeler's abdomen. See *Keeler v. Superior Court of Amador County*, 2 Cal. 3d 619; 470 P.2d 617 (1970).

[66] The court's choice of language in *Keeler v. Superior Court of Amador County* (1970) seemed to invite the state legislature to reconsider the scope of its murder statute. "In this proceeding for writ of prohibition we are called upon to decide whether an unborn but viable fetus is a 'human being' within the meaning of the California statute defining murder (Pen. Code Section 187). We conclude that the Legislature did not intend such a meaning, and that for us to construe the statute

overturned the murder conviction of a man who beat a pregnant woman with a stick and his fists, causing the stillbirth of an eight-month fetus, because the legislature had not criminalized fetal killings, leading to a statutory revision of its criminal laws in 1977.[67] The 1986 enactment of Minnesota's fetal murder statute also was prompted by a 1985 state supreme court's ruling that the common law meaning of "human being" did not include fetuses.[68]

Higher courts (both in states and at the federal level) have generally upheld the constitutionality of statutes making third-party fetal killings a crime. For example, an Illinois man who stomped on the abdomen of his seventeen-year-old stepdaughter and killed her five-and-a-half-month-old fetus, tried to argue that his "intentional homicide of an unborn child" conviction violated the Equal Protection Clause because it failed to distinguish between a viable and a nonviable fetus. The appellate court affirmed his conviction, holding, "It is unnecessary to prove the unborn child is a person or human being. The statute only requires proof that, whatever the entity within the mother's womb is called, it had life and, because of the acts of the defendant, it no longer does" (*People of the State of Illinois v. Robert Ford, Jr.* 1991). In another case, a Georgia man appealed his feticide conviction all the way to the U.S. Eleventh Circuit Court of Appeals but was unable to convince the court that the statute was unconstitutionally vague because it included the term "quick."[69]

Summary

As we have seen, fetal policies differ substantially regarding prenatal drug use and third-party acts of violence against pregnant women. Most state legislatures have passed laws that treat drug abuse by pregnant women as a public health matter, but a few have emphasized punitive statutes. Although none has passed laws making drug use by pregnant women a separate criminal offense, prosecutors in some states have aggressively pursued criminal charges against drug-using pregnant women, while others have chosen not to consider it a criminal matter.

---

contrary and apply it to this petitioner would exceed our judicial power and deny the petitioner due process of law."

[67] Justice Barham in his majority opinion noted that Louisiana's criminal code did not include fetal killings as part of the murder statute nor did the state have a feticide statute like many other states. Then, in explaining why the court could not extend the existing statutes by judicial fiat to cover third-party fetal killings, Barham wrote, "In the first place, this Court cannot create a crime; only the legislature may. In the second place, the articles of the Criminal Code expressly cannot be extended by analogy so as to create crimes not provided for herein" (*State of Louisiana v. Arthur Ray Gyles*, La. 313 S. 2d 799 [1975]).

[68] See *State v. Soto*, 378 N.W.2d 625, 630 (Minn. 1985) and *State of Minnesota v. Justin L. Bauer*, 471 N.W.2d 363 (1991 Minn. App.); the first case prompted the legislative action and the second summarizes the history of fetal prosecutions and legislative action in the state.

[69] *Smith v. Newsome*, 815 F.2d 1386 (1987 U.S. App). A similar argument was rejected by the supreme court of Minnesota in *State of Minnesota v. Sean Patrick Merrill*, 450 N.W.2d 318 (1990 Minn.).

When it comes to third-party fetal killings, the interstate discrepancies are even greater. As of January 1998, half of the states had statutes or case law criminalizing third-party fetal killings, with maximum penalties from three years' incarceration to death. Thus a person can be convicted of first-degree murder and sentenced to death in Cincinnati, Ohio, for killing a fetus of any gestational age, but one hundred miles south in Louisville, Kentucky, the killing of a nine-month-old fetus is not a crime.

In many cases, the intrastate disparities in treatment of potentially harmful actions against fetuses are often as glaring as the interstate differences. Although both prenatal drug exposure and prenatal battering can result in physical and developmental problems and even death, states regard the two situations very differently. Despite the absence of laws criminalizing substance abuse by pregnant women vis-à-vis their fetuses, at least thirty-four states have enhanced existing statutes, particularly child abuse laws, to cover fetal abuse situations. I found no evidence of analogous interpretive creativity in cases where the fetus is harmed or possibly killed by violent acts of a third party. Roughly half of the states that have prosecuted women for drug use while pregnant have no statutes or case law that make it a criminal offense for a person to knife, shoot, stomp, or beat a fetus to death.[70] In other words, a woman in these states can give birth to a healthy baby but be prosecuted for a criminal offense on the basis of a positive toxicology screen, but a man who intentionally stomps a pregnant woman in the abdomen, leading to the stillbirth of an eight-month-old fetus, cannot be charged for killing the fetus. Most of the states that do allow criminal charges to be filed in third-party fetal killing cases also have historically prosecuted women for drug use during pregnancy.[71]

Making sense of these disparate policy responses seems almost impossible, although some points are worth considering. Notably, the morality policy framework posited by Meier and other policy scholars must recognize that legislative and judicial policymaking are different and that, perhaps paradoxically, the latter is far more susceptible to the "politics of sin" and "rush to Armageddon." As we have seen, the most punitive of the prenatal drug-exposure policies have been implemented by the courts rather than state legislatures. Also, any explanation of the differential responses to the two fetal policies under consideration must take into account the role of unconscious gender bias. How else can we explain policies that send pregnant women to prison for using drugs but do not even charge men who batter and kill fetuses with a crime?

---

[70] The following states have women prosecuted for using drugs while pregnant but do not have statutes or case law that make it a crime for a third party to kill a fetus: Alabama, Alaska, Connecticut, Idaho, Kentucky, Nebraska, New York, North Carolina, Oregon, Texas, Virginia, Wisconsin, and Wyoming.

[71] Of the twenty-six states that have case or statutory law that criminalizes third-party fetal killing, all but seven (Arkansas, Iowa, Louisiana, Minnesota, New Hampshire, New Mexico, and Rhode Island) have pursued criminal charges against substance-abusing pregnant women.

CHAPTER 5

Explaining Fetal Policies across the States

Searching for the Common Thread in Fetal Policies

Despite their common moral component, the three fetal policies engender very different politics and policy outcomes. Abortion politics appears to fit the profile of a contested morality policy, with different camps deeply divided over their moral convictions, but the actual policy enactments may or may not reflect the relative strength of pro-life and pro-choice sentiment in the states. Characterizing the other two fetal policy issues as morality policies is even more dubious. Drug-using pregnant women and individuals who commit acts of violence against pregnant women and fetuses are universally condemned, but only the former has appeared prominently on state policy agendas. Moreover, efforts to channel public anger against substance-abusing pregnant women into the passage of new criminal laws have been largely unsuccessful. Instead, states have adopted a range of policies, both punitive and public health–oriented, outside the criminal justice system—hardly a "rush to Armageddon." In the context of fetal battering/third-party fetal killing, the one-sided morality policy framework is completely inapplicable. Despite publicity campaigns by the surgeon general of the United States and the March of Dimes, the public has collectively yawned.

This lack of a common morality politics does not necessarily render the policies totally unconnected. It is still important to try to identify common threads linking the policies together. For example, do state policies in the three areas reflect public sentiment about the value of fetal life? No opinion polls have explicitly measured the value society places on fetal life, so it can be ascertained only indirectly through survey questions about abortion. This chapter begins by probing whether any relationship exists between responses to a general abortion question and state laws controlling a woman's access to abortion services. Then I examine links between the same responses and state policies on prenatal drug exposure and prenatal battering/killing. Finally, I focus on the congruence among the three fetal policies' value of fetal life, measured by the competing propositions formulated by the fetal rights and women's rights narratives discussed in Chapter 1.

Public Opinion and State Abortion Policies

Scholars (Wright, Erikson, and McIver 1987; Erikson, Wright, and McIver 1993) generally have found that states' policies reflect the views of their residents. This should be particularly true for politically prominent issues such as abortion.[1] Whether such a relationship extends to policy and opinion on fetal abuse and third-party fetal killings is less obvious. If antiabortion sentiments among pro-life lawmakers are part of a general reverence for "unborn" human life, those attitudes should extend to all fetal policy issues. The absence of any such relationship would indicate the absence of a comprehensive pro-life (pro-fetus) ideology.

To assess pro-life attitudes in the states, I used the 1988–90 National Election Series (NES) Senate Panel Study, which included responses to questions about abortion from nearly all fifty states.[2] Also, as noted in Chapter 3, the 1989 *Webster* decision profoundly altered the political mobilization of abortion interest groups (i.e., both pro-life and pro-choice forces became fully engaged.)[3] According to Tatalovich and Daynes (1993), *Webster* was a lightning rod that sparked interest group activity; 65 pro-life groups and 316 pro-choice organizations cosponsored amicus curiae briefs. The discrepancy in numbers is misleading because most of the pro-life organizations focus solely on abortion while nearly all of the pro-choice groups are multi-issue organizations.

Responses to the NES's question, "Do you think abortion should be legal under all circumstances, only legal under certain circumstances, or never legal under any circumstances?" will be used to explore linkages between public opinion and state fetal policies.[4] The wide interstate variation in support for

[1] Nearly all of the substantial body of research on the determinants of state abortion policies (Goggin and Kim 1992; Berkman and O'Connor 1993; Cohen and Barrileaux 1993; Goggin and Wlezien 1993; Hansen 1993; Meier and McFarlane 1993) have used public opinion polls or their proxies as independent predictors, and most have found a significant relationship.

[2] Because state-level public opinion data were previously unavailable, scholars (Berkman and O'Connor 1993; Hansen 1993) used proxies, such as NARAL membership and percentage of Catholics, to measure pro-life sentiment. Others (Cohen and Barrilleaux 1993; Cook, Jelen, and Wilcox 1993) have used data sets that include public opinion data from some but not all states. The 1988–90 NES data used in this study cover nearly all fifty states and were compiled by Wetstein (1996: 78–79).

[3] Although *Webster* dramatically affected interest group activity, the impact of court decisions on public opinion about abortion is short-lived and does not usually alter long-term attitudes (Wlezien and Goggin 1993).

[4] In scaled dimensional studies of attitudes toward abortion, Guth, Smidt, Kellstedt, and Green (1993) used a similar question to assess levels of pro-life and pro-choice sentiment.

legal abortion under all circumstances facilitated assessing differing degrees of support for pro-life or pro-choice positions. Moreover, as Christopher Wlezien and Malcolm Goggin (1993) point out, responses to this question have not varied significantly since 1973. Roughly 23 percent of respondents consistently support a woman's right to have an abortion under all circumstances. The measure of the overall character of state abortion laws used here was derived in Chapter 3 and indicates the restrictiveness of the laws as of January 1998 (Lexis). Because state abortion laws are constantly undergoing revision, January 1998 is used as the comparison point.

The expected inverse relationship between support for abortion and the restrictiveness of state abortion laws was not consistent across all states or on all types of abortion laws. The tenuousness of the linkage between public opinion and actual abortion laws can be seen in the abortion laws in Kentucky and Colorado, the states with the lowest (12 percent) and highest (48 percent) levels of public support for unrestricted abortion.

Despite strong pro-life sentiment, Kentucky's abortion laws are less restrictive than many other states'. Although it is one of the forty-one states that prohibit postviability abortions, its ban is less stringent than in eight of them. It lacks a pre-*Roe* abortion proscription, and the legislature has not chosen to enact a new one, such as those passed by Utah and Louisiana in 1991. Kentucky also is one of thirty-one states allowing intact dilation and extraction (partial birth) abortions. In its overall abortion prohibitions, Kentucky falls in the middle of the pro-choice/pro-life continuum; twenty-three states are more strict and twenty-six are less so. In its restrictions on abortion, however, Kentucky is one of the strictest states, including conscience-based exemptions for medical personnel and health care facilities, husband notification, a mandatory waiting period, informed consent that mandates a description of abortion risks and the gestational age of the fetus, and a requirement that insurance companies exclude abortion coverage unless the insured pays for an optional rider. Overall, the pro-life content of Kentucky's abortion laws fell in the eighty-second percentile (i.e., the ninth most restrictive).

Colorado's laws were far less restrictive than Kentucky's but less pro-choice than would be expected, given the strong public support for abortion rights. Although it is one of only six states that have banned neither partial birth nor postviability abortions, its pre-*Roe* ban (unless the woman's life or health is threatened, or the pregnancy is the result of rape or incest, or if the child would have serious physical deformities or defects) remains on the books. Colorado's abortion laws include conscience-based exemptions, husband consent requirements, a prohibition on abortion coverage by public employees' insurance providers, and severe limits on public funding of abortions for indigent women. Overall, Colorado ranked in the sixty-fourth percentile of pro-choice states (i.e., the eighteenth most favorable to the pro-choice position).

Table 5.1. Public opinion and state laws banning abortion

Type of ban	States divided into quartiles according to public opinion about abortion			
	Strong pro-choice	Weak pro-choice	Weak pro-life	Strong pro-life
General ban				
No	9 states (69.2%)	8 states (66.7%)	10 states (76.9%)	6 states (50%)
Yes	4 states (30.8%)	4 states (33.3%)	3 states (23.1%)	6 states (50%)
Partial birth				
No	10 states (76.9%)	7 states (58.3%)	8 states (61.5%)	6 states (50%)
Yes	3 states (23.1%)	5 states (41.7%)	5 states (38.5%)	6 states (50%)
Postviability				
No	6 states (46.2%)	1 state (8.3%)	0 states	2 states (16.7%)
Yes	7 states (53.8%)	11 states (91.7%)	13 states (100%)	10 states (83.3%)

Note: States were assigned to quartiles based on the percentages of respondents who agreed that abortion should be legal under all circumstances in the 1988–90 NES Senate Panel Study. The top figures are the numbers of states in each quartile that have adopted or not adopted a particular ban. The bottom figures are the percentages of states in that quartile that have adopted or not adopted a particular ban.

The Overall Relationship between Pro-Life Sentiment and State Abortion Policies

The remaining states are similar to Kentucky and Colorado. Pro-life states typically have stringent abortion laws, and pro-choice states typically place fewer restrictions on abortion, but the relationship is far from clear. Incremental increases in the percentage of the public opposed to abortion do not necessarily correlate to additional restrictions, as demonstrated by the relationship between the prevalence of different types of abortion bans and the degree of support for abortion rights as measured by responses to the NES survey question. For illustrative purposes, the states are divided into quartiles based on their population's support for the pro-choice position—strong pro-life, weak pro-life, weak pro-choice, and strong pro-choice. Table 5.1 shows that weak pro-life states are less likely to ban abortion unequivocally than are strong pro-choice states. Differences between weak pro-choice and weak pro-life states diminish regarding bans on partial birth abortions and postviability abortions. Weak pro-choice and weak pro-life states are more likely to prohibit postviability abortions than strong pro-life states.

Similar anomalies arise concerning a state's adoption of specific abortion re-

Table 5.2. Public opinion and state laws restricting abortion

Restrictiveness of laws	States divided into quartiles according to public opinion about abortion			
	Strong pro-choice	Weak pro-choice	Weak pro-life	Strong pro-life
Not restrictive	7 states (53.8%)	1 state (8.3%)	3 states (23.1%)	1 state (8.3%)
Some restrictions	4 states (30.8%)	5 states (41.7%)	3 states (23.1%)	1 state (8.3%)
Restrictive	2 states (15.4%)	2 states (16.7%)	4 states (30.8%)	3 states (25%)
Very restrictive	0 states	4 states (33.3%)	3 states (23.1%)	7 states (58.3%)

Note: States were assigned to quartiles based on the percentages of respondents who agreed that abortion should be legal under all circumstances in the 1988–90 NES Senate Panel Study. The top figures are the numbers of states in each quartile that fall into each category of restrictiveness. The bottom figures are the percentages of states in that quartile that are in each category of restrictiveness.

strictions. But pro-life states are more likely than pro-choice states to adopt restrictive abortion laws for both adults and minors. Table 5.2 shows the relationship between public opinion in the states and the measure of overall restrictiveness developed in Chapter 4. In the most surprising incongruity between public sentiment and the character of abortion laws, four states from the pro-life end of the continuum (one strong and three weak pro-life states) have minimal restrictions on abortion.

Public Opinion and State Polices toward Prenatal Drug Exposure

The few surveys of public attitudes toward drug-abusing pregnant women cannot serve as surrogates to assess the value accorded fetal life in each state. First, none includes state-level public opinion data from every state. Second, the nearly universal approbation accorded pregnant addicts cannot be used to explain differences in value accorded fetal life. One need not believe that the fetus is fully human from the point of fertilization to oppose in utero exposure to narcotics. Responses to the NES general abortion question better measure pro-life attitudes in the states.

The large variance in responses to prenatal drug exposure make it difficult to ascertain which of those accord greater or lesser value to fetal life. But it is quite simple to distinguish between states that do and do not have laws designed to address the problem and to argue that the former accord the fetus greater value than the latter. The states in these two categories only weakly correspond to those where public opinion is pro-life and pro-choice. Antiabortion Kentucky should be far more active than pro-choice Colorado in legislating about prenatal drug exposure, but each has two laws on the subject. The

Table 5.3. Public opinion and fetal abuse prosecutions, 1985–98

Whether there has been a prosecution	States divided into quartiles according to public opinion about abortion			
	Strong pro-choice	Weak pro-choice	Weak pro-life	Strong pro-life
No	6 states (46.2%)	5 states (41.7%)	1 state (7.7%)	4 states (33.3%)
Yes	7 states (53.8%)	7 states (58.3%)	12 states (92.3%)	8 states (66.7%)

Note: States were assigned to quartiles based on the percentages of respondents who agreed that abortion should be legal under all circumstances in the 1988–90 NES Senate Panel Study.

difference lies in the mix of policies they adopted. Kentucky is more punitive than Colorado, requiring that medical personnel report positive toxicology screens in pregnant women and newborns, although it also has developed a pilot drug-treatment program. In contrast, Colorado has focused entirely on public health–oriented measures—preventive drug education and a pilot drug-treatment program.

The Overall Relationship between Pro-Life Sentiment and Prenatal Drug Policies

In general, states in the most pro-life quartile are somewhat more likely than others to have adopted prenatal drug-exposure laws, both punitive and public health–oriented measures. Moreover, strong pro-choice states are just as likely as weak pro-life states to have such policies. There also are no significant differences in the policies adopted in the states. Both pro-life and pro-choice states have enacted punitive as well as public health–oriented measures.

The pro-life and pro-choice states do differ considerably in whether they have prosecuted drug-using pregnant women since 1985. Local district attorneys in pro-life states are far more likely than those in pro-choice states to use existing criminal statutes, such as child abuse laws, to prosecute these women, but whether they are motivated by their own pro-life convictions or public sentiment is an open question. Table 5.3 shows the relationship between public opinion on abortion and fetal abuse prosecutions in the states.

Public Opinion and Policies toward Third-Party Fetal Killing

Since no surveys assess public opinion about policies toward third-party fetal killing (one more indication of its relative absence from the policy agenda), I continue to use the general NES abortion question as a surrogate for atti-

Table 5.4. Public opinion and third-party fetal killing prosecutions

Whether there has been a prosecution	States divided into quartiles according to public opinion about abortion			
	Strong pro-choice	Weak pro-choice	Weak pro-life	Strong pro-life
No	6 states (46.2%)	3 states (25%)	5 states (38.5%)	2 states (16.7%)
Yes	7 states (53.8%)	9 states (75%)	8 states (61.5%)	10 states (83.3%)

Note: States were assigned to quartiles based on the percentages of respondents who agreed that abortion should be legal under all circumstances in the 1988–90 NES Senate Panel Study.

tudes on the value of fetal life. Examining policies toward fetal killing in the strongest pro-life (Kentucky) and pro-choice (Colorado) states to determine whether such policies reflect differences in the treatment of third-party fetal killings, I found they treat fetal killings identically. Both are common law states that follow the born alive rule, meaning that criminal liability does not attach for killing a fetus that dies before birth.

Even though twenty-three states statutorily criminalize third-party fetal killings, the likelihood that a particular state has such a law is not related to public sentiment about abortion. Still, prosecutions are more likely in the strong pro-life states than in any other quartile. Again, this may be connected to the personal beliefs of district attorneys or their responses to pro-life sentiment in the broader community. Table 5.4 shows the relationship of abortion opinion and prosecutions for fetal killings.

Summing Up the Impact of Public Opinion

We now know that public opinion cannot predict state fetal policies, although pro-life sentiment is somewhat related to the restrictiveness of state abortion laws. Moreover, pro-life attitudes on abortion do not predict even whether states will have laws governing prenatal drug exposure and third-party fetal killings. The nature of the policy process, in which policy outcomes result from political competition among organized interest groups and do not reflect public sentiment, often weakens the relationship between opinion and policy.[5] Strong pro-choice and pro-life interest groups have been active in all of the states since *Roe*.

Although the views of the interest groups are quite different from those held

[5] Public actions by pro-life and pro-choice interest groups affect public opinion differently. According to Wlezian and Goggin (1993), very visible actions by the pro-life side cost it more than 1 percent of public support, but pro-choice actions did not affect public opinion in either direction. They believe the difference is owing to the type of actions rather than the policy aims of the groups. Confrontational conduct, such as blockades of clinics, triggered a strong negative response, while the more low-key actions favored by pro-choice groups did not affect attitudes.

by the general public, they wield enormous power within the Republican and Democratic parties, both of which have used candidates' positions on abortion as litmus tests (Rozell and Wilcox 1996). Because much of the South is still Democratic, the party has been far more split than the Republicans on the question of abortion. For example, in 1997 a Democratic member of the Alabama state assembly introduced a resolution commending the antiabortion group Alabama Citizens Action Program and its director for their help in passing bans on postviability and partial birth abortions. The resolution passed both chambers and was signed by the governor (Act No. 97–306, 1997 Ala. Adv. Legis Serv. 309).

Assessing the Fetal Rights and Women's Rights Narratives

Although public opinion is a poor predictor of state enactment of laws on prenatal drug exposure and third-party fetal killing, the relationship between the stringency of state abortion laws and their responses to the other two fetal issues may still be significant. After all, the fetal laws all come from the same legislative bodies and may implicitly reflect their views about the importance of protecting fetal life from various possible harms. We can compare the narratives put forth by fetal rights proponents and women's rights proponents and the actual conditions in the different states. Although neither can be definitively proven correct or incorrect on the basis of these comparisons, it is possible to ascertain whether the evidence is consistent with a particular side's story or not. If the laws are not consistent, then one can infer that the narrative is probably not an accurate or a full chronicle of reality.

Because fetal rights proponents premise their argument on the moral imperative of saving "human" life, they must meet a higher evidentiary standard than their opponents. If the fetal rights story about the need to protect innocent fetal life reflects its proponents' views, then antiabortion states should have laws that protect the fetus from in utero drug exposure and prenatal battering/fetal killing. Moreover, since the fetal rights proponents' argument is premised on a moral imperative, their concern with saving the lives of fetuses should outweigh secondary considerations, such as the cost of policies, and their positions should be consistent across the three policy areas. Why would an unborn child threatened by abortion be any more deserving of protection than one at risk of being battered by its father or exposed to drugs in utero?

Conversely, the women's rights story holds that antiabortion activists are really using their campaign against abortion only as a subterfuge to attack women's rights. If it is accurate, states should differ in the protection they accord fetuses, with policymakers in antiabortion states caring deeply about fetal life threatened by the actions of the woman and caring less when that life is threatened by third parties (i.e., typically men who commit acts of violence against pregnant women and their fetuses). In subsequent sections I assess the validity of the narratives by empirically testing the following propositions derived from them. See Chapter 1 for a discussion of the reasoning behind each of the alternative propositions.

Fetal Rights Propositions

Proposition 1a: Antiabortion states treat the fetus as a "person" in other areas of the law, regardless of the gender and/or status of the individual responsible for harming it.

Proposition 2a: Antiabortion states are more likely to adopt policies to combat prenatal drug use and third-party killings than other states.

Proposition 3a: Antiabortion states are more likely to support a wide range of policies that improve the health and well-being of society's weakest and most vulnerable "persons."

Women's Rights Propositions

Proposition 1b: Antiabortion states do not consistently treat the fetus as a "person" in other areas of the law.

Proposition 2b: Differences in abortion law are a function of women's political, social, and economic status, which is generally lower in antiabortion states than in pro-choice states.

Proposition 3b: Antiabortion states are not more likely to support a wide range of policies that improve the health and well-being of society's weakest and most vulnerable "persons."

Proposition 1: Do Anti-Abortion States Consistently Treat the Fetus as a Person?

The two narratives generate very different propositions about the expectation that states with antiabortion laws would treat the fetus as a "person" in their laws governing in utero drug exposure and third-party fetal killing. Because the underlying imperative in the fetal rights story is premised on the moral necessity of protecting fetal life, these states' concern for fetal well-being should carry over into the two other fetal policy areas. If the women's rights narrative is accurate, antiabortion states would not consistently treat the fetus as a person in the other policy areas. Because the focus of the women's rights story is the subjugation of women, its proponents would expect antiabortion forces more vehemently to advocate fetal rights when the person harming the fetus is its mother than when it is a third party (i.e., male). They would expect antiabortion states to favor policies aimed at in utero drug exposure over fetal battering/third-party fetal killing.

Again the states were divided into quartiles based on the degree to which their abortion laws reflect the pro-life position. Overall, the women's rights proposition—antiabortion states are more concerned about prenatal drug exposure than third-party fetal killings—is strongly supported. Of the fourteen states with strong pro-life abortion laws, 78.6 percent passed laws to deal with prenatal drug use but only 57.1 percent criminalized third-party fetal killings. Even though Delaware, Idaho, Kansas, Kentucky, Nebraska, and Wisconsin are among the most solid antiabortion states in the country, they had not criminalized third-party fetal killings before January 1998, and all except Idaho have passed prenatal drug-exposure laws. At least four of them (Idaho, Kentucky, Nebraska, and Wisconsin) have prosecuted pregnant addicts for exposing their children prenatally to narcotics.[6] Because prenatal narcotics exposure often produces no lasting harm, fetal rights proponents' aggressive stance toward drug use during pregnancy seems paradoxical, when compared to the lack of concern about third-party fetal battering/killing.

The differences in responses to the two types of fetal harms are even more striking among the eleven weak pro-life states. Roughly one-third (36.4 percent) have statutes making third-party fetal killing a crime, compared to 63.6 percent with prenatal drug-exposure laws. Three (Massachusetts, Missouri, and Tennessee) have prenatal drug laws and no statutes on third-party fetal killings,[7] but no weak pro-life states have fetal-killing statutes in the absence of prenatal drug laws. In addition, the weak pro-life states aggressively have pursued criminal charges against drug-abusing pregnant women; all but Arkansas and Montana have taken such action.

The weak pro-choice states are more likely than either the weak or strong pro-life states to have criminalized third-party fetal killings. Of the thirteen weak pro-choice states, more than three-fourths (76.9 percent) have prenatal drug-exposure statutes and 61.5 percent have fetal-killing statutes. Their laws also are most consistent with regard to enhancing the well-being of fetuses through policies designed to deal with both prenatal drug exposure and third-party fetal killings. More than half of the weak pro-choice states (Arizona, California, Florida, Georgia, Iowa, Illinois, and Minnesota) have both types of laws, and only two (Maine and Wyoming) have neither. Colorado, Connecticut, and Virginia have prenatal drug-exposure laws but no third-party killing statutes, while New Mexico has only the latter.

Probably the most notable characteristic of the final group of states—the most pro-choice category—is their relative lack of legislative activism; 41.7 percent have prenatal drug-exposure laws and 25 percent have fetal-killing laws. Seven (Hawaii, Maryland, New York, North Carolina, Texas, Vermont, and West Virginia) have neither prenatal drug-exposure laws nor third-party

---

[6] The following heavily pro-life states have prosecuted pregnant women for exposing their fetuses to illegal narcotics: Idaho, Indiana, Kentucky, Michigan, Mississippi, Nebraska, North Dakota, Ohio, Utah, and Wisconsin. Prosecutions may not reflect a whole state's views on prenatal drug exposure because it is the province of local district attorneys to determine whether to prosecute. Therefore I believe that more attention should be paid to the actual statutes adopted by state legislatures.

[7] Massachusetts and Missouri are expanded common law states; their courts, by judicial fiat, have extended their murder statutes to encompass third-party fetal killings.

fetal killing statutes. Only three (New Hampshire, Oklahoma, and Washington) have both types of laws while two (New Jersey and Oregon) have prenatal drug-exposure laws but not fetal-killing statutes.

Both pro-life and pro-choice states are more likely to have laws directed at combating prenatal drug exposure than laws regarding third-party fetal battering/killing. I believe this is a function of the low political salience of the latter, which, in turn, can be attributed to the unwillingness of fetal rights proponents to pursue this issue in a manner comparable to their actions on the other two fetal issues. Women's rights proponents would not be expected to place fetal battering/killing on the policy agenda because they are afraid that any law that accords value to fetal life will be used as a wedge in the struggle over abortion.

Overall, the evidence strongly supports the women's rights proposition that antiabortion states do not consistently treat the fetus as a person in other areas of the law. Although antiabortion states often enacted policies to aid infants exposed to narcotics in utero, they were far less interested in combating third-party fetal battering and killing. For a comparison of fetal laws in the fifty states, see Table 5.5.

Proposition 2: Do Antiabortion States Care about the Fetus or Women's Status?

The evidence on this proposition is somewhat more mixed, although again it is more consistent with the women's rights narrative. On the one hand, fetal rights proponents can point out that states with strongly restrictive abortion laws are significantly more likely than those with a strong pro-choice orientation to have passed laws to deal with the problems of drug use by pregnant women and to criminalize third-party fetal killings. Yet this relationship does not hold for the weak pro-life and weak pro-choice states. On the other hand, the women's rights argument that antiabortion states are antiwomen is supported by the data. Women's political, social, and economic status is generally lower in antiabortion states than in pro-choice states.

With respect to the other two fetal policies, the differences are dramatic between states with the most and least restrictive abortion laws. Strong pro-life states are nearly twice as likely as the strongest pro-choice states to have laws designed to combat prenatal drug exposure. Although the gap is not as wide, the strongest antiabortion states are still over a third more likely to have third-party fetal killing statutes. But the differences between the strongest antiabortion and the weak pro-choice states is statistically insignificant; roughly the same proportion of weak pro-choice states have prenatal drug-exposure laws and fetal killing laws as have the strongest antiabortion states. These weak pro-choice states are substantially more likely to have these laws than are states with weak pro-life abortion laws. See Table 5.5 for a summary of state-by-state differences.

Several points are worth noting. First, the quartiles of states with the most extreme abortion laws (both in pro-life and pro-choice directions) are quite different from their more moderate counterparts, perhaps because their views of all fetal policies are mediated through an abortion lens, rendering legislators in strong pro-choice states reluctant to accord the fetus status or value in any venue and strong pro-life states eager to do so. Second, states with weak pro-choice or weak pro-life abortion laws have decoupled their responses to the problems of prenatal drug exposure and third-party fetal battering/killing from abortion. The fact that weak pro-choice states are far more likely than are weak pro-life states to pass laws designed to protect a fetus threatened by prenatal drug exposure and to punish third-party acts of violence against it indicates that pro-choice/pro-life attitudes alone cannot explain fetal policymaking. What other factors, then, explain the existence of these laws?

Women's rights proponents believe they have the answer: pro-life rhetoric about the need to protect unborn babies is simply a smoke screen to cover up a broad-based attack on women's rights. We cannot accurately determine the conscious and unconscious motivations of state legislators, at least not without a great deal of psychoanalysis, but we can determine whether women's status is inversely related to the restrictiveness of abortion statutes. If so, that would suggest that the women's rights story is a plausible, if only partial, explanation.

To test the women's rights proposition, variables designed to measure women's political, social, and economic status in each state were created. I used two indicators of women's political status—the percentage of women state legislators and the NOW Index of Women's Rights Laws in the states. The first measures the extent to which women are able to participate meaningfully in the political system (i.e., have a seat at the table), while the second indicates their legal status.[8] Conceptually, social status is more illusive than political status, but I developed two independent measures of women's social status—education (the percentage of women with four years of college education) and whether the state had enacted a law requiring insurers to cover minimum hospital stays for women following childbirth.[9] Several indicators of women's economic status were used. Most of them measured different aspects of women's participation in the business world—the percentage of women in the workforce, the earnings ratio of full-time employed women to men, the percentage of women in professional and managerial occupations, and the proportion of businesses owned by women. Economic status separate from employment or business was measured by the percentages of women in poverty and of women without health insurance.[10]

All but one (the dichotomous measure of insured minimum hospital stay

---

[8] For a discussion of the legal index of women's rights in the states, see NOW Legal Defense and Education Fund 1987.

[9] The compilation of state laws concerning minimum hospital stays following childbirth was done by the American Political Network, Inc. 1996.

[10] The economic measures were developed by the Institute for Women's Policy Research and compiled from Bureau of Labor Statistics and Census Bureau data. See Institute for Women's Policy Research 1996.

Table 5.5. Comparison of fetal laws across the states (as of January 1998)

State	Overall abortion laws[a]	Prenatal drug exposure	Drug treatment and mandatory reporting	Third-party fetal killings
Northeast				
Connecticut	pro-choice (9)	public health		
Maine	pro-choice (8)			
Massachusetts	pro-life (14)	mixed	reporting	murder (judicial ruling)
New Hampshire	strong pro-choice (2)	public health		first-degree assault
New Jersey	strong pro-choice (2)	public health		
New York	strong pro-choice (2)			
Pennsylvania	pro-life (14)	public health	treatment	homicide of an unborn child
Rhode Island	strong pro-life (16)	public health	treatment	manslaughter
Vermont	strong pro-choice (2)			
Midwest				
Illinois	pro-choice (7)	mixed	treatment, reporting	homicide of unborn child
Indiana	strong pro-life (19)	punitive	reporting	feticide
Iowa	pro-choice (6)	mixed	reporting	feticide
Kansas	strong pro-life (15)	mixed	treatment, reporting	manslaughter
Michigan	strong pro-life (20)			murder
Minnesota	pro-choice (8)	mixed	treatment, reporting	murder (judicial ruling)
Missouri	pro-life (11)	mixed	treatment, reporting	
Nebraska	strong pro-life (18)	public health	treatment	homicide of unborn child
North Dakota	strong pro-life (17)	public health	treatment	murder
Ohio	strong pro-life (19)	mixed		murder of unborn child
South Dakota	pro-life (14)	public health		
Wisconsin	strong pro-life (17)	mixed	reporting	
South				
Alabama	pro-life (11)			
Arkansas	pro-life (10)	public health		first-degree battery

State				
Delaware	strong pro-life (15)	public health	treatment	manslaughter
Florida	pro-choice (6)	public health	treatment	feticide
Georgia	pro-choice (8)	public health	treatment, reporting	feticide
Kentucky	strong pl(16)	mixed	treatment	
Louisiana	strong pro-life (23)	public health	treatment	manslaughter
Maryland	strong pro-choice (5)	public health	treatment	
Mississippi	strong pro-life (15)		reporting	manslaughter
North Carolina	strong pro-choice (5)	public health	treatment	
Oklahoma	strong pro-choice (4)	mixed	treatment	murder (judicial ruling)
South Carolina	pro-life (13)	public health	treatment	
Tennessee	pro-life (13)			
Texas	strong pro-choice (4)	mixed	treatment, reporting	
Virginia	pro-choice (8)			
West Virginia	strong pro-choice (5)	mixed	treatment, reporting	
West				
Alaska	pro-life (10)	public health	treatment	manslaughter
Arizona	pro-choice (8)	mixed	treatment, reporting	murder
California	pro-choice (9)	public health	treatment	
Colorado	pro-choice (8)			
Hawaii	strong pro-choice (1)			
Idaho	strong pro-life (15)	mixed	treatment	manslaughter
Montana	pro-life (14)			injury to pregnant woman
Nevada	pro-life (11)			
New Mexico	pro-choice (7)	mixed	reporting	
Oregon	strong pro-choice (1)		reporting	
Utah	strong pro-life (20)	punitive		murder
Washington	strong pro-choice (2)	public health	treatment	manslaughter
Wyoming	pro-choice (7)			

[a] Numbers in parentheses denote scores that rank the restrictiveness of abortion laws. See Table 3.5.

laws) of the women's rights variables are continuous, so I aggregated total points awarded states on the basis of the pro-life content of their abortion laws rather than dividing by quartiles as in the preceding sections. Higher scores reflect the degree to which abortion laws epitomize the pro-life view (i.e., more restrictive). The presence or absence of minimum hospital stay laws will be measured against quartiles of abortion laws.

The two measures of women's political status in the states—the percentage of women serving in state legislatures and the degree to which state laws protect the rights of women—were negatively correlated with pro-life abortion laws. Although this correlation generally supports the women's rights narrative (i.e., women's status in antiabortion states is lower than that in pro-choice states), neither political variable is statistically significant (although both approach the .1 level).

The two indicators of women's social status—women's education and minimum hospital stays—also were inversely related to the pro-life content of state abortion statutes. States with a higher proportion of women with four years of college education tend to be pro-choice while those with fewer educated women are more likely to restrict or ban abortions. The coefficient is significant at the .01 level. Given that mandated insurance coverage of minimum hospital stays protects both the health of both the woman and the newborn, one would expect pro-life and pro-choice states to share a common interest in this policy, but that is not the case. Fifty-eight percent of the strong pro-choice states, but only 21.4 percent of strong pro-life states, require insurers to cover hospital stays.

Aside from the workforce participation variable, all of the economic status variables relating to women's employment had coefficients that were significant and inversely correlated with the pro-life content of state laws. The coefficient of the earnings ratio of female to male workers variable was significant at the .001 level. The other two variables—percentage of women in professional and managerial occupations and the percentages of businesses owned by women—had negative coefficients significant at .01 and .05 levels. The two non-employment-related measures of women's economic status were less strongly related to the content of state abortion laws. The percentage of women without health insurance variable was not significant, but the poverty measure was positive, as expected, and weakly significant. Overall, the workforce participation rates of women in the antiabortion and pro-choice states are comparable, but the former received lower pay relative to men. Also, a lower proportion of women in pro-life than pro-choice states own businesses or have professional occupations and more are below the poverty line. See Table 5.6 for a summary of the correlations.

There is significantly more support for the women's rights narrative than for the fetal rights one. Although states with strong antiabortion laws are more likely than those with strong pro-choice abortion laws to have enacted laws designed to combat prenatal drug exposure and third-party battering,

Table 5.6. Correlations between restrictiveness of abortion laws and women's political, social, and economic status in the states

| | Restrictiveness of abortion laws | |
Measures of women's status	Pearson's r	Significance
Percent of women in state legislature	−.266	.114
Index of women's rights in laws	−.212	.139
Percent of women with four years of college	−.397[c]	.004
Percent of women in workforce	.007	.961
Earnings ratio of female to male full–time workers	−.457[c]	.001
Percent of women in managerial and professional occupations	−.390[c]	.005
Percent of businesses owned by women	−.309[b]	.029
Percent of women in poverty	.257[a]	.071
Percent of women without health insurance	−.068	.637

[a] Significant at the .1 level (2 tailed)
[b] Significant at the .05 level (2 tailed)
[c] Significant at the .01 level (2 tailed)
N = 50

the difference is minimal. Weak pro-choice states are almost as likely to have these laws as are the strong pro-life states, and they are far more likely than are the weak pro-life states. In contrast, the evidence showing that antiabortion states accord women lower status than pro-choice states is very strong.

Proposition 3: Do Antiabortion States Support Policies to Aid Vulnerable "Persons"?

The strength of the fetal rights position is its moral imperative that we, as a society, must protect and care for our weakest and most vulnerable "persons." Its power can be seen in the overwhelming public support for criminal prosecutions of women whose substance abuse harms their children prenatally. The question, however, is whether it actually drives policymaking in states with strong antiabortion laws or is invoked only when women potentially harm their fetuses. Women's rights proponents argue the latter and believe that pro-life states are not consistently committed to aiding society's weakest and most vulnerable members.

To test this proposition, I picked the group that most closely resembles fetuses—children. The applicable indicators are divided into three categories: general measures of infant health, indicators of state responsiveness to the needs of particularly vulnerable infants and children, and a comprehensive indicator of overall state support for children as a class.

I used two measures of the general well-being of infants at birth: the percentage of children born to mothers who received adequate prenatal care and the percentage of low-birth-weight babies. The first gauges a state's commitment to maximizing infant health.[11] The second is a common indicator of babies' health at birth.[12] If the fetal rights position is truly driven by the need to care for fetuses, pro-life states should try more than pro-choice states to ensure that pregnant women receive adequate medical care and to minimize the prevalence of low-birth-weight babies. If the women's rights story is correct, these variables and the content of state abortion laws should be unrelated.

The second category of variables flows directly from the fetal rights narrative's moral argument that fetuses are especially deserving of society's protection because they constitute an innocent group that is especially weak and vulnerable. I used similar reasoning to devise variables measuring state policies toward weak and vulnerable children, many of whom were at risk of physical harm or death while in utero.

Because adoption is often presented to pregnant women as an alternative to abortion, I included two measures of state commitment to the placement of children in adoptive families. It is easy to place healthy infants in adoptive families, but most of the children available for adoption are older and many have suffered physical or sexual abuse and neglect. These special needs children are usually far more difficult to place in adoptive families because they have been abused or neglected or have physical, emotional, or mental disabilities. Many people cannot afford the extremely high cost of providing the medical and psychological assistance required by special needs children. Currently, there are approximately one hundred thousand special needs children cleared for adoption (Warren 1997, A1, A30, A31). Congress in 1980 passed the Adoption Assistance Program, a joint state and federal government effort granting monthly stipends to assist adoptive families in covering the costs of care for special needs children. Because they vary from state to state, the monthly maximum stipends in each state tend to reflect that state's commitment to placing special needs children in permanent homes. If the fetal rights narrative is correct, there should be a strong positive correlation between antiabortion laws and special needs adoption stipends. I created two adoption variables: the monthly maximum stipends available to adoptive families with two-year-old and nine-year-old special needs children.[13]

---

[11] The American College of Obstetricians and Gynecologists defines adequate prenatal care as receiving prenatal care within the first four months of a pregnancy and attending at least 80 percent of the recommended number of medical appointments. The percentages were compiled by the Alan Guttmacher Institute from National Center for Health Statistics and published by the Annie E. Casey Foundation (1995).

[12] Low-birth-weight babies are defined as those weighing less than 5.5 pounds at birth. The percentages of low-birth-weight babies per state were compiled by the Annie E. Casey Foundation (1995) from data provided by the National Center for Health Statistics.

[13] Figures on the monthly maximum stipends available to adoptive parents of special needs children were provided by the North American Council on Adoptable Children (NACAC), which conducted a state-by-state survey in 1996. Although unpublished, they were made available by the staff at the NACAC.

Many children languish in the foster care system because they either have not been cleared for adoption or no adoptive families are available, so I added the average monthly foster care rates paid in the states as another measure of each state's commitment to its most vulnerable children. Again, the focus was on subsidies to foster parents of two- and nine-year-old children.[14]

The limited number of young women with unplanned pregnancies who placed their children for adoption or in foster care system required that I analyze state aid to needy children who remain with their birth mothers. I created two measures of state commitment to improving the well-being of poor children. The first of these, the average level of welfare given to poor women with dependent children, measures a state's willingness to aid poor families with children.[15] Again, a positive correlation between pro-life abortion laws and welfare levels would be consistent with the fetal rights story. Moreover, restricting the amount of welfare that a poor woman can receive also may lead such women to choose abortion over continuing a pregnancy. Researchers at Rutgers University found that a "family cap" that excludes coverage of children conceived while a woman is on welfare leads to higher abortion rates among welfare recipients. New Jersey's family cap increased that state's annual number of abortions among welfare recipients by roughly 240 (Lewin 1998, A10).

Because welfare is only one form of aid to poor children, a second and more comprehensive measure of state commitment to providing assistance to poor children was included—the level of state spending per poor child.[16] If the arguments put forth by fetal rights activists is an accurate reflection of their underlying motivations, there should be a positive relationship between pro-life abortion statutes and state expenditures per poor child.

Finally, I measured the level of general commitment to children regardless of need because fetal rights proponents often cite the state's in loco parentis role to justify public intervention to protect fetuses or as a broad-based responsibility to ensure the well-being of children. Most state actions are directed at specific subpopulations of children, however, necessitating the choice of per pupil spending for those enrolled in kindergarten through twelfth grade as a surrogate for state concern for children as a whole, because all children are required by law to attend school.[17]

Contrary to the expectations generated by the fetal rights narrative, there was not a positive relationship between the measures of children's well-being and the pro-life content of state abortion statutes. Only the percentage of ba-

[14] The figures on the average monthly rates paid to foster parents were provided by the North American Council on Adoptable Children from an unpublished 1996 survey.

[15] Figures on the average level of welfare payments per state were obtained from the Bureau of the Census 1996.

[16] The 1995 figures on state expenditures per poor child were compiled by the Urban Institute and listed in *State and Local Sourcebook 1999*.

[17] The per pupil spending figures were compiled by Hovey 1996.

bies born to mothers who received adequate prenatal care was positively associated with pro-life abortion laws, and even it was statistically insignificant. The percentage of low-birth-weight babies was higher in pro-life states than in pro-choice states, but it did not reach statistical significance. There was a highly significant inverse relationship between the adoption subsidy variables and the pro-life content of state abortion laws. The foster care payment rates also were negatively associated with the pro-life content of abortion laws, but only one was significant. The indicators of state willingness to aid needy children who remained with their mothers (the average size of state welfare payments and state expenditures per poor child) were also negatively correlated with the pro-life content of state abortion laws. In other words, pro-life states want to prevent women from having abortions but seem unwilling to provide a decent level of support for those children after their birth.

The final measure of state willingness to aid children—the level of education spending per child enrolled in kindergarten through twelfth grade—also was negatively correlated with the pro-life content of state abortion statutes. Contrary to what the fetal rights story would predict, pro-choice states are more committed to providing for the society's weakest and most vulnerable than are pro-life states. See Table 5.7 for a summary of the correlations.

A Comparison of the Evidence

Although correlations do not determine causation, their aggregation suggests that one position is more valid than the other. A summary of the evidence, proposition by proposition, leads to the probable conclusion that the women's rights perspective is empirically stronger.

In Proposition 1 we examined whether antiabortion states consistently treat the fetus as a person in other areas of the law, regardless of the gender or status of the individual who harms it. The moral foundation of the fetal rights narrative is the fetus's humanity, requiring full protection of the law. If pro-life legislators are primarily motivated to protect fetal (i.e., "human") life, pro-life states should consistently treat the fetus as a person. In contrast, the women's rights story is morally driven by the belief that antiabortion rhetoric is really a subterfuge for pervasive attacks on women's rights. If women's rights proponents are correct, antiabortion states should more aggressively pursue fetal rights when harm comes from a woman than a man. I found that antiabortion states were far more likely to protect the fetus from harms traceable to maternal actions than those usually caused by males. To assert that third-party fetal killing is a more grievous act than drug use by pregnant women is axiomatic, yet pro-life states were more likely to legislate against the former than the latter. The evidence is strikingly clear—antiabortion states do not treat the fetus consistently across fetal policy domains.

Proposition 2 also considers other evidence estimating the motives of lawmakers in antiabortion states. Again, human motives can only be inferred through actions—in this case, legislative actions. While strong antiabortion states are more likely than strong pro-choice states to have addressed the two

Table 5.7. Correlations between restrictiveness of abortion laws and state responsiveness to the needs of children

Concern for children	Restrictiveness of abortion laws	
	Pearson's r	Significance
Percent of babies born to women who got adequate prenatal care	.149	.302
Percent of low-birth-weight babies	.082	.573
Adoption subsidy for a special needs two-year-old child	−.415[b]	.003
Adoption subsidy for a special needs nine-year-old child	−.422[b]	.002
Foster care rate for a two-year-old child	−.164	.254
Foster care rate for a nine-year-old child	−.238[a]	.097
Average welfare benefit	−.252[a]	.077
Spending per poor child	−.273[a]	.055
Spending per pupil	−.271[a]	.057

[a] Significant at the .1 level (2 tailed)
[b] Significant at the .01 level (2 tailed)
$N = 50$

other fetal problems, this pattern does not hold for weak pro-life and weak pro-choice states. In fact, chances are greater that weak pro-choice states, not weak pro-life states, have enacted these laws, and they pass both prenatal drug laws and third-party fetal killing laws at roughly the same rate as strong pro-life states. In addition, women's status is consistently lower in antiabortion states than in pro-choice states, indicating that lawmakers in the former are more interested in attacking women's rights than protecting fetal life. Although the evidence about motives is somewhat murky, it generally also supports the women's rights narrative.

Finally, with respect to Proposition 3, no evidence was found that pro-life states have adopted a comprehensive range of policies designed to protect and assist the weakest and most vulnerable in our society. Instead, the opposite appeared to be true. I examined policies toward the group most closely related to fetuses—born children. Pro-choice states were more likely to favor adoption and to provide aid to needy children. Simply, pro-life states make it difficult for women to have abortions, but they do not help these women provide for the children once born. Pro-life states also spend less money per pupil on kindergarten through twelfth grade education.

On all three of the propositions, the evidence was generally consistent with the narrative put forth by women's rights proponents. There was virtually no support for the fetal rights story, but I do not mean to denigrate the sincerity of pro-life lawmakers who attribute their antiabortion actions to a desire to save unborn babies. I suspect that many pro-life individuals are unaware of the effect of some of their other beliefs on policies toward born and unborn children. For example, the belief that women should be primarily responsible for the welfare of children may lead them to overlook the ways that males harm the fetus.

People often hold contradictory beliefs, such as simultaneously supporting increases in many domestic programs and major tax cuts.[18] Such cognitive political dissonance can lead to unconscious policy hierarchies. For example, individuals with pro-life views may also strongly believe that government waste is a serious problem and vote for a politician who promises to cut public sector spending without thinking of the effects of these cuts on governmental services, such as prenatal care, adoption subsidies, and the like, that are generally "pro-life." The remainder of this chapter explores influences on abortion policymaking in the states and, to a lesser extent, the other two fetal policies.

Modeling Abortion Policymaking in the States

As I show in the preceding sections, many states with pro-life abortion laws have adopted other policies that do not support increased regard for fetal life threatened by parties other than a pregnant woman. Their policies often contradict fetal rights proponents' claim that they want to protect the most needy and vulnerable. In many policy domains, the relationship between pro-life abortion policies and more generalized regard for life was inverse. I also found significant indirect corroboration for the women's rights argument that support for fetal rights is part of a sweeping assault on women's rights. Of course, causality cannot be "proven" by correlations (e.g., just because it is more likely to rain on days when prisoners are executed in Texas does not mean that rainy days cause executions).

Although this is not the first attempt to explain the abortion policies adopted in the fifty states, my research design is unique. First, the dependent variable is the composite measure of the pro-life content of state abortion laws that is developed in Chapter 3. As a single composite measure of state abortion policies, it parsimoniously gauges the cumulative thrust of abortion laws.[19] Second, because I want to ascertain the relative strength of the two competing narratives, I have added several new independent variables. Some were used to test the propositions generated by the narratives, but others are used only to develop an explanatory model of abortion policymaking across the states. Again, the variables are divided according to their association with one or the other narrative.

[18] See the 1996 American National Election Study for examples of the prevalence of incompatible beliefs in the general public.

[19] Most previous research on interstate differences in abortion laws has simply sought to explain the number of new enactments after a particular court abortion ruling. States with more enactments are classified as more restrictive while those with fewer are classified as less so, an approach that fails to consider the substantive content of the enactments. As I demonstrate in Chapter 3, informed consent laws vary dramatically across states. I have therefore measured the restrictiveness of state abortion laws on the basis of their substantive content rather than simply the number of enactments.

Explanatory Variables

Public opinion about abortion probably most directly reflects pro-fetal-rights sentiment in the various states. In addition to the 1988–90 NES public opinion variable measuring attitudes toward abortion in the states, two other public opinion variables based on the 1996 NES survey were used: the percentages of respondents who believe that abortion should never be permitted and those who believe it should always be the personal choice of the woman.[20] The polarizing conflict over abortion has often involved activists who are not representative of the general public's views, so I tried to measure the strength of pro-life interest groups in the states. Unfortunately, none of these groups was willing to provide their membership figures.[21] Although I developed a proxy measure—the percentage of the population belonging to a pro-life church—it potentially confounds the relationship between pro-life sentiment and opposition to women's equality.[22]

Most of the pro-life churches also are on record as opposing equal rights for women.[23] At their 1998 convention, the sixteen-million-member strong Southern Baptists, the largest Protestant pro-life denomination, amended their Baptist Faith and Message to read: "A wife is to submit graciously to the servant leadership of her husband even as the church willingly submits to the headship of Christ." It also said that a wife "has the God-given responsibility to respect her husband and to serve as his helper in managing her household and nurturing the next generation" (Stammer 1998, A1 and A26). Although no Baptist is required to agree with it, the Faith and Message Statement is a major Baptist theological proclamation, and ministers, church employees, and seminary professors are expected to abide by it (Niebuhr 1998, A1). The rapidly growing movement among evangelical Christian men, Promise Keepers, also believes that women should defer to their husbands. Even though their stadium rallies with forty to sixty thousand men have attracted most of the attention, Promise Keepers are committed to furthering their agenda by organizing ten thousand groups in local communities across the country (Ross and Cokorinos 1997, 6).

---

[20] The 1996 American National Election Study had an N of 1,714 and included responses from forty-one states. To include all fifty states, I gave the missing states and those with extremely small sample sizes the percentage figures for their geographic region (Pacific, Mountain, West North Central, East North Central, Middle Atlantic, New England, West South Central, East South Central, and South Atlantic).

[21] I did devise dichotomous variables reflecting the presence or absence of particular pro-life groups in a state, but none explained any of the variance. Equivalent measures of pro-choice presence in the states were also ineffective.

[22] The major pro-life religious bodies were identified through primary materials compiled in Melton 1989. Membership figures for each state were obtained from Bradley and Green 1992.

[23] Many pro-life conservative churches also have a poor record on the issue of wife beating, which, as I have shown, not only affects women but also is a major cause of fetal harms. According to Nason-Clark (1997), the response of conservative churches has been "a pervasive holy hush."

To measure the explanatory power of the women's rights story, 1996 NES data on the percentage of respondents who believed that women and men should have equal roles in society was used.[24] I believe it is the most direct attitudinal measure of equal rights for women. Other indicators of women's status in the states (i.e., the political, social, and economic variables used in the preceding sections) were also useful predictors. Because abortion and fetal rights often involve questions of sexual morality, it was important also to devise a measure of attitudes about sex. In the absence of public opinion poll data measuring views about the morality of various sexual practices,[25] the presence or absence of state laws requiring sex education about sexually transmitted diseases and HIV was used as an indicator of sexual attitudes in the states.[26]

Political institutions and elected officials play an important policymaking role in a representative democracy. As noted in Chapter 3, pro-life groups have devoted lots of attention over the past decade to electing state legislators who share their views about abortion. States with a strong pro-life legislature and a pro-life governor should have enacted more proscriptions and restrictions on abortion than states with pro-choice control of the state legislature and governor's office. Although previous researchers have tried to measure pro-life sentiment in state legislatures by either using party affiliation or pro-life views of state legislators,[27] I felt it was important to assess the views of both the state legislature and the governor. Case studies of abortion policymaking in Louisiana, Massachusetts, Minnesota, North Carolina, and Pennsylvania have shown that governors can play a key role in passing or halting abortion legislation (Borrelli 1995; Day 1995; Halva-Neubauer 1995; Nossiff 1995; Strickland 1995). For this reason, I created an ordinal variable reflecting the degree to which the state legislature and governor's office are controlled by officials with pro-life or pro-choice views about abortion.[28] This variable superficially

[24] This variable was created in the same manner as the 1996 NES abortion public opinion variable discussed in note 20.

[25] In the past decade, the NES and other public opinion pollsters have asked a variety of questions about the sexual practices of homosexuals and equal rights for homosexuals but not questions about heterosexual sexual practices. For obvious reasons, these questions are not directly relevant to the issue of sexual practices that could result in the birth of a child.

[26] Data on state sexuality education laws were provided by NARAL 1995a.

[27] Party control variables have not been very effective predictors of votes on abortion laws because a Democratic Party majority in the state legislature does not necessarily reflect whether that body is pro-life or pro-choice. Even today most southern state legislatures are controlled by Democrats who, unlike their more liberal nonsouthern Democratic counterparts, tend to be far less pro-choice. For example, most of Louisiana's extremely stringent abortion laws were enacted during periods when the Democrats controlled both chambers of the legislature and the governor's office. For an analysis of abortion politics in Louisiana, see Day 1995.

[28] NARAL (1995b) compiled data on the positions of all state legislatures and governors on abortion. Using these data, I developed the following ordinal ranking of states: 0 = governor and state legislature favor banning abortion, 1 = governor and one chamber clearly favor banning abortion, 2 = governor and legislature closely split over whether abortions should be banned, 3 = governor and legislature favor restricting but not banning abortion, and 4 = governor and legislature are pro-choice.

appears to measure the strength of the fetal rights narrative but is confounded by pro-life politicians' disproportionate opposition to equal rights for women. For example, Randall Terry, founder of Operation Rescue, is now heading up a group of congressional candidates called the Patrick Henry Men, who advocate women's subservience to men and vehemently oppose homosexuality (Gottlieb 1998). Michael Russo (1995, 176–77) found that pro-life candidates for the California state assembly typically classify themselves as "pro-family," which means they tend to support the conservative "family values" agenda of groups such as the Christian Coalition and the Traditional Values Coalition that are strongly opposed to equal rights for women.

Findings

None of the abortion public opinion variables were significant, but public opinion about whether women and men should have equal rights was highly significant. This public opinion variable was significant even when an additional measure of women's status—the ratio of women's per capita income to that of men—was included in the model. As postulated by the women's rights narrative, these measures are inversely related to the restrictiveness of state abortion laws. The sex education variable's negative relationship to abortion restrictiveness indicates that sexual morality, separate from the question of whether the fetus is or is not a person, affects abortion policymaking. The percentage of the population belonging to pro-life churches is significant, although the relationship between church membership and pro-life abortion laws may be spurious because pro-life churches also tend to favor traditional roles for women and oppose equal rights. Finally, control of the state legislature and the governor's office matters. These findings are presented in Table 5.8.

Although the model explained nearly half of the variance in abortion laws, the results are more ambiguous with respect to the relative power of the two narratives. The impact of public opinion on women's rights and women's income relative to men's on the restrictiveness of state abortion statutes signifies that pro-life lawmaking at least partially reflects uneasiness over women's changing role in society. The negative relationship between sex education in schools and restrictiveness of abortion laws similarly captures a reaction against changes in sexual morality and behavior. Certainly, the connection between these changes and women's greater sexual freedom through better contraception is undeniable. Since most sex education in high schools involves the prevention of unwanted pregnancies (and, by extension, abortions) and sexually transmitted diseases and HIV (both of which can be transmitted in utero to the fetus), opposition to these efforts is hardly pro-fetus. The statistical insignificance of the abortion public opinion variables also indicates that the fetal rights narrative is flawed. At the same time, the impact of pro-life churches is significant, although it is difficult to interpret whether that is primarily driven by pro-life or anti-women's-rights sentiments. Although the women's rights variables explain more of the variance, the restrictiveness of state abor-

Table 5.8. Regression model explaining the restrictiveness of state abortion laws

Variable	Coefficient	Significance
Public opinion about women's role	−.275 (−.140)	.018[b]
Earnings ratio of female to male full-time workers	−.221 (−39.810)	.083[a]
Sex education in schools	−.209 (−3.010)	.055[a]
Percent belonging to pro-life churches	.242 (.117)	.032[b]
Pro-choice views of state legislature and governor	−.335 (−1.498)	.017[b]

Note: The upper coefficients are the standardized coefficients from OLS regression and the lower ones (in parentheses) are the unstandardized ones.

[a] Significant at the .1 level
[b] Significant at the .05 level
$N = 50$
$R^2 = .512$
Adjusted $R^2 = .456$

tion laws is also affected by which side controls the state legislature and governor's office and the strength of conservative pro-life/antiwomen's-rights churches.

None of the fetal rights variables or the women's rights variables explain differences in case or statutory laws dealing with prenatal drug exposure and third-party fetal killings. Speculation is pointless, but a few factors are worth noting. First, because many of the state laws criminalizing third-party fetal killings originated in the nineteenth and early twentieth centuries, it would be remarkable if variables measuring current phenomena were significant. Second, no state has passed new criminal laws directed at prenatal drug exposure; state legislatures have enacted civil laws and some courts have applied existing criminal statutes to women who abuse drugs while pregnant. Judicial activism and its determinants are far more important in this area than in abortion policymaking, where state legislatures have responded to court abortion rulings by passing new abortion laws.

Summary

This chapter begins by searching for a common thread to explain the three fetal policy areas. Despite the policies' shared moral considerations, the preceding two chapters show that the morality policy framework was more useful heuristically than as a link between fetal politics and policy outcomes. We next considered the possibility that abortion policies, fetal abuse statutory and case law, and decisions over the criminalization of third-party fetal killings simply mirror public views about the value of fetal life. Because pollsters have never asked whether respondents believe that fetuses should be treated identically to born life or any other question that places a particular value on fetal life, I chose to use responses to the 1988–90 NES survey question about whether abortion should be legal and, if so, under what conditions.[29] Although state abortion laws reflect to some extent state attitudes toward abortion, there was no connection between those views and state laws governing either drug use by pregnant women or third-party fetal killings. Fetal abuse prosecutions, but not third-party fetal killing prosecutions, did appear to be related to pro-life abortion sentiment.[30] In short, public opinion about the value of fetal life (as measured by respondents' views about abortion) did not unite the three fetal policies.

The rest of the chapter tests the validity of the competing narratives promulgated by fetal rights proponents and women's rights advocates. I begin by showing how three sets of competing propositions can be logically derived from the two narratives and then tested each set to determine which was empirically stronger. Though the moral imperative in the fetal rights stance is based on the claim that the fetus is a person fully deserving protection as a born human being, antiabortion states are inconsistent in their regard for fetal life. They are far more interested in protecting fetuses from in utero drug exposure than from third-party acts of violence and killings. Six of the states with the strongest antiabortion laws in the country do not make it a crime for a third-party to kill a fetus. Pro-life states are ambivalent in their concern about threats to fetal health by drug-abusing pregnant women or violent individuals. Although the strong pro-life states are more likely than the strong pro-choice states to have policies to deal with prenatal drug exposure and third-party fetal killings, there is virtually no difference between the weak pro-choice states and strong pro-life states.

States with pro-life abortion laws are consistent in according lower political, social, and economic status to women. Pro-life states (i.e., those claiming to be most concerned with fetal well-being) are far less likely than pro-choice states to require insurance companies to cover minimum hospital stays after childbirth, a measure that protects the health of both the woman and the newborn baby.

Finally, I examine whether antiabortion laws were part of a broader commitment to the protection of society's weakest and most vulnerable members

---

[29] Although I used responses to the 1988–90 NES abortion question because it marked a key period in abortion activism, I also examined whether responses to abortion questions in the 1996 NES survey were more closely correlated with state abortion laws. They were less closely related.

[30] State prosecution of women for fetal abuse was related to whether the judiciary was elected or appointed. States with elected judges were far more likely to have prosecuted drug-using pregnant women. The likelihood of third-party fetal killing prosecutions, however, was not affected by the means used to choose judges.

that is ostensibly central to the fetal rights story. The evidence in this case was overwhelmingly contrary. Pro-life states are less likely than pro-choice states to provide adequate care to poor and needy children. Their concern for the weak and vulnerable appears to stop at birth.

The evidence provides far greater support for the women's rights narrative than for the fetal rights one. The regression model showed that opposition to women's changing roles in society was a stronger predictor of the chances a state would adopt restrictive abortion laws. Concern for fetal life by pro-life activists and legislators may not be hypocritical; unacknowledged factors, most notably views about women's place in society, also powerfully influence abortion policymaking. A concern for fetal life does not equally motivate policymaking in the three areas.

CHAPTER 6

Where Do We Go from Here?

Federalism and Fetal Personhood

On May 26, 1998, the Supreme Court denied certiorari in the South Carolina Supreme Court's 3–2 decision in *Whitner v. South Carolina* (1996) and a companion case, *Melissa Ann Crawley v. South Carolina* (1998).[1] By declining to review these decisions, the Court allowed rulings that the definition of a "child" in South Carolina's child abuse and endangerment statutes includes a viable fetus to stand. Consistent with cases in which certiorari is denied, the Supreme Court did not explain its reasoning. We do not know whether the justices considered the issues raised in the cases to be insufficiently important to merit judicial review or whether they thought the issues were not yet "ripe," preferring to wait until matters became clearer as states grappled with the question.

Whatever the motivation, the justices opened the way for increasing disparities in the ways states treat fetuses. Based on *Whitner*, a woman in South Carolina may be sentenced to a maximum of ten years in prison for child abuse (i.e., using illegal narcotics while pregnant)[2] even though the child shows no adverse effects, but in nearby Kentucky, whose high court has ruled that the fetus is not legally a person covered by child abuse statutes, a woman has not committed a crime even if her drug use results in severe physical and mental

---

[1] The high-profile *Whitner* case is discussed in Chapter 4. In the second case, which generated far less publicity, a woman was sentenced to five years in prison for child endangerment because her son, Antwon, tested positive for cocaine shortly after his birth in 1992. Even though Melissa Crawley has been drug-free since 1995 and her son is completely healthy, the Supreme Court's decision means that she will have to serve her sentence. When asked about the case, South Carolina attorney general Charles Condon indicated that it might not be in the best interests of Antwon and the three other children for Crawley to be imprisoned but stated, "Her situation made a sympathetic case. But who am I to change the law?" See Associated Press 1998.

[2] A positive toxicology screen showing the presence of crack cocaine in the newborn baby was the basis for Whitner's conviction (*Whitner v. State*, 1996).

handicaps to the child. The absurd incongruity of such disparities will probably multiply as more states attempt to define the fetus as a person or a child, at least until the Supreme Court decides the merits of the issue.

The Supreme Court's refusal to act also may be interpreted as encouraging ongoing efforts to dismantle *Roe*, which while holding that states may have a compelling interest in protecting the fetus in the third trimester because it is "potential life," implicitly denied the fetus personhood status. Justice A. J. Toal, writing for the South Carolina Supreme Court, clearly states that the *Whitner* majority believed viable fetuses to be legal persons, based on the "plain meaning of the word 'person' in light of existing medical knowledge concerning fetal development" (*Whitner v. State*, 1996). The U.S. Supreme Court's denial of certiorari allowed *Whitner* to become the law in South Carolina, but it does not apply in other states. If the Court subsequently considers and upholds a lower court ruling like *Whitner*, the distinction between "potential life" and fetal personhood status would vanish or, at the very least, be blurred significantly. By refusing to use *Whitner* to revisit *Roe*, either by reaffirming that viable fetuses are "potential life" or by holding that viable fetuses are legally persons, the Court simultaneously left its options open and encouraged antiabortion forces.

Conservative judicial scholars probably will support the denial of certiorari in *Whitner* because it allows states to use their police power to regulate maternal behavior. In the past conservatives, such as Bruce Fein (1992), Richard Erb and Alan Mortensen (1993), and Lino Graglia (1995), have attacked *Roe* on federalist grounds, arguing that abortion and reproductive rights should be decided through democratic processes at the state level. For example, Erb and Mortensen (1993, 643) charge that the Supreme Court has usurped the policymaking role of state legislatures: "Value judgments, such as abortion, are best left to the state legislatures to address through the political process." The Supreme Court should "admit its error and overrule those cases which have resulted in usurpation of state police power" (Erb and Mortensen 1993, 643).[3] The Court's decision to let *Whitner* stand is consistent with this view of state-national relations in the fetal rights area.[4]

[3] Traditionally, the Supreme Court has arbitrated disputes over the propriety of state or federal government authority. The Court's views on the boundaries between state and federal jurisdiction have shifted over time. At the founding, the Court adopted a nationalist stance in cases such as *Martin v. Hunter's Lessee* (1816), *McCulloch v. Maryland* (1819), and *Cohens v. Virginia* (1821). In the late antebellum era, however, it approached a "dual federalist" position by upholding state sovereignty in several important cases—*Swift v. Tyson* (1842), *License Cases* (1847), and, finally, the infamous *Dred Scott v. Sandford* (1857). During the New Deal era the Court returned to a more nationalist (i.e., "cooperative federalist") stance. In recent years, the pendulum has swung back toward a states'-rights perspective. For example, in 1995, the Court invalidated a federal regulation under the Commerce Clause for the first time in sixty years (*U.S. v. Lopez*, 1995). Then, in 1997, the Court unanimously rejected arguments that terminally ill people have a "right to die" and upheld state laws against doctor-assisted suicide (Savage 1997, A1).

[4] Advocates of states' rights base their belief in state government sovereignty over public welfare on the premise that states are closer to the people and therefore are more responsive to their needs and wishes. See Peltason 1991 and Rossum and Tarr 1995.

The States'-Rights Approach to Fetal Personhood

Although predicting the direction of future Supreme Court decisions is highly risky, speculating about its implication is a worthwhile pastime. The Court can continue to grant states wide latitude in regulating abortion and extending rights to the fetus without overturning *Roe*, decide formally to reject *Roe* and extend personhood status to the fetus, or formally reaffirm *Roe* and strengthen women's rights to privacy and equal protection. The current political climate and Court composition militates in favor of the first course. Although state courts and legislatures have more autonomy under the states'-rights approach to determine fetal rights and regulate reproductive decisions, that freedom can lead to state policies favorable to the abortion rights side.[5]

The states'-rights approach may be a misnomer because the Court has been reluctant to intervene when Congress impedes women's access to abortion, short of an outright ban. In the past the judiciary has allowed Congress to restrict poor women's access to legal abortions by limiting the conditions under which Medicaid funds may be used to pay for the procedure. The Court has not overturned federal laws that hinder members of the armed forces and their dependents from obtaining safe, legal abortions,[6] nor has it intervened against congressional attempts to halt the development and sale of RU486 (mifepristone), a drug taken orally that can nonsurgically end a pregnancy during the first trimester.[7] It thus seems unlikely that the Court will overturn congressional restrictions on access to abortion such as the Child Custody Protection Act that came close to passage in the 105th Congress; the legislation would make it a federal crime, punishable by up to a year in prison and a fine of as much as $100,000, to take a minor across state lines to obtain an abortion in circumvention of parental notification/consent laws in the home state.[8]

The states'-rights approach will probably lead to a continued erosion of *Roe* by the passage of new abortion restrictions or bans, greater fetal rights in civil law, and enormous disparities in the rights accorded the fetus in different states and across policy areas.

---

[5] For example, on March 23, 1998, the Supreme Court denied certiorari in an Ohio case overturning a ban on partial birth abortions. The Supreme Court declined to review the Sixth Circuit Federal Court's decision in *Women's Medical Professional Corp. v. Voinovich*, Nos. 96-3157/3159 (6th Cir. Nov. 18, 1997).

[6] Since 1995 members of the armed forces and their dependents have been prohibited from obtaining abortions in overseas military hospitals, even when they pay for the procedures themselves. They must choose between convenient but potentially dangerous abortions in nonmilitary facilities (i.e., in the local country) or inconvenient and often delayed procedures in the United States (NARAL 1998b, 1998c.)

[7] For a brief chronology of the conflict over RU 486, see Feminist Majority Foundation 1996 and Haney 1998.

[8] The NRLC worked with congressional staffers in drafting the Child Custody Protection Act (Center for Reproductive Law and Policy 1998b, 122).

New Assaults on Abortion Rights

According to a recent study, antiabortion organizations associated with the Christian right raise more than $40 million annually. These funds have been used to develop "advocacy organizations that are using the legal system to undermine constitutionally protected reproductive health care choices" (Center for Reproductive Law & Policy 1998b, 1). The most common activities of the twelve pro-life legal advocacy groups profiled in the study are the provision of legal counsel to abortion protesters, litigation in abortion and fetal rights cases, and the crafting of model state and federal legislation dealing with abortion. By providing approved continuing legal education courses, promoting Christian student advocacy groups at law schools, and working with conservative Christian law schools, such as Regent University School of Law which was founded by Pat Robertson in 1986, pro-life legal advocacy groups are extending their reach far beyond their current membership.

Since late 1994 pro-life groups have experienced a dramatic upsurge in their effectiveness in getting measures adopted both at the national and state levels. NARAL (1998, iii) labeled members of the 104th and 105th Congresses as "the most anti-choice since *Roe*" on the basis of a record number of antiabortion votes.[9] They classified only 131 of the 435 members of the House of Representatives and 33 senators as fully supportive of the pro-choice position on abortion. Of the eighty-one votes on reproductive issues since 1995, abortion rights supporters prevailed on only ten (Carey 1998a, 127).

The success of pro-life groups at the national level has not led to a diminution of effort at the state level. In 1997 state legislatures considered 84 percent more antiabortion measures than in the preceding year and enacted almost three times more of them. Nearly two-thirds (thirty-two) of the states passed restrictive abortion statutes in 1997, compared to only nine states in 1996 (NARAL 1998d, v–vi). The trend is not abating. In 1998 twenty-seven states enacted a total of sixty-two new laws restricting abortion (NARAL 1999, ix). In addition to their aggressive efforts to enact further restrictive laws and bans on late-term abortions, pro-life supporters in the states have recently launched two new efforts designed to curtail abortion providers' business through both civil penalties and criminal sanctions.

The Use of Civil Penalties

A long-range strategy of some pro-life legal groups is to drive abortion providers out of the business by making medical malpractice insurance either prohibitively expensive or even unavailable. Although two relatively small legal advocacy groups started filing medical malpractice suits in the mid-1980s

---

[9] In 1996 the NRLC through its political action committee contributed more than $2 million to over one hundred pro-life congressional candidates (Long 1997, 93).

against physicians who perform abortions, the tactic only recently became widespread. In 1993 Life Dynamics Incorporated (LDI), a legal organization that uses self-described "guerrilla" tactics to make abortion unavailable instead of illegal, launched a campaign to get personal injury lawyers throughout the country to file medical malpractice suits on behalf of women harmed by abortion. LDI has provided thousands of attorneys with free materials about how to go about filing such suits and claims to have a network of more than six hundred attorneys willing to file these cases (Center for Reproductive Law & Policy 1998b, 96).

Pro-life organizations and legislators also have mounted a campaign to expand the group of possible litigants who can file civil claims against abortion providers. In 1997 pro-life legislators in at least fifteen states introduced bills to allow fathers to recover monetary damages through civil suits if a partial birth abortion is performed without their consent;[10] most also would award damages to parents whose minor daughters had partial birth abortions without their consent.[11] As of November 1999, at least fourteen states had enacted such measures. The states whose partial birth abortion bans allow civil actions for monetary damages differ with respect to which parties have legal standing. Six states (Alabama, Arizona, Georgia, Idaho, South Dakota, and Wisconsin) allow the father of the fetus and parents of the woman if she is under eighteen or a minor to sue for civil damages. Florida, Mississippi, Oklahoma, and South Carolina have similar laws but only allow the father of the fetus to sue if he is married to the woman. Illinois allows the parents of the woman but not the father of the fetus to sue if the woman is under eighteen years. Iowa allows the father of the fetus to sue as well as the parents of the woman if she is either under eighteen years or unmarried. The remaining two states, Louisiana and Rhode Island, allow suits by the woman, the father of the fetus, and the woman's parents if she is a minor or under eighteen. The popularity of such bills almost certainly will grow in coming years, and civil damage suits by fathers and parents of minors could well extend beyond partial birth abortion statutes. At the federal level, H.R. 1122, Partial Birth Abortion Ban Act of 1999 would allow the woman's parents to sue for civil damages if she is under eighteen. The fetus's father could also sue under this act if he is married to the woman.

---

[10] Pro-life lawyers also have filed injunctions on behalf of fathers who want to prevent their girlfriends from having abortions. For example, in 1995 lawyers from the Rutherford Institute helped a teenage boy obtain a temporary injunction that prevented his girlfriend from obtaining an abortion (Center for Reproductive Law and Policy 1998b, 136). All of these actions are part of a broader "fathers' rights" movement that seeks to give men greater control over decisions about abortions and questions of fetal health. See Harris 1986 and Apollo 1989.

[11] The states that considered legislation to allow fathers or parents of minors to obtain monetary damages for the loss of fetal life because of a partial birth abortion in 1997 are Alabama, Arizona, Colorado, Delaware, Florida, Georgia, Illinois, Louisiana, Maine, Mississippi, North Carolina, Oklahoma, Rhode Island, South Carolina, and South Dakota.

The Use of Criminal Sanctions against Abortion Providers

Pro-life legislators also have introduced (and, in many states, passed) bills that make abortion providers subject to very harsh criminal sanctions for performing partial birth abortions, a top legislative priority of the NRLC since 1993. As of November 1999 thirty states had passed laws that made anyone who performs partial birth abortions subject to felony charges, with extremely harsh penalties—for example, up to twenty years in prison, a $25,000 fine, or both, in Nebraska or life imprisonment in Wisconsin.[12] Somewhat ironically, three of the states (Alabama, Montana, and Nebraska) that make performing a partial birth abortion a felony do not have case or statutory law criminalizing third-party fetal killing.

The language in the partial birth abortion bans is extremely vague, leaving a great deal of discretion to prosecutors and judges to determine which procedures are permissible and which are not. The ambiguous phrasing of the bans has resulted in ongoing litigation. These laws would make it extremely difficult for abortion providers to operate.[13] There are two reasons why the courts have held that these bans are too vague. First, although the laws ostensibly ban only a single procedure, a dilation and extraction abortion, the statutory language defining the prohibited act is so broad that it bans virtually all common abortion procedures.[14] Second, because the language used to define the banned procedures is unclear, physicians do not have adequate warning about what is and is not criminal.[15]

Even though the targeting of partial birth abortions by pro-life forces has been an extremely effective public relations tool for winning converts to their side, the vagueness in the language and the stringency of the provisions are beginning to affect public opinion. Several recent polls show that public senti-

[12] As of November 1, 1999 partial birth abortion bans were in effect in ten states (Indiana, Kansas, Mississippi, North Dakota, Oklahoma, South Carolina, South Dakota, Tennessee, Utah, and Virginia) and being enforced after viability in Alabama and Georgia. The laws in the following sixteen states had been blocked by federal or state courts: Alaska, Arizona, Arkansas, Florida, Idaho, Iowa, Kentucky, Louisiana, Michigan, Missouri, Montana, Nebraska, New Jersey, Ohio, Rhode Island, and West Virginia (Center for Reproductive Law and Policy 1999). On October 26, 1999 the Seventh Circuit Court of Appeals issued a 5–4 decision upholding the constitutionality of partial birth abortion bans in Illinois and Wisconsin. Because only a month earlier, similar laws in Arkansas, Iowa, and Nebraska were struck down by a federal appeals court in St. Louis, it is likely that the issue will end up being addressed by the Supreme Court in the next few years (Associated Press 1999).

[13] After U.S. District Court judge John C. Shabaz refused to grant an injunction to prevent the Wisconsin partial birth ban from going into effect, doctors in the state refused to perform abortions because the law was too vague and they were afraid of prosecution (NARAL 1998a). Another court ended up blocking the law.

[14] See *Planned Parenthood v. Alaska*, No. 3AN-97-6019 CIV, slip op at 10 (Alaska Super. Ct. Mar. 13, 1998) and *Hope Clinic v. Ryan*, 995 F.Supp. 857 (N.D. Ill. 1998).

[15] See *Evans v. Kelley*, 977 F.Supp. 1283 (E.D. Mich. 1997) and *Carhart v. Stenberg*, 11 F. Supp. 2d 1099 (D. Neb. 1998). U.S. Dist., LEXIS at 114.

ment has begun to swing toward opposition. One recent poll found that respondents by a 44–34 percent margin supported President Clinton's veto of the federal ban on partial birth abortions; another found that respondents by a 65–23 margin believed there should be exceptions when "the woman's doctor determines that the procedure is necessary to prevent serious harm to the woman's health" (Center for Reproductive Law & Policy 1998c, 3).

Ever greater obstacles are impeding the paths of women seeking legal abortions, as was acknowledged by Supreme Court Chief Justice William Rehnquist in his opinion in *Casey* (1992): "*Roe* continues to exist, but only in the way a storefront on a western movie set exists: a mere facade to give the illusion of reality."[16]

New Efforts to Expand Fetal Rights/Personhood

Fetal rights proponents have led efforts to grant additional rights to the fetus in nonabortion contexts. I have chronicled the developments related prenatal drug exposure, so I focus here on the recent evolution of fetal personhood with respect to third-party acts of violence and civil law.

During 1998 and 1999 the criminalization of third-party fetal killing/battering emerged as a pro-life issue in a number of states and at the national level. Wisconsin and Tennessee adopted new third-party fetal killing laws in 1998 and the following year Arkansas revised its statute, changing the offense from first-degree battery to murder, manslaughter, or negligent homicide.[17] The Wisconsin statute, similar to the 1997 Ohio and Pennsylvania laws, makes it an offense to kill an "unborn child" at any state of prenatal development, whereas Arkansas and Tennessee use twelve weeks' gestational age and viability respec-

---

[16] Chief Justice Rehnquist issued his own separate opinion, which partly concurred with and partly dissented from the majority opinion in *Casey*.

[17] The 1998 Wisconsin law, which covers all stages of prenatal development, makes individuals who "cause the death of an unborn child with intent to kill that unborn child, kill the woman who is pregnant with that unborn child or kill another" liable for first-degree intentional homicide prosecution, a Class A felony (Wis. Stat. 940.01, 1998). When mitigating circumstances are present, the offense is second-degree intentional homicide, a Class B felony (Wis. Stat. 940.05, 1998). Embryos and fetuses in Wisconsin also are included in the list of victims of first-degree reckless homicide, second-degree reckless homicide, homicide by negligent handling of dangerous weapons, explosives, or fire, homicide by intoxicated use of vehicle or firearm, and homicide by negligent operation of a vehicle (Wis. Stat. 940.02, 940.06, 940.08, 940.09, 940.10). The new Tennessee law includes a viable fetus as a "victim" in its first-degree murder, second-degree murder, voluntary manslaughter, vehicular homicide, and reckless homicide statutes (Tenn. Code Ann. 39-13-214, 202, 211, 213, and 215). First-degree murder is a capital offense in Tennessee (Tenn. Code Ann. 39-13-202, 1999). The revised Arkansas law makes a person who kills a fetus of twelve weeks' or greater gestational age liable for prosecution under their murder, manslaughter, and negligent homicide provisions (Fetal Protection Act, H.B. 1329 enacted April 9, 1999 to revise Arkansas Code 5-1-102 [13], 5-2-501 [1], 5-10-101 through 5-10-105, 5-61-101, 5-61-102, 20-16-704, and 20-16-806).

tively as their demarcation points. At the national level, pro-life forces in Congress introduced H.R. 2436, the "Unborn Victims of Violence Act of 1999," which would revise federal laws dealing with acts of violence that occur on federal property, involve the military justice system and other acts of violence that have been made federal offenses to criminalize fetal killing.[18] The bill was modeled after the Arkansas statute but defined the term "unborn child" as "a member of the species homo sapiens, at any stage of development, who is carried in the womb" (H.R. 2436 Sec. 1841 [D] [d]). On September 30, 1999 the House of Representatives passed H.R. 2436 by a 254–172 margin.

Even though H.R. 2436 explicitly excluded abortion, it is clear that its supporters were more concerned with scoring points in the abortion debate than with actually punishing individuals whose acts of violence against pregnant women result in fetal deaths. The use of the term unborn child as well as the decision to cover embryos and fetuses at all stages of prenatal development are inflammatory and not conducive to building a national consensus about the need to protect pregnant women and their fetuses from violence. The anti-abortion motivations of pro-life legislators and lobbyists is evident in their responses to a proposed substitute amendment offered by Representative Zoe Lofgren (D–CA). In the Judiciary Committee and subsequently on the House floor, Lofgren offered a substitute measure, The Motherhood Protection Act, which would increase the penalty for assaults on pregnant women that occurred while committing a federal crime, but would not recognize the fetus as a separate legal entity.[19] After the Lofgen alternative was defeated on a 20–8 vote in the Judiciary Committee, the original measure was sent to the floor by a 14–11 vote. The National Right to Life Committee in a September 30, 1999 letter to House members explicitly urged them to only support H.R. 2436. The letter stated that if "contrary to our expectation the Lofgren Amendment is actually adopted the NRLC urges you to vote *no* on final passage" (National Right to Life Committee 1999). In other words, the NRLC only wanted the criminalization of third-party fetal killing if the statute included language that would strengthen their position in the abortion debate. They would rather

---

[18] Representative Lindsey Graham (R-SC), who received a 100 percent approval rating from the Christian Coalition in 1998, is the primary sponsor of H.R. 2436, the Unborn Victims of Violence Act of 1999. The bill was favorably voted out of the Judiciary Committee September 14, 1999 and approved by the House by a 254–172 margin on September 30, 1999. The Senate version of the bill, S. 1673, sponsored by Senator Mike DeWine (R-OH), was not considered before adjournment but it will almost certainly be taken up in 2000. Like his counterpart in the House, DeWine is a strong proponent of socially conservative legislation. He earned a 91 percent approval rating from the Christian Coalition in 1998. See Barone and Ujifusa (1999) for interest group approval scores.

[19] The Motherhood Protection Act would have substantially increased the penalties associated with harming or killing a fetus while committing a federal offense. If the assault harmed the fetus but did not kill it, the perpetrator could be sentenced to a maximum of twenty years' imprisonment. If the assault resulted in the death of the fetus, the perpetrator could receive a sentence of life imprisonment (*Congressional Quarterly Weekly Report* 1999).

have no action taken than to have a bill passed that granted further protection to fetuses but that stopped short of personhood status. On the floor, Lofgren's bill was defeated 201–224.

It is important to remember that the vast majority of third-party fetal killings are caused by acts of domestic violence, which rarely occur in settings that would be covered by H.R. 2436. Despite their newly professed concern with protecting pregnant women and unborn human life from violence, most pro-life activists in Congress have consistently opposed measures designed to combat domestic violence. The most obvious example is their failure to support the 1994 Violence Against Women Act (H.R. 3355), which provided $1.62 billion over six years to combat violence against women.[20] More recently, pro-life legislators have been notably absent from the campaign to pass legislation (H.R. 357 and H.R. 1248) to re-authorize these programs. For example, Representative Lindsay Graham (R–SC), the primary sponsor of the Unborn Victims of Violence Act, is missing from the list of 175 co-sponsors of H.R. 357 and 156 co-sponsors of H.R. 1248. Also missing are other prominent pro-life supporters of the Unborn Victims of Violence Act, such as Representatives Charles Canady (R–FL), Christopher Smith (R–NJ), and Henry Hyde (R–IL). There is little overlap between the members who voted in favor of the Unborn Victims of Violence Act and the sponsors of the two re-authorization measures.

In addition to running the political risk of being labeled hypocrites for professing concern for unborn victims of violence while not supporting the major initiative that provides assistance to victims of domestic violence (both born and unborn), these politicians are also running a serious risk of being out of touch with their constituents. Not only has the public awareness of the problem of domestic violence increased, due at least in part to the O. J. Simpson murder trial, there is also a high degree of support for increased public spending on initiatives directed at reducing domestic violence and assisting the victims. A survey of 1,000 randomly selected people drawn from throughout the United States found that nearly 90 percent said they would support legislation to increase funding for battered women's programs and 69 percent said they would personally give money to an organization working on the issue (Klein, Campbell, Soler, and Ghez 1997, 51).[21]

[20] Even though it has only been in existence a few years, the Violence Against Women Act has registered dramatic successes. For example, police and city officials in New Orleans used the $1.5 million in federal funding over the past two years to completely revamp their domestic violence training for police officers and increase services for battered women. Bridget Bain, a spokesperson for the mayor described the changes in how police treat batterers: "Rather than try to mediate or give him a cooling off period, we've found that a pro-arrest policy could relieve some of the domestic violence incidents." During the same period, the city's overall murder rate was cut in half (Baldauf 1999, 3). Since the Violence Policy Center recently found that Louisiana has by far the highest per capita rate of women being murdered by men, efforts to address violence against women in that state need to be encouraged (Baldauf 1999, 3).

[21] At least part of the heightened public support can be traced to a multi-year national public education campaign launched in mid-1994 by the Family Violence Prevention Fund, which has re-

Connections between the civil status of the fetus and criminal law take two forms. The first and most widely recognized involves prosecutors in criminal cases arguing that civil laws and precedents that accord the fetus personhood status or near personhood status should be applied to criminal law. For example, the majority opinion in *Whitner* (1996) refers to South Carolina's wrongful death statute as a basis for fetal personhood in criminal law. The second link is relatively new. Legislators, frustrated as higher courts (outside of South Carolina) have not upheld criminal convictions of drug-abusing pregnant women because the fetus lacks legal personhood, have tried to rewrite their civil laws to expand the conditions under which individuals may be involuntarily committed so that pregnant women who abuse drugs or alcohol can be confined until they give birth.

Developments in Tort Law

According to Christina Fletcher (1996, 1), the understanding of fetal rights in civil tort law has been quietly transformed over the past two decades in two important ways: the extension of personhood status to the fetus in wrongful death cases, and statutes barring tort claims for wrongful life or wrongful birth.[22] Both of these have contributed to the trend of viewing the fetus as a person with independent rights in civil law. According to Judith Rosen (1989, 57), the right-to-life movement hopes to use these developments in civil law as a springboard toward defining the fetus as a person, regardless of the gestational age, in all areas of the law.

Most states no longer limit tort damages in wrongful death actions to compensation for the parents for the loss of a pregnancy. Increasingly, courts assign a separate legal identity to the fetus, thereby allowing for recovery rights independent of the parents. Only ten states in late 1996 still adhered to the born alive rule that prohibits the award of tort damages in wrongful death cases to a fetus; in the rest the fetus has independent recovery rights (Fletcher 1996, 10). In wrongful death tort action, the modern trend allows recovery

---

ceived more than $40 million in donated media space for public service announcements in magazines and newspapers and on radio and television (Klein, Campbell, Soler, and Ghez 1997, 93-95). Magazines as disparate as *People, Self, Emerge,* and *Men's Fitness,* have run articles about domestic violence. Not all of the media stories and public service announcements have included a discussion of the adverse consequences of fetal battering, but a fair number have. During the fall of 1999, the beleaguered tobacco company Phillip Morris began running a series of public service announcements designed to improve their corporate image. One featured a very obviously pregnant woman talking about prenatal battering and the need to provide assistance to pregnant women whose partners were abusing them. The ad, which began airing on October 13, has been shown on all of the major networks; it has been given particularly heavy play during football games (interview with Phillip Morris spokesperson, November 8, 1999).

[22] The second area of civil law that remains unchanged, that dealing with the legal rights and status of the fetus, is property law governing inheritance. Developments regarding fetal rights in property law are summarized in Chapter 2.

rights to fetuses at ever earlier gestational ages—moving from the born alive rule to viable fetuses, previable fetuses, and finally, to embryos from conception. In 1980, Georgia became the first state to assign independent recovery rights in wrongful death cases to a nonviable, in this case a "quick," fetus.[23] More recent cases have dropped the quick requirement and simply allowed tort recovery for "nonviable" fetuses.[24] According to Fletcher (1996, 11), four states (Missouri, Pennsylvania, South Carolina, and West Virginia) permit wrongful death recovery from the moment of fertilization or conception.

At the same time, some courts have barred tort actions for damages in wrongful life and wrongful birth cases. Typically, the parents assert that a medical practitioner failed to inform them that their fetus was not healthy, thereby denying them the choice to continue the pregnancy or abort an unhealthy fetus.[25] *Gleitman v. Cosgrove* (1967) was the first major "wrongful life/wrongful birth" case (Jackson 1995, 539). The plaintiff was born with hearing, speech, and sight defects caused by his mother's exposure to German measles while pregnant. Even though the physician knew that she had been exposed, he told her it would not affect the health of her child. Rather than seeking damages because the physician's negligence had caused him to face an abnormal life, the plaintiff argued that "the best possibility he could have obtained was nonexistence." The court concluded that it was incapable of determining the relative value of a life with defects versus no life (Dawe 1990, 490).

Then in *Curlender v. Bio-Science Laboratories* (1980) a court for the first time ruled that "wrongful life" was grounds for a tort action by an individual harmed while in utero (Beasley 1992, 234).[26] The court held that a child born with Tay Sachs disease, which can cause mental retardation, high susceptibility to diseases, convulsions, partial blindness, a shortened life span, and a range of other severe physical impediments, could sue to recover damages for pain and suffering caused by her "wrongful life" (Blank 1993, 140; Jackson 1995, 570).

A few years later the California Supreme Court in *Turpin v. Sortini* (1982) developed the "special benefits" rule, which holds that damages can be recovered for wrongful conduct even though the actions may have conferred a net

[23] See *Shirley v. Bacon*, 267 S.E.2d 809 (Ga. 1980).

[24] Recent court cases allowing wrongful death tort recovery on behalf of nonviable fetuses include *Conner v. Monkem Co.*, 898 S.W.2d 89 (Mo. 1995); *Wiersma v. Maple Leaf Farms*, 543 N.W.2d 787 (S.D. 1996); *Farley v. Sartin*, 466 S.E.2d 522, 533 (W. Va. 1995); *Smith v. Mercy Hospital and Medical Center*, 203 Ill. App. 3d 465, 560 N.E.2d 1164, 148 Ill. Dec. 567 (Ill. App. Ct. 1990).

[25] The first use of the term "wrongful life" in a tort action occurred in *Zepeda v. Zepeda*, 190 N.E.2d 849 (Ill. 1963), a case that did not involve an unhealthy fetus or child. Instead, the plaintiff charged that his biological father had "caused" him to have a "wrongful life" because he was illegitimate. The basis for the case was not negligence but fraud. Although the court agreed that the defendant had committed a tortious act, the claim for damages was denied on public policy grounds (i.e., it would open up the judicial system to a flood of tort actions based on harms resulting from illegitimacy, racial/ethnic identity, or poor socioeconomic conditions) (Leightman 1982, 730; Dawe 1990, 487; Laudor 1994, 1700).

[26] See *Curlender v. Bio-Science Laboratories*, 106 Cal. App. 3d 811 (1980).

benefit to the person, thus avoiding the *Gleitman* argument that courts cannot determine whether nonexistence is preferable to a less than perfect life.[27] The court held that parents should be entrusted with deciding whether a child should be born (Kearl 1983, 1280). Applying the special benefits rule, it awarded the plaintiff funds needed to pay for medical expenses but not for general damages (Shepherd 1995, 763). The New Jersey Supreme Court reached a similar conclusion in another case where in utero exposure to German measles resulted in the birth of a child with physical defects, ruling that a child with birth defects could sue to recover medical expenses but not for damages for a less than normal life.[28]

Pro-life groups feared that even these few and very limited claims provided an opening that would eventually expand the definition of and devalue human life.[29] The Catholic Church began a multifaceted campaign against wrongful life and wrongful birth actions asserting that God does not make mistakes. As part of a 1985 public relations campaign, the Catholic Health Association of the United States placed a full page ad in *Newsweek* magazine denouncing wrongful life tort actions and arguing that all human life is "rightful" (Fletcher 1996, 8).

More important, pro-life groups began encouraging states to ban wrongful life/wrongful birth suits. One of the most influential pro-life groups, Americans United for Life, developed and disseminated model legislation barring wrongful life/wrongful birth tort actions. After such legislation was introduced into state legislatures, many pro-life groups lobbied and testified in support of its passage. For example, the Pennsylvania Catholic Conference wrote a paper titled "Why the Senate Should Concur in the Wrongful Birth/Wrongful Life Amendments to Senate Bill 750" and submitted it to the relevant senate committee (Fletcher 1996, 8).[30] In testimony before the Pennsylvania House, a representative of the Catholic Conference again argued that wrongful life and wrongful birth torts should be prohibited. According to Julie Kowitz (1995, 256), the actions of the Catholic Church were instrumental in convincing the state's legislators to adopt the ban.[31] By 1996, thirteen states had passed statutes prohibiting wrongful life,

[27] The wrongful life claim was based on medical advice that was given to James and Donna Turpin, whose first child appeared to have hearing problems. A specialist in hearing and speech disorders told them their child's hearing was within the normal range for her age and there was no sign of genetic problems. Based on this advice, the parents conceived a second child, who was born with a cleft palate and hearing impairment. The first child also developed hearing problems. See *Turpin v. Sortini*, 643 P.2d 954, 956 (Cal. 1982).

[28] *Procanik v. Cillo*, 97 N.J. 339, 478 A.2d 755 (1984).

[29] Many groups representing disabled people also are opposed to wrongful life/wrongful birth claims because they encourage eugenics policies that allow people to pursue the "perfect" child and devalue individuals with disabilities (Kowitz 1995, 255; Shepherd 1995, 762).

[30] In "Why the Senate Should Concur in the Wrongful Birth/Wrongful Life Amendments to Senate Bill 750" the Pennsylvania Catholic Conference argued that allowing these suits amounted to "telling doctors treating pregnant women to practice eugenic abortion or pay the damages" (Reprinted in Fletcher 1996, 8).

[31] Title 42, section 8505(b) of the Pennsylvania Consolidated Statutes states: "A person shall be deemed to be conceived at the moment of fertilization. There shall be no cause of action or award

wrongful birth, or both tort actions (Fletcher 1996, 64).[32] The statutes in Idaho, Minnesota, Missouri, North Dakota, Pennsylvania, and Utah explicitly bar both wrongful life and wrongful birth suits because they oppose claims that appear to favor abortion over life (Fletcher 1996, 65).

Pro-life groups have also actively defended these statutes against court challenges and filed legal briefs opposing wrongful life/wrongful birth suits in other states. For example, seven pro-life groups filed amicus curiae briefs in *Hickman v. Group Health* (1986), a case that unsuccessfully challenged Minnesota's 1982 law barring wrongful life and wrongful birth claims: Americans United for Life/Legal Defense Fund, the Catholic Health Association of the United States, the Catholic League for Religious and Civil Rights, the Minnesota Conference of Catholic Health Facilities, the Minnesota Catholic Conference, the National Right to Life Committee, and the Rutherford Institute.[33] Even though this was the only wrongful life/wrongful birth case to reach a higher court, not a single pro-choice organization filed an amicus curiae brief supporting the plaintiff's argument that the Minnesota statute unconstitutionally provided no remedy for those harmed by a physician's failure to provide information regarding the health of a fetus.

Taken together, these two developments in fetal tort law add up to a "backdoor approach" to regulating abortion. Allowing independent recovery rights to the fetus in wrongful death cases moves it closer to full legal personhood status and provides a framework for similar civil actions in abortion cases. For example, Louisiana adopted a statute making abortion providers liable for tort damages caused by the procedure up to three years after the abortion, even if the woman signed a consent form. The statutory definition of "damages" not only applies to the woman but also to the "unborn child."[34] The assignment of these rights at ever earlier gestational ages—moving from the born alive rule, to viable fetuses, to previable fetuses, and finally to embryos from fertilization is an additional attack on women's abortion rights.

---

of damages on behalf of any person based on a claim that, but an act or omission of the defendant, a person once conceived would or should not have been born."

[32] The states with laws banning wrongful life, wrongful birth, or both tort actions are California, Idaho, Indiana, Kansas, Maine, Michigan, Minnesota, Missouri, North Carolina, North Dakota, Pennsylvania, South Dakota, and Utah (Fletcher 1996, 65).

[33] The Rutherford Institute, which describes itself as a "nonprofit legal and educational organization specializing in the defense of religious freedom, the sanctity of human life, and family autonomy" (Rutherford Institute, "Publications and Litigation Report," reprinted in Center for Reproductive Law and Policy 1998b,135), is arguably the most extreme of the Christian right legal advocacy groups. Two of the founding board members of the institute, R. J. Rushdoony and Howard Ahmanson, have been closely connected with the Christian Reconstructionist movement, which favors a return to a Bible-based legal system that would prescribe capital punishment for a wide range of "crimes," including homosexuality, adultery, blasphemy, astrology, and witchcraft (Center for Reproductive Law & Policy 1998b, 31, 32, 136).

[34] Even though enforcement of the Louisiana partial birth statute was permanently blocked by U.S. District Court Judge G. Thomas Porteous, these efforts will almost certainly continue (Center for Reproductive Law & Policy 1999).

Finally, statutes barring wrongful life/wrongful birth tort action not only protect physicians against damage claims for their failure to inform pregnant women of potential physical and mental fetal defects, but they also restrict abortion. Women uninformed of possible risks to the health of their fetus are far less likely to consider terminating pregnancies.

The Use of Civil Detention against Pregnant Women

Over the past decade, fetal rights proponents have become increasingly frustrated by their inability to pass new criminal laws permitting prosecution of pregnant substance abusers for exposing their fetuses in utero to harmful drugs and alcohol and by the tendency of higher courts to overturn convictions based on expansive interpretations of existing statutes to include these "crimes." Some (Mathieu 1995, 1996; Wexler 1996) have proposed mandatory outpatient drug treatment or, even under some conditions, civil commitment as a "compromise" alternative. The use of civil commitment laws not designed to control substance abuse by pregnant women has been rejected by higher courts, which have held that legislatures, not courts, make new laws. For example, in Wisconsin, fetal rights proponents were appalled by their supreme court's reversal of a juvenile court decision that allowed the state to take custody of a cocaine-using woman's fetus. The justices argued that extending the existing involuntary commitment statute to cover pregnant substance-abusing women would usurp the role of the legislature.[35] Fetal rights proponents were equally appalled when a New York trial court judge ruled in *Matter of the Retention of Tanya P.* filed in Supreme Court, New York County, 1A Part 39 (1995), that a mentally ill pregnant woman could not be involuntarily committed to prevent her from using crack cocaine and thereby harming her fetus.

In 1988 Minnesota adopted a measure allowing involuntary commitment of pregnant women who abused hard drugs such as cocaine and heroin (Minn. Stat. 253B 1997). Marijuana was specifically excluded, and a recent attempt to add alcohol to the list of proscribed substances failed. Fewer than one hundred women have been involuntarily committed to residential drug-treatment centers under this law, with average stays of less than a month (Pasternak 1998b, A13).[36]

Although the effectiveness of the Minnesota law has never been analyzed, fetal rights proponents decided it could be used as a model for new civil commitment statutes that would get around the difficulties they were having with higher courts overturning their use of existing laws to commit pregnant addicts involuntarily. In the 1997–98 legislative session, at least twelve states

[35] See *State ex rel. Angela M. W. v. Kruzicki*, No. 95-2480-W, 209 Wis. 2d 112, 561 N.W.2d 729 (1997).

[36] According to Pearson and Thoennes (1995, 52) nothing in the statute requires that those involuntarily confined get drug treatment. At least one woman was involuntarily committed for several months to a locked hospital ward for people with eating disorders.

considered legislation to allow pregnant women to be civilly committed. South Dakota and Wisconsin passed civil commitment laws far more draconian than Minnesota's. South Dakota now allows the involuntary commitment until delivery of pregnant women who use drugs or alcohol (South Dakota Codified Laws Section 34–20A-70, 1998), and Wisconsin authorizes the state to take custody of drug- and alcohol-exposed fetuses (Wisconsin ALS. 292, 1997). In addition to punishing a class of people for engaging in the otherwise legal consumption of alcohol, the Wisconsin law confers custody rights to the state as early as conception. Because the state obviously cannot take separate physical custody of a fetus, a pregnant woman is civilly committed to a residential drug-treatment center.

These laws defy modern principles of civil rights and civil liberties. There are many reasons to oppose civil commitment laws,[37] but the central problem is their underlying unproven assumption that state coercion is necessary to force pregnant addicts (and, in some cases, pregnant women who drink alcohol) into treatment. In fact, all of the evidence indicates that pregnancy itself motivates female addicts to seek treatment (Moss 1990; Ooms and Herendeen 1990; Walker, Eric, Pivnick, and Drucker 1991). The basic problem is not so much pregnant addicts' lack of motivation but a severe shortage of drug-treatment facilities that will accept pregnant women (Feig 1990; Moss 1990; Paltrow 1991; Romney 1991; Chavkin, Paone, Freidmann, and Wilets 1993; Breitbart, Chavkin, Layton, and Wise 1994; Chavkin 1996). According to Wendy Chavkin (1996, 53), budget cuts in drug-treatment funds at the local, state, and federal levels have made a bad situation even worse.

These laws may be an example of poor policymaking caused by legislators' failure to consult with experts in the field before passing them. That, however, is not necessarily the case. In the Wisconsin legislature's debate over its civil commitment law, representatives from Wisconsin social service agencies testified in committee hearings about an acute shortage of drug-treatment slots and further stated that the number of pregnant addicts voluntarily seeking treatment far exceeded the number of slots available in the state (Pasternak 1998b, A13). When pressed, even the bill's sponsor acknowledged that this deficiency was a serious problem (Pasternak 1998b; A13). Chavkin (1996) argues that proposals to revise state civil commitment laws without adequate drug-treatment programs are "symbolic."

What is the purpose of focusing public attention on controversies that have symbolic resonance but little concrete meaning? I would suggest that these symbolic debates serve to divert attention from what is really happening—the assault on the state's obligation to provide basic services. Moreover, the issue as framed is a mat-

---

[37] The journal *Politics and the Life Sciences* included a symposium on these proposals in its 1996 issue. Although many of the articles contain useful information, the critiques by Chavkin (1996), Daniels (1996), Peretz and Schroedel (1996), Strickland (1996), and Woliver (1996) are representative of scholarly responses.

ter of individual culpability, and this inverts the reality of the systemic social refusal to provide meaningful care. This is where the danger comes in. These symbolic debates camouflage, and thus permit, the reduction of services. We might better advance the well-being of women and children by advocating that their needs
be met. (Chavkin 1996, 53)

The abrogation of women's fundamental rights for "symbolic" reasons is an
appalling but inescapable conclusion. My purpose, however, is not to malign
the intent of pro-life and fetal rights proponents. Legislators often are unaware
of the consequences of seemingly unconnected policy decisions (such as budget
cuts that worsen an existing shortage in drug-treatment slots and profound
concern about the health and well-being of unborn children). Others, such as
the sponsor of the Wisconsin law, may sincerely believe these measures mark a
first step and they will be able later to convince their colleagues to fund additional drug-treatment facilities (Pasternak 1998b, A13). That view is not only
naive in light of current budgetary trends (i.e., continuing cutbacks in drug-
treatment funds during a period of budgetary surpluses), but it sets a dangerous precedent by violating a women's fundamental rights without even ap-
proximating a "compelling state interest."

Civil detention laws that allow the involuntary commitment of substance-
abusing pregnant women fail to meet the two basic tests required to sustain
governmental regulation of a fundamental right such as reproduction. First, a
state must show that its specific action is necessary. Although *Roe* (1973),
Webster (1989), and *Casey* (1992) found a compelling state interest in fetal
health at some point in a pregnancy, Wisconsin radically extends the reasoning
of these cases by authorizing state intervention to protect the fetus from conception. This would allow a woman's fundamental rights to be abrogated to
protect the rights of a cell-sized embryo, elevating its rights above those of a
living human being. Second, the state's action must be narrowly tailored to
serve a compelling governmental interest (i.e., prove that its interest could not
be met through another, less restrictive means). The cutbacks in funding for
drug-treatment programs makes such a showing difficult. These laws constitute a very serious attack on women's rights to due process, privacy, bodily integrity, self-sovereignty, and equal protection and cannot be justified on compelling state interest grounds.[38]

[38] Even though Rubenfeld (1991, 603) argues that "scant jurisprudence exists" on what the con-
cept of "compelling state interest" means, I would argue that the Court has often applied a double
standard that discriminates against women in its use of the term. In one of the earliest relevant
cases, *Buck v. Bell* (1927), Justice Holmes wrote that Virginia had a "compelling state interest in
preventing the procreation of children who will become a burden on the state" that justified its involuntary sterilization of an eighteen-year-old woman who was mistakenly characterized as "fee-
ble minded." *Buck v. Bell* was not reversed until 1942, when an Oklahoma statute mandating
sterilization for criminals convicted of three felony offenses was ruled unconstitutional. Because
the law allowed exceptions for embezzlement, liquor law violations, and political offenses, the
Court held that it violated the Fourteenth Amendment's guarantee of equal protection. In a unanimous decision, Justice Douglas argued that the law was unfairly applied to certain criminals, such
as appellant Jack Skinner, who raided chicken coops, while those who committed financial crimes

Broader Effect of Extending Fetal Rights Back to Fertilization

The civil detention proposals, similar to the developments in tort law discussed in the preceding section and the new fetal homicide laws, surreptitiously constitute a backdoor approach to banning abortion. By creating more and more opportunities by which the fetus is or nearly is a person at ever earlier gestational ages, fetal rights proponents undermine public and legal support for abortion at any stage in a pregnancy and foster the creation of a civil and criminal law system that assigns rights to the fetus beginning at fertilization or conception. Not only will abortion statutes violate this new general legal principle, but so will many popular forms of contraception such as the IUD,[39] oral contraceptives, and "morning after" pills.[40] These forms of birth control do not prevent fertilization. Instead, they prevent the implantation of a fertilized egg (e.g., embryo) in the woman's uterine wall, which typically occurs between five and seven days after fertilization. Groups such as the National Right to Life Committee, which date life from fertilization, consider these contraceptives to be very early abortifacients,[41] but most physicians and scientists consider implantation, rather than fertilization, the beginning of

---

were not sterilized. See *Skinner v. State of Oklahoma* (1942). The Court's willingness to ignore both the "strict scrutiny standard" typically invoked when fundamental rights are infringed or the "least restrictive alternative" requirement in abortion cases where the women's rights are pitted against the state's "compelling interest" in fetal life can be considered a continuation of the tendency to treat women's rights as less valuable than those of men. Only in cases involving women's reproductive rights has the Court used a separate and unequal standard in the application of "compelling state interest."

[39] The copper in some forms of IUDs works by inhibiting the sperm from fertilizing an egg, but fertilization still sometimes occurs. Then the copper affects the chemical balance in the uterine wall, thereby preventing the fertilized egg from implanting on the uterine wall (Office of Population Research 1998b).

[40] "Morning after" pills are oral contraceptives, such as Ovral or Levlen, which halt conception if taken within seventy-two hours of intercourse. These drugs are also referred to as "emergency contraception," and depending on the point in a menstrual cycle, they halt or delay ovulation or alter the lining of the uterus to prevent the implantation of a fertilized egg. Although Ovral and Levlen are legally available in the United States as ordinary contraceptives, no company has applied to the Food and Drug Administration (FDA) for approval to market them for postcoital use. Both the FDA and the American College of Obstetricians and Gynecologists have declared them safe, however, and they are widely used as "emergency contraception" in Europe (Office of Population Research 1998a, c). The recent success of an eighteen-month pilot project involving more than 900 Washington state pharmacists make it likely that the drugs will be available soon. Pharmacists who chose to participate in the trial were allowed to prescribe the drugs to women without their having to see physicians. Nearly 12,000 prescriptions were written. If 30 percent of those women would have ended up pregnant, the program prevented more than 3,000 unwanted pregnancies, many of which probably would have ended up being aborted. Even though the Washington State Pharmacy Association was initially concerned about a backlash from right-to-life groups, these fears turned out to be groundless (Montgomery 1999).

[41] In "When Does Life Begin?" the NRLC states, "Starting at birth and traveling back in time, the life of each human being can be traced to the beginning of his or her own individual life: fertilization" (National Right to Life Committee 1998).

pregnancy (Office of Population Research 1998a). The logical evolution of fetal rights at ever earlier stages of gestational development represents not only the possible return to pre-*Roe* abortion bans but also the pre-*Griswold* era of state criminalization of contraception. In 1998 South Dakota passed a law allowing pharmacists to refuse to fill prescriptions that they believe would interrupt a pregnancy at any stage. The law was passed after a pharmacist refused to fill an emergency contraception prescription for a rape victim (Barfield 1998; Brown 1998).

The extension of fetal rights back to fertilization also can have a chilling effect on medical research and treatments that use fetal tissue. Because most fetal tissue is obtained from aborted fetuses, pro-life groups are adamantly opposed to its use in medical research.[42] Research into promising new treatments for a range of medical conditions (Parkinson's disease, Huntington's disease, diabetes, and Alzheimer's disease) requiring the use of fetal tissue cells declined in the late 1980s and early 1990s when pro-life groups convinced Congress to halt federal funding for medical research using tissue from aborted fetuses. The ban was reversed by President Clinton shortly after he took office in 1993.[43] The increase in pro-life sentiment among members of Congress heightens the chances of the ban's reenactment after Clinton leaves office.

In the twenty years since the birth of Louise Brown, the first "test tube baby," (a child conceived in a petri dish), in vitro fertilization (IVF) and related procedures such as gamete intrafallopian transfer (GIFT) and zygote intrafallopian transfer (ZIFT) have become increasingly common. In all three procedures, women are treated with hormones such as Pergonal that stimulate the ovaries and induce the production of multiple eggs (or follicles). When undergoing these hormonal treatments, a woman must be carefully monitored to prevent hyperstimulation of the ovaries that causes abdominal swelling that can reach the size of a basketball. The methods and sites of fertilization differ by procedure. In IVF the eggs are fertilized in a laboratory and a few days later surgically placed in the woman's uterus. GIFT fertilization does not occur in the laboratory; the eggs and sperm are surgically placed in the fallopian tube. ZIFT is a cross between IVF and GIFT; fertilization occurs in the laboratory, but the fertilized eggs are then inserted into the fallopian tubes.[44]

Because these assisted reproductive technologies are extremely expensive, have relatively low success, and pose long-term medical risks to women, physicians try to increase the odds of live birth in a cycle of hormonal treatments by

[42] Although some fetal tissue could be collected from nonaborted fetuses that are not carried to term (i.e., miscarriages and ectopic pregnancies), medical researchers opposed President George Bush's proposal to create a nation fetal tissue bank to collect fetal tissue from these sources because the tissue was of poor quality (Robertson 1994, 208).

[43] For a discussion of the ethical issues involved in fetal tissue research, see Robertson 1994, 207-17.

[44] For an understandable description of the different types of assisted reproductive technologies, see Wisot and Meldrum 1997.

inserting more embryos during IVF and ZIFT than can be safely carried to term or, in GIFT, inserting more eggs into the fallopian tubes than can be safely carried to term; typically four to six embryos or eggs are implanted in the woman. The procedures generally fail (i.e., do not result in a live birth or births),[45] but they occasionally succeed too well (i.e., too many embryos become attached to the uterus). The physician thereupon usually recommends "selective reduction"—abortion of one or more of the embryos to improve the chances that the others will be healthy at birth (Roan 1996, A1).[46] Most physicians will recommend that the number of fetuses be reduced to two or three (Robertson 1994, 204). The abortion of the extra fetuses is unaffected by postviability abortion bans because it occurs between the gestational ages of ten to twelve weeks.[47] If previable fetuses are persons, however, selective reductions would be criminal.

Also, contingent on a woman's response to the hormone-stimulating drugs, a physician may be able to harvest more eggs than could possibly be implanted. Extra usable eggs are typically fertilized, frozen, and stored for possible use during a later cycle, causing irreversible damage to some. If personhood status is accorded from fertilization, physicians who permit the fertilization of extra eggs and freeze the embryos for subsequent use would be liable for wrongful death tort actions or criminal charges for those destroyed in the process of freezing and thawing.

Enormous Disparities in Legal Status of the Fetus

Not all state laws and court rulings have or will extend fetal personhood back to the point of fertilization. By granting states autonomy in deciding whether and how fetal life should be protected, the Supreme Court allowed the disparities between states and across policy areas to persist and expand, as demonstrated in the range of legislative enactments on abortion. As of January 1998, five states (Connecticut, Maine, Maryland, Nevada, and Washington) had adopted laws declaring that the state could not interfere with a woman's right to terminate a pregnancy before fetal viability (or, in Nevada, before a gestational age of twenty-four weeks), but ten states had passed laws declaring the opposite intent—to protect the "unborn."[48] Courts in fifteen states have

---

[45] A recent U.S. and Canadian study found less than a 20 percent success rate per IVF cycle. For a discussion of the study and findings, see Society for Assisted Reproductive Technology, American Society for Reproductive Medicine 1995.

[46] The incidence of cerebral palsy is six times higher in multiple births than in single births and the chances of birth defects are twice as high (Roan 1996, A16).

[47] According to Robertson (1994, 203), a transabdominal injection of potassium chloride is directly injected into the heart or thorax of each fetus chosen for termination. The choice of which ones to abort is usually made on technical grounds (i.e., which ones are easiest to reach). For a more detailed discussion of the procedure, see Evans, May, and Fletcher 1992.

[48] The ten states with statutes declaring their intent to protect "unborn" human life are Arkansas, Illinois, Kentucky, Louisiana, Missouri, Montana, Nebraska, North Dakota, Pennsylvania, and Utah.

ruled that their state constitutions provide greater protection than the United States Constitution for women's reproductive choices.[49]

A state's current laws provide some basis for predicting the future direction of its fetal politics, but changes in political mobilization may alter a state's course. For example, Patricia Richard (1995, 147) described Ohio as "steering for middle ground" in its abortion statutes, but it has subsequently adopted some of the country's most stringent abortion laws. Increased pro-life activism led it to become the first state to ban partial birth abortions. In contrast, Washington was always considered a rock-solid pro-choice state. In 1991, Initiative 120, which stated, "Every woman has the fundamental right to choose or refuse to have an abortion. . . . The state may not deny or interfere with a woman's right to choose to have an abortion prior to viability of the fetus, or to protect her life or health," was almost defeated because its supporters made a series of tactical mistakes. After a vote recount, the initiative won by less than half a percent (Hanna 1997, 153).[50]

A Fetal Rights Continuum

Existing fetal case and statutory laws reveal huge disparities in the rights accorded fetuses. Case and statutory laws can be sorted into a fetal rights continuum, ranging from consistently pro–fetal rights states to consistently anti–fetal rights states. At the pro–fetal rights pole are Utah and North Dakota, which consistently accord personhood or near personhood status to the fetus in all policy domains, have legislatively declared their commitments to protect the "unborn," and have among the most restrictive abortion statutes in the nation. In addition, both states have prosecuted drug-abusing pregnant women and have criminalized third-party fetal killings. They also allow wrongful death tort recovery from conception and prohibit wrongful life/wrongful birth tort actions. Indiana and Michigan are close, lacking only the general declaration affirming the sanctity of unborn life but with case and statutory laws that consistently accord rights to the fetus.

At the opposite end of the continuum are pro-choice New Jersey and Vermont, whose courts have ruled that their constitutions more fully protect women's reproductive rights than does the federal Constitution and whose case and statutory laws consistently deny legal rights to the fetus. Hawaii also is a strong pro-choice state, with case and statutory laws that consistently do not accord rights to the fetus but a constitution that does not exceed the federal Constitution in guaranteeing reproductive rights for women.

[49] The fifteen states whose constitutions accord greater protection for reproductive choice than the federal Constitution are Alaska, California, Connecticut, Florida, Idaho, Illinois, Massachusetts, Minnesota, Montana, New Jersey, New Mexico, Oregon, Tennessee, Vermont, and West Virginia.

[50] For a discussion of pro-choice groups' missteps in the Initiative 120 campaign, see Hanna 1995.

All of the other states are rife with inconsistencies. For example, Idaho's abortion laws are among the most stringent in the country, but its constitution is more protective of reproductive rights than the United States Constitution. It also prohibits wrongful life/wrongful birth tort actions. Even though district attorneys in the state have prosecuted drug-using pregnant women for child abuse, Idaho does not criminalize third-party fetal battering/killing at any gestational age. Washington, which NARAL labels one of the four strongest pro-choice states in the country, criminalizes third-party fetal killings and has historically prosecuted pregnant addicts.

A few examples illustrate the intrastate inconsistencies. Physicians who perform partial birth abortions in Alabama, Montana, and Nebraska, can be charged with felonies, but those same states do not criminalize the killing of a nine-month-old fetus by stabbing, stomping, shooting, or bludgeoning it.

The Link between Fetal Rights and the Antiabortion Movement

Despite these disparities, fetal rights are generally expanding across policy areas. Women's rights proponents with paranoid tendencies might want to think of 1950s videos that fast-forward to show maps of the world being swallowed up in red—the inexorable march of communism across the globe—as analogous. Antiabortion legal advocacy groups, most notably Americans United for Life and the National Right to Life Committee, have developed and promulgated model fetal rights and antiabortion laws and actively pursued changes in civil and criminal law through litigation to enhance fetal rights and close abortion clinics. Its statement of purpose reads, "AUL focuses on strategic initiatives that will help to change public policy and public opinion on the issues of abortion and assisted suicide in the short term, while laying the groundwork for more comprehensive protection for human life over the long term" (Americans United for Life 1998a). Even most strong pro-choice states over the past fifteen years have adopted laws that extend legal rights to fetuses. Despite the importance of model pro-life legislation in furthering this transformation, most supporters of abortion rights have not connected recent changes in civil law, such as bans on wrongful life/wrongful birth torts, and women's reproductive rights.

Stealth and High-Profile Attacks on Reproductive Rights

The attention to fetal rights beyond the abortion context does not imply a diminution of antiabortion activity. Although the focus in this book is on legally permissible political activities, nonlegal forms of antiabortion protest continue. Nearly one-fourth of all clinics that perform abortions experienced acts of severe violence, such as death threats, stalking, bomb or arson threats, bombings, arson, invasions, blockades, or chemical attacks, in 1998 (Jackman, Onynago, and Gavrilles 1999, 1). In 1998 clinics in Alabama, North Carolina, and California were bombed and similar attacks were foiled in North Dakota and Texas (Jackman, Onynago, and Gavrilles 1999, 7). There also was a sharp increase in the number and severity of chemical attacks. In the late spring and early summer of 1998, antiabortion activists sprayed butyric acid into nineteen abortion clinics in Florida, Louisiana, and Texas, and employees and patients had to be treated for nausea, breathing difficulties, and other injuries. Experts who track clinic violence are concerned because the chemical used in these attacks is more dangerous than those used in attacks in the 1980s and early 1990s. Kathy Spillar, national coordinator of the Feminist Majority Foundation, said, "We believe that there is an orchestrated campaign of terror that is spreading now across three states" (Havemann 1998, A02; Healy 1998, A12).

Because radical antiabortion groups, such as Operation Rescue, have had their assets seized and some members imprisoned for violating federal anti-racketeering laws, they have recently begun devoting a significant amount of attention to grooming the next generation of activists. Summer camps where teenagers divide their time between Bible study, street ministry, and abortion clinic picketing have been highly successful. At a recent two-week San Clemente camp, the adult leaders included Jeff White, formerly of Operation Rescue, and Reverend Joseph Foreman, who while head of Missionaries to the Pre-Born wrote a petition endorsing the use of antiabortion violence (Gottlieb 1998).

Even though the legal efforts to restrict abortion are far less dramatic than the individual acts of violence that grabbed media attention in 1998, their impact may be far more important in the long run. Fetal rights advocates concomitantly engage in efforts to enact laws that incrementally restrict abortion, conducting a "stealth" attack on reproductive choice because the scope of each individual constraint is often relatively small and may appear eminently reasonable. After all, few people oppose the idea of "informed consent" (i.e., providing the information necessary to decide whether to continue or terminate a pregnancy).[51] Few people realize the cumulative magnitude of restrictions quietly adopted over the past decade.

Pro-life groups also have vigorously campaigned to ban late-term and partial birth abortions, seeking to change the public's overall perception of abortion by shifting the focus from first trimester abortions to the brutal crushing of fully formed babies' skulls. At the same time, they are doing everything they can to prevent the distribution of RU 486 (mifepristone), a postcoital means to terminate a first trimester pregnancy. Like the postcoital oral contraceptive described in an earlier section, RU 486, if taken early, halts the implantation of a

---

[51] To enhance the public appeal of informed consent measures, Americans United for Life advocates call them "women's-right-to-know" laws—a clever play on words to gain support from women's rights proponents. The organization also has a booklet titled *Women's Right to Know Legislative Guide* that includes a model "informed consent" bill and talking points to be used with the media and in debates (Americans United for Life 1998b).

fertilized egg in the uterine lining. If taken later, it induces a miscarriage. Because it is a nonsurgical abortifacient, pro-life groups believe that it allows pregnant women to avoid the moral implications of their actions and the public scrutiny and harassment associated with visiting an abortion clinic (Robertson 1994, 65).

In the late 1980s, pro-life groups threatened the firm that markets mifepristone in Europe with a massive economic boycott if it sold the drug in the United States, causing the firm to drop its plans to distribute the drug in this country. In 1989 the Food and Drug Administration (FDA) prohibited the importation of the drug for personal use. Shortly after taking office in 1993, President Clinton issued an executive order instructing the FDA to reevaluate its import ban, but the company with marketing rights still refused to seek approval for licensing and testing in the United States. In 1994, it transferred patent rights to the Population Council, which quickly began clinical trials, the first step toward FDA approval. The clinical trials involving 2,121 women from across the country found that mifepristone triggered miscarriages 92 percent of the time and without any serious side effects (Haney 1998). In 1996 the FDA found the test results satisfactory and labeled mifepristone "approvable" but delayed final approval until a manufacturer was found. The process stalled at that point because no major drug manufacturers were willing to alienate antiabortion groups (Krieger 1998, A1). Finally, in 1998 a new pharmaceutical company, Danco, offered to market the drug and indicated it had obtained a manufacturer but refused to disclose any details about production. Mifepristone is expected to reach the American market in 2000. If the drug is marketed in the United States, pro-life groups will lose a major public relations battle because the public's image of abortions will radically change from the gruesome images conjured by partial birth abortions to a much less troubling image. As Robertson (1994, 64) wrote, "Preventing a fertilized egg from implanting or interrupting implantation shortly after an embryo has developed is less morally or symbolically problematic than surgically destroying a much more developed fetus."

The Price of Fetal Rights—A Curtailment of Women's Rights

Nearly all extensions of fetal rights are paid for by a curtailment of women's fundamental rights that extends far beyond the abortion context. At first, the diminution in reproductive rights affected only a few categories of women seeking abortions—poor women, public employees, minors, and members of the armed forces and their dependents—but it has spread more broadly to limit a range of medical and lifestyle choices by pregnant women. Again, the process started with attacks on the rights of a limited number of groups—pregnant addicts, pregnant women whose religion prohibits medical interventions such as cesarean sections or blood transfusions, and nonpregnant women working in hazardous environments. In each case, the argument has been that the state has a compelling interest in protecting the fetus that supersedes the woman's rights to due process, privacy, bodily integrity, self-sovereignty, and equal protection. More than ten years ago, women's rights proponents argued that these extensions of fetal rights constituted a slippery slope that placed the rights of all women at risk. The new involuntary civil detention laws that permit the confinement of women who legally consume alcohol indicate that the footing is becoming treacherous indeed.[52]

Even some strong fetal rights proponents have become concerned about the antiwomen character of the pro-life movement. While not discounting the pro-life movement's concern with "innocent human life," Robertson (1994, 66) argues that it has a "latent agenda" that "appears to be the control of women—punishing them for their sexuality and keeping them in certain reproductive and family roles." Although women's rights proponents might question the latency of the pro-life movement's antipathy toward women's rights, I believe that Robertson correctly ascribes both motives to the pro-life movement. My research and statistical analyses in Chapter 5 found more support for the women's rights narrative than for the fetal rights one, but I believe that many in the movement are driven by the moral imperative that the fetus is a person whose vulnerability makes it especially deserving of the state's protection.

An Opportunity to Find Common Ground

Even though society is no closer to reaching a consensus about the value that should morally and legally be accorded fetal life, there are some possibilities for moving forward on this extraordinarily contentious issue. If the pro-life movement's opposition to women's rights is "latent" rather than dominant, an opportunity exists to move away from symbolic political gestures and demagoguery and to unite all who share a genuine concern for the most vulnerable and needy members of our society. Fetal politics in the strongest pro-life and pro-choice states appear to be driven by concerns about the effect that one's position on the policy under consideration had on abortion rather than by its effectiveness and suitability to a particular problem, but a more normal process of weighing alternative proposals by merit was more typical in the less polarized states.

Several recent developments provide pro-life and pro-choice individuals with an opportunity to forge a new fetal politics that more closely resembles policymaking in the less polarized states. But first, the stereotype that equates pro-choice sentiments with being antilife must be discarded. As discussed in

---

[52] A comment by the lead defense attorney in the *Whitner* case summarized these fears: "There are not enough jail cells in South Carolina to hold the pregnant women who have a drug problem, drink a glass of wine with dinner, smoke cigarettes, fail to take prenatal vitamins, or decide to go to work despite their doctor's advice that they should stay in bed—all of whom could be guilty of the crime of child neglect" (NARAL 1997a).

Chapter 5, the evidence shows that pro-choice states are committed to protecting and caring for the most vulnerable members of our society. Pro-choice states were far more likely than pro-life states to support the adoption of special needs children and to provide adequate funding for children in the foster care system. They also provide greater assistance to poor children. Moreover, a large proportion of these states have laws dealing with the problem of prenatal drug exposure, and many criminalize third-party fetal killing. The weak pro-choice states were at least as committed as strong pro-life states and more committed than weak pro-life states to combating these threats to fetal health. Pro-life individuals whose primary motivation is the protection of innocent human life can find a common ground with many who hold pro-choice views.

That shared commitment provides an opportunity for both sides to address constructively the serious threats to fetal well-being from in utero drug exposure and third-party acts of violence. These problems can be ameliorated if politicians and groups on both sides would forget about sound bytes and legal precedents for future abortion lawsuits and instead focus on proven solutions. No silver bullet will eliminate drug use by pregnant women, but the evidence overwhelmingly shows that drug-treatment programs, particularly longer-term residential programs with child care facilities, do work. The studies also show that pregnancy itself motivates addicts to seek treatment, but most are turned away from centers because of the severe shortage of available treatment. Rather than focusing on incarceration or civil commitment (without increasing the availability of treatment options), responsible leaders on both sides of the debate should be demanding to know why we do not have drug treatment on demand for pregnant addicts.

Furthermore, the problem of fetal battering and third-party fetal killings can be addressed within the criminal justice system without further polarization over abortion. Again, the question is whether the aim is to protect fetal life or to establish legal precedents that can be applied to abortion. If the aim is to send a strong message that acts of violence against the fetus will not be tolerated, there is no reason why separate categories of criminal offenses applicable to third-party actions that harm or kill the fetus cannot be established. For example, in New Hampshire it is a Class A felony for a person to "purposely or knowingly cause injury to another resulting in miscarriage or stillbirth," and in New Mexico, a third party who kills a fetus can be charged with the crime of "injury to a pregnant woman." Feticide can be defined as a criminal offense. None of these alternatives implicitly or explicitly classifies the fetus as a legal person, but they establish that these actions will be prosecuted. These state laws, similar to the Lofgren bill that was rejected by the House of Representatives concretely address the problem without inflaming the abortion debate. Moreover, because most fetal killing occurs as a result of domestic violence, it is imperative that laws such as the Violence Against Women Act be re-authorized.

Finally, the development of postcoital oral contraceptives and drugs, such as mifepristone, that interrupt implantation of the embryo at an early stage provide an opportunity to defuse the entire abortion debate. Although some pro-life groups believe that human life begins at fertilization, most people neither consider the destruction of an embryo to be the equivalent of killing a born human being nor view it in the same light as a postviability abortion. Ovral and Levlen, which can be taken within seventy-two hours of unprotected intercourse to prevent pregnancy, already are available in the United States, and RU 486 is expected to reach the market in 2000. These drugs provide us with an opportunity to back away from the precipice and put much of the abortion conflict behind us. We should take advantage of that opportunity and use our energies to solve real problems, such as ensuring that every child in our country has a decent, loving home.

References

Abbott, Jean, Robin Johnson, Jane Koziol-McLain, and Steven R. Lowenstein. 1995. "Domestic Violence Against Women: Incidence and Prevalence in an Emergency Department Population." *Journal of American Medical Association* 273(22) (June 14): 1763–1767.

Abortion Rights Activist. 1998. "Louisiana Heart Patient Transported to Texas for Abortion." October 20. http://www.cais.com/agm/main/news/la-heart-2.html.

"Abuse of Viable Fetus Ruled a Crime." 1996. *National Law Journal* 18 (July 29): A8.

Alaska Attorney General. 1981. Opinion J-66-81681. October 70.

Amaro, Hortensia, Lisa E. Fried, Howard Cabral, Barry Zuckerman, and Suzette Levenson. 1988. "Violence toward Pregnant Women and Associated Drug Use." Paper presented at the American Public Health Association Annual Meeting.

American Bar Association. 1994. *Uniform Probate Code.* St. Paul, Minn.: West Publishing Company.

"The American Holocaust." 1983. Palm Springs, Calif.: Center for the Documentation of the American Holocaust.

American National Election Study. 1996. http://csa.berkeley.edu:7502/D3/NES96new/Doc/ns96.html.

American Political Network, Inc. 1996. *American Health Line 50-State Report: Summer 1996.* Alexandria, VA.: National Journal Company.

Americans United for Life. 1996a. "Viable Unborn Child Protection Act."

———. 1996b. "Women's Right to Know Model Bill." *Women's Right to Know Legislation Guide.*

———. 1998a. "Welcome to the AUL Home Page." http://www.unitedforlife.org/

———. 1998b. "Woman's Right to Know." http://www.unitedforlife.org/wrtk.html.

Amicus Brief of 167 Distinguished Scientists and Physicians, Including 11 Nobel Laureates, for *Webster v. Reproductive Health Services.* 1988. No. 88-605, October Term.

Andrews, Lori B. 1986. "The Legal Status of the Embryo." *Loyola Law Review* 32: 357–409.

Annas, George. 1986. "Pregnant Women as Fetal Containers." *Hastings Center Report* 16: 13–14.

Annie E. Casey Foundation. 1995. *Kids Count Data Book: State Profiles of Child Well-Being.* Baltimore: Annie E. Casey Foundation.

Apollo, Kevin M. 1989. "The Biological Father's Right to Require a Pregnant Woman to Undergo Medical Treatment Necessary to Sustain Fetal Life." *Dickinson Law Review* 94(1): 199–229.

Ashbrook, Debra L., and Linda C. Solley. 1979. *Women and Heroin Abuse: A Survey of Sexism in Drug Abuse Administration*. Palo Alto, Calif.: R and E Research Associates.

Associated Press. 1998. "Ex-Drug User Fighting Sentence." *Augusta Chronicle Online*, February 22.

——. 1999. "Late-Term Abortion Issue Likely Bound for U.S. Supreme Court." CNN.com. October 27.

Attorney General of California. 1982. 65 Op. Attorney General of California 261.

Attorney General of Delaware. 1977. Statement of Policy. March 24.

Attorney General of Kansas. 1991. Opinion of Kansas Attorney General, No. 91-130. October 15.

Balch, Burke. 1989. "NRLC Proposes a Post-*Webster* State Legislative Program." *National Right to Life News*, October 19: 6–7.

Baldauf, Scott. 1999. "A State's Challenge to Domestic Violence." *Christian Science Monitor*, November 15, 3.

Barfield, Deborah. 1998. "A Pharmacist's Conscience Issue." *Newsday*, May 18.

Barone, Michael, and Grant Ujifusa. 1999. *The Almanac of American Politics 2000*. Washington, D.C.: National Journal.

Barry, Ellen M. 1985. "Quality of Prenatal Care for Incarcerated Women Challenged." *Youth Law News* 6(6): 1–4.

——. 1989. "Recent Developments: Pregnant Prisoners." *Harvard Women's Law Journal* 12: 189–205.

——. 1996. "Women Prisoners and Health Care: Locked Up and Locked Out." In *Man-Made Medicine: Women's Health, Public Policy, and Reform*, edited by Kary L. Moss. Durham, N.C.: Duke University Press.

Bassin, Donna, Margaret Honey, and Meryle Mahrer Kaplan. 1994. *Representations of Motherhood*. New Haven: Yale University Press.

Baumgartner, Frank R., and Byran D. Jones. 1993. *Agendas and Instability in American Politics*. Chicago: University of Chicago Press.

Beasley, Michele E. 1992. "Wrongful Birth/Wrongful Life: The Tort Progeny of Legalized Abortion." In *Abortion, Medicine and the Law*, edited by J. Douglas Butler and David F. Walpert. New York: Facts on File.

Beck, William W., Jr. 1989. *Obstetrics and Gynecology*. 2d ed. Baltimore: National Medical Series.

Becker, Barrie, and Peggy Hora. 1993. "The Legal Community's Response to Drug Use during Pregnancy in the Criminal Sentencing and Dependency Contexts: A Survey of Judges, Prosecuting Attorneys, and Defense Attorneys in Ten California Counties." *Southern California Review of Law and Women's Studies* 2(2): 527–75.

Behrman, Richard E., Carol S. Larson, Deanna S. Gomby, Eugene M. Lewit, and Patricia H. Shiono. 1991a. "Analysis." *The Future of the Children* 1 (Spring): 9–16.

——. 1991b. "Recommendations." *The Future of the Children* 1 (Spring): 8–9.

Bentley, Perry Mack. 1983. "Feticide: Murder in Kentucky?" *Kentucky Law Journal* 71: 933–51.

Berenson, Abbey B., Norma J. Stiglich, Gregg S. Wilkinson, and Garland D. Anderson. 1991. "Drug Abuse and Other Risk Factors for Physical Abuse in Pregnancy." *American Journal of Obstetrics and Gynecology* 164(6): 1491–99.

Berkman, Harvey. 1995. "Mr. Hyde's Other Side: Principles, Now Power." *National Law Review*. January 23, A1.

Berkman, Michael B., and Robert E. O'Conner. 1993. "Do Women Legislators Matter?

Female Legislators and State Abortion Policy." In *Understanding the New Politics of Abortion*, edited by Malcolm L. Goggin. Newbury Park, Calif.: Sage.

Berman, David R. 1997. *State and Local Politics*. 8th ed. Armonk, N.Y.: M. E. Sharpe.

Berrien, Jacqueline. 1990. "Pregnancy and Drug Use: The Dangerous and Unequal Use of Punitive Measures." *Yale Journal of Law and Feminism* 2(2): 239–50.

Bertin, Joan E., and Laurie R. Beck. 1996. "Of Headlines and Hypotheses: The Role of Gender in Popular Press Coverage of Women's Health and Biology." In *Man-Made Medicine: Women's Health, Public Policy, and Reform*, edited by Kary L. Moss. Durham, N.C.: Duke University Press.

Beyle, Thad L. 1995. *State Government*. Washington, D.C.: Congressional Quarterly Press.

Bingol, Nesrin, Carlotta Schuster, Magdalena Fuchs, Silvia Iosub, Gudrun Turner, Richard K. Stone, and Donald S. Gromisch. 1987. "The Influence of Socioeconomic Factors on the Occurrence of Fetal Alcohol Syndrome." *Advances in Alcohol and Substance Abuse* 6(4): 105–18.

Black, Henry Campbell, Joseph R. Nolan, and Jacqueline M. Nolan-Haley. 1990. *Black's Law Dictionary*. 6th ed. St. Paul: West Publishing.

Blake, Judith. 1977. "The Supreme Court's Abortion Decisions and Public Opinion in the United States." *Population and Development Review* 3(1–2): 45–62.

Blanchard, Dallas A., and Terry J. Prewitt. 1993. *Religious Violence and Abortion: The Gideon Project*. Gainesville: University Press of Florida.

Blank, Robert. 1993. *Fetal Protection in the Workplace*. New York: Columbia University Press.

Blum, R., M. Resnick, and T. Stark. 1987. "The Impact of a Parental Notification Law on Adolescent Abortion Decision Making." *American Journal of Public Health* 77: 619–27.

——. 1990. "Factors Associated with the Use of Court Bypass by Minors to Obtain Abortions." *Family Planning Perspectives* 22: 158–60.

Bohn, Diane K. 1990. "Domestic Violence and Pregnancy: Implications for Practice." *Journal of Nurse-Midwifery* 35(2): 86–98.

Boling, Patricia. 1995. *Expecting Trouble: Surrogacy, Fetal Abuse, and New Reproductive Technologies*. Boulder: Westview Press.

——. 1996. "Mandating Treatment for Pregnant Substance Abusers Is the Wrong Focus for Public Discussion." *Politics and the Life Sciences* 15(1): 51–52.

Bond, John R., and Charles A. Johnson. 1982. "Implementing a Permissive Policy: Hospital Abortion Services after *Roe v. Wade*." *American Journal of Political Science* 26(1): 1–24.

Borrelli, MaryAnne. 1995. "Massachusetts: Abortion Policymaking in Transtition." In *Abortion Politics in American States*, edited by Mary C. Segers and Timothy A. Byrnes. Armonk, N.Y.: M. E. Sharpe.

Bourgeois, Philippe, and Eloise Dunlop. 1993. "Exorcising Sex-for-Crack: An Ethnographic Perspective from Harlem." In *Crack Pipe as Pimp*, edited by Mitchell S. Ratner. New York: Lexington Books.

Bower, Lisa C. 1995. "The Trope of the Dark Continent in the Fetal Harm Debates: `Africanism' and the Right to Choice." In *Expecting Trouble: Surrogacy, Fetal Abuse, and New Reproductive Technologies*, edited by Patricia Boling. Boulder: Westview Press.

Boyd, Martha Anne. 1990. "Towards a Policy of Involuntary Commitment to Force Female Addicts into Drug Treatment Programs in California." M.P.A. thesis, California State University, Chico.

Bradley, Martin B., and Norman M. Green Jr. 1992. *Churches and Church Membership in the United States*. Atlanta: Glenmary Research Center.

Bragg, Rick. 1997. "Bomb Blasts Rock Abortion Clinic in Atlanta; 6 Are Injured." *New York Times*, January 17, A15.

Breitbart, Vicki, Wendy Chavkin, Christine Layton, and Paul Wise. 1994. "Model Programs Addressing Perinatal Drug Exposure and HIV Infection: Integrating Women's and Children's Needs." *Bulletin of the New York Academy of Medicine* 71(2): 236–51.

Brodie, Janet Farrell. 1994. *Contraception and Abortion in 19th Century America*. Ithaca: Cornell University Press.

Brown, Angela K. 1998. "New Pharmacy Law Heightens Abortion Controversy in South Dakota. *Sioux Falls Argus Leader* May 15, Al.

Brown, LaRay 1992. "Women and Children Last: Barriers to Drug Treatment for Women." *Health/PAC Bulletin* 22(Summer): 15–19.

Bureau of the Census. 1996. *The American Almanac, 1996–1997: Statistical Abstract of the United States*. Austin, Tex.: Hoover's.

California Department of Alcohol and Drug Programs. 1994. *Evaluating Recovery Services: The California Alcohol and Drug Treatment Assessment*. Chicago: National Opinion Research Center at the University of Chicago and Lewin-VHI.

Campbell, John. 1984. "Work, Pregnancy, and Infant Mortality among Southern Slaves." *Journal of Interdisciplinary History* 14(4): 793–812.

Campbell, Jacqueline C., Catharine Oliver, and Linda Bullock. 1992. "Why Battering during Pregnancy." Unpublished manuscript.

Carey, Mary Agnes. 1998a. "*Roe v. Wade*'s Challenge at 25: Hang on to the Votes." *Congressional Quarterly Weekly Report*, January 17, 127–28.

——. 1998b. "Testimony by Parents Gives an Emotional Edge to Hearings on Abortion Bills." *Congressional Quarterly Weekly Report*, May 23, 1394.

Carmody, Dianne C., and Kirk R. Williams. 1987. "Wife Assault and Perceptions of Sanctions." *Violence and Victims* 2(1): 25–38.

Carney, Eliza Newlin. 1995. "Maryland: A Law Codifying *Roe v. Wade*." In *Abortion Politics in American States*, edited by Mary C. Segers and Timothy A. Byrnes. Armonk, N.Y.: M. E. Sharpe.

Cartoof, Virginia, and Lorraine Klerman. 1986. "Parental Consent for Abortion: Impact of the Massachusetts Law." *American Journal of Public Health* 76: 397–421.

Cassidy, Keith. 1996. "The Right to Life Movement: Sources, Development, and Strategies." In *The Politics of Abortion and Birth Control in Historical Perspective*, edited by Donald T. Critchlow. University Park: Pennsylvania State University Press.

Center for Reproductive Law & Policy. 1996. "Punishing Women for Their Behavior during Pregnancy: A Public Health Disaster." In *Reproductive Freedom in Focus*. New York: Center for Reproductive Law & Policy.

——. 1997. "South Carolina Jury Rejects Claim That Hospital Policy Violated Rights of Pregnant Women." http://204.168.19.126/rfnviol.html.

——. 1998a. "Sea Change Occurs as 17 Courts Find `Partial Birth Abortion' Bans Unconstitutional." New York: Center for Reproductive Law & Policy.

——. 1998b. *Tipping the Scales: The Christian Right's Crusade against Choice*. New York: Center for Reproductive Law & Policy.

——. 1998c. "Combating the `Partial Birth Abortion' Myth: Where Do the People Stand?" *Reproductive Freedom News* 7(8): 1–4.

——. 1999. "Banson Partial-Birth Abortion and Other Abortion Methods." *CRLP Publications*, September 20, 1–3.

Chasnoff, Ira J. 1989. *National Hospital Incidence Survey*. Chicago: National Association for Perinatal Addiction Research and Education.

Chasnoff, Ira J., Dan Griffith, Catherine Freier, and James Murray. 1992. "Cocaine/Poly-drug Use in Pregnancy: Two Year Follow-Up." *Pediatrics* 89(2): 284–89.

Chasnoff, Ira J., Dan Griffith, Scott MacGregor, Kathryn Dirkes, and Kayreen A. Burns. 1989. "Temporal Patterns of Cocaine Use during Pregnancy." *Journal of the American Medical Association* 261(12): 1741–44.

Chasnoff, Ira J., Harvey J. Landress, and Mark E. Barrett. 1990. "The Prevalence of Illicit Drug or Alcohol Use during Pregnancy and Discrepancies in Mandatory Reporting in Pinellas County, Florida." *New England Journal of Medicine* 322(17): 1202–6.

Chavkin, Wendy. 1990a. "Drug Addiction and Pregnancy: Policy Crossroads." *American Journal of Public Health* 80(4): 483–87.

———. 1990b. "*Webster*, Health, and History." *Public Historian* 12(1): 53–56.

———. 1996. "Mandatory Treatment for Pregnant Substance Abusers: Irrelevant and Dangerous." *Politics and the Life Sciences* 15(1): 53–54.

Chavkin, Wendy, Dennis W. Paone, Patricia Freidmann, and Ilene Wilets. 1993. "Reframing the Debates: Towards Effective Treatment for Inner City Drug Using Mothers." *Bulletin of New York Academy of Medicine* 70(1): 50–68.

Cicchese, Michael. 1998. "Couple to Bury Fetuses." *Inland Valley Daily Bulletin*, September 25, A1 and A4.

Clary, Freddie. 1982. "Minor Women Obtaining Abortions: A Study of Parental Notification in a Metropolitan Area." *American Journal of Public Health* 72: 283–90.

Cohen, Jeffrey E., and Charles Barrilleaux. 1993. "Public Opinion, Interest Groups, and Public Policy Making: Abortion Policy in the American States." In *Understanding the New Politics of Abortion*, edited by Malcolm L. Goggin. Newbury Park, Calif.: Sage.

Colorado Attorney General. 1985. Opinion of the Attorney General. February 6.

Condit, Celeste Michelle. 1990. *Decoding Abortion Rhetoric*. Urbana: University of Illinois Press.

Condit, Deidre Moira. 1995. "Fetal Personhood: Political Identity under Construction." In *Expecting Trouble: Surrogacy, Fetal Abuse, and New Reproductive Technologies*, edited by Patricia Boling. Boulder: Westview Press.

Condon, Charles Molony. 1995. "Clinton's Cocaine Babies." *Policy Review* (Spring): 12–15.

Congressional Quarterly Weekly Report. 1999. "For the Record House Votes." October 2.

Cook, Elizabeth Adell, Ted G. Jelen, and Clyde Wilcox. 1992. *Between Two Absolutes*. Boulder: Westview Press.

Coombs, Robert H., Lincoln J. Fry, and Patricia C. Lewis. 1976. *Socialization in Drug Abuse*. Boston: Schenkman.

Council on Scientific Affairs, American Medical Association. 1992. "Induced Termination of Pregnancy before and after *Roe v. Wade*." *Journal of the American Medical Association* 268(22): 3237.

"Courts Disagree on Mother's Liability." 1991. *National Law Journal* 13 (May 30): 30.

Coutinho, Absalom. 1998. "Questions and Answers By Fr. Absalom Coutinho." http://www.thegospeltruth.org/questions.html.

CRLP Press. 1999. "Louisiana's 'Partial-Birth Abortion' Ban Struck Down by Federal Court." March 4. New York: Center for Reproductive Law & Policy.

Curran, William J. 1983. "An Historical Perspective on the Law of Personality and Status with Special Regard to the Human Fetus and the Rights of Women." *Milbank Memorial Fund Quarterly/Health and Society* 61(1): 58–75.

Daniels, Cynthia R. 1993. *At Woman's Expense*. Cambridge, Mass.: Harvard University Press.

——. 1996. "A Million (Missing) Men: A Commentary on Mathieu's Compromise on Pregnancy and Substance Abuse." *Politics and the Life Sciences* 15(1): 54–56.

Daunt, Tina, and Josh Meyer. 1998. "Controversies Weigh Down Block's Bid for Re-election." *Los Angeles Times*, March 3, A1 and A17.

Davis, John Jefferson. 1984. *Abortion and the Christian*. Phillipsburg, N.J.: Presbyterian and Reformed Publishing Company.

Davis, Nanette J. 1985. *From Crime to Choice*. Westport, Conn.: Greenwood Press.

Dawe, Timothy J. 1990. "Wrongful Life: Time for a 'Day in Court.' " *Ohio University Law Review* 51: 473–98.

Day, Christine L. 1995. "Louisiana: Religious Politics and the Pro-Life Cause." In *Abortion Politics in American States*, edited by Mary C. Segers and Timothy A. Byrnes. Armonk, N.Y.: M. E. Sharpe.

Daynes, Byron W. 1988. "Pornography: Freedom of Expression or Social Degradation?" In *Social Regulatory Policy: Moral Controversies in American Politics*, edited by Raymond Tatalovich and Byron W. Daynes. Boulder: Westview Press.

Dearwater, Stephen R., Jeffrey H. Coben, Jacquelyn C. Campbell, Gregory Nah, Nancy Glass, Elizabeth McLoughlin, and Betty Bekemeier. 1998. "Prevalence of Intimate Partner Abuse in Women Treated at Community Hospital Emergency Departments." *Journal of the American Medical Association* 280 5: 433–38.

De Leon, George, and Nancy Jainchill. 1991. "Residential Therapeutic Communities for Female Substance Abusers." *Journal of the New York Academy of Medicine* 67 (May–June): 277–90.

Dinsmore, Janet. 1992. "Pregnant Drug Users: The Debate over Prosecution." Washington, D.C.: American Prosecutors Research Institute.

Dobash, R. Emerson, and Russell Dobash. 1979. *Violence against Wives*. New York: Free Press.

Dolan, Maura. 1997. "State Justices Strike Down Abortion Consent Law." *Los Angeles Times*, August 8, A1 and A14.

Dye, Thomas. 1987. *Understanding Public Policy*. Englewood Cliffs, N.J.: Prentice-Hall.

Easton, David. 1965. *A Systems Analysis of Political Life*. New York: Wiley.

Egley, Charles C., David E. Miller, Juan L. Granados, and Catherine Ingram-Fogel. 1992. "Outcome of Pregnancy during Imprisonment." *Journal of Reproductive Medicine* 37 (February): 131–34.

Eisenberg, Sue E., and Patricia L. Micklow. 1979. "The Assaulted Wife: 'Catch 22' Revisited." *Women's Rights Law Reporter* 3: 138–61.

Eisenstein, James. 1973. *Politics and the Legal Process*. New York: Harper & Row.

Ellwood, William N. 1994. *Rhetoric in the War on Drugs: The Triumphs and Tragedies of Public Relations*. Westport, Conn.: Praeger.

Englehart, H. Tristram. 1983. "Viability and the Use of the Fetus." In *Abortion and the Status of the Fetus*, edited by William B. Bondeson, H. Tristram Engelhardt Jr., Stuart F. Spicker, and Daniel H. Klinship. New York: Reidel.

Epstein, Lee, and Thomas G. Walker. 1992. *Constitutional Law for a Changing America: Institutional Powers and Constraints*. Washington, D.C.: Congressional Quarterly Press.

Erb, Richard A., and Alan W. Mortensen. 1993. "Wyoming Fetal Rights—Why the Abortion 'Albatross' Is a Bird of a Different Color: The Case for Fetal-Federalism." *Land and Water Law Review* 28(2): 627–59.

Erikson, Robert, Gerald Wright, and John McIver. 1993. *State House Democracy:*

Public Opinion and Policy in the American States. New York: Cambridge University Press.

Evans, Mark, Marlene May, and John Fletcher. 1992. "Multifetal Pregnancy Reduction and Selective Termination." In *Textbook of Operative Obstetrics*, 2d ed., edited by L. Iff, J. L. Apuzzio, and A. N. Vintzileos. New York: Pergamon Press.

Farkas, Kathleen J., and Theodore V. Parran Jr. 1993. "Treatment of Cocaine Addiction during Pregnancy." *Clinics in Perinatology* 20 (March): 24–45.

Feig, Laura. 1990. *Drug Exposed Infants and Children: Service Needs and Policy Questions*. Washington, D.C.: Office of Human Services Policy, U.S. Department of Health and Human Services.

Fein, Bruce. 1992. "Does Congress Know No Limits?" *Texas Lawyer*, March 23, 19.

Feldman, Harvey W., Frank Espada, Sharon Penn, and Sharon Byrd. 1993. "Street Status and the Sex-for-Crack Scene in San Francisco." In *Crack Pipe as Pimp*, edited by Mitchell S. Ratner. New York: Lexington Books.

Feminist Majority Foundation. 1996. "The Fight to Make RU 486 Available to U.S. Women." Washington, D.C.: Feminist Majority Foundation.

Fletcher, Christina. 1996. *Emerging Fetal Rights and Civil Law*. Master's thesis, Claremont Graduate School.

Fowler, Paul. 1987. *Abortion*. Portland: Multnomah Press.

Franklin, Charles H., and Liane C. Kosaki. 1989. "Republican Schoolmaster: The U.S. Supreme Court, Public Opinion, and Abortion." *American Political Science Review* 83(3): 751–71.

Freidman, Lawrence M. 1977. *Law and Society: An Introduction*. Englewood Cliffs, N.J.: Prentice-Hall.

FY 1995. Labor, Health, and Human Services and Education Appropriations Act, Pub. L. 103-333, sect. 509.

Gallagher, Janet. 1987. "Prenatal Invasions & Interventions: What's Wrong with Fetal Rights." *Harvard Women's Law Journal* 10 (Spring): 9–58.

Gallup, George, Jr. and Frank Newport. 1990. "Negative Reaction to U.S. Involvement in Vietnam Reaches Record High." *Gallup Poll Monthly*, May.

Garson, D. David. 1986. "From Policy Science to Policy Analysis: A Quarter Century of Progress." In *Policy Analysis and Perspectives, Concepts and Methods*, edited by William Dunn. Greenwich, Conn.: JAI Press.

Garton, Jean. 1984. *Language of Illusion: The Abortion Slogans*. Lewiston, N.Y.: Life Cycle Books.

Gelles, Richard J. 1988. "Violence and Pregnancy: Are Pregnant Women at Greater Risk of Abuse?" *Journal of Marriage and Family* 50: 841–47.

Gersham, Bennett L. 1992. "The New Prosecutors." *University of Pittsburgh Law Review* 53: 393–458.

Ginsburg, Faye D. 1989. *Contested Lives: The Abortion Debate in an American Community*. Berkeley: University of California Press.

Glantz, Leonard. 1976. "Legal Aspects of Fetal Viability." In *Genetics and the Law*, edited by Aubrey Milunsky and George Annas. New York: Plenum Press.

Glink, Shona. 1991. "The Prosecution of Maternal Fetal Abuse: Is This the Answer?" *University of Illinois Law Review* 2: 533–80.

Goggin, Malcolm L. 1993. *Understanding the New Politics of Abortion*. Newbury Park, Calif.: Sage.

Goggin, Malcolm L. and Jung-Ki Kim. 1992. "Interest Groups, Public Opinion, and Abortion Policy in the American States." Paper presented at the annual meeting of the Western Political Science Association, San Francisco.

Goggin, Malcolm L., and Christopher Wlezen. 1993. "Abortion Opinion and Policy in the American States." In *Understanding the Politics of Abortion*, edited by Malcolm L. Goggin. Newbury Park, Calif.: Sage.

Goldberg, Wendy G., and Michael C. Tomlanovich. 1984. "Domestic Violence Victims in the Emergency Department." *Journal of the American Medical Association* 251 (24): 3259–64.

Goldman, John J. 1998. "Abortion Doctor Killed by Sniper in Upstate New York." *Los Angeles Times*, October 25, A1, A14, and A16.

Goldstein, Leslie Friedman. 1979. *The Constitutional Rights of Women*. New York: Longman.

Gomez, Laura E. 1997. *Misconceiving Mothers: Legislators, Prosecutors, and the Politics of Prenatal Drug Exposure*. Philadelphia: Temple University Press.

Gordon, Linda. 1977. *Woman's Body, Woman's Right: A Social History of Birth Control in America*. New York: Grossman.

Gorman, Michael J. 1993. "Ahead to Our Past: Abortion and Christian Texts." In *The Church and Abortion*, edited by Paul T. Stallsworth. Nashville: Abington Press.

Gorman, Tom. 1998. "ACLU Protests Release of Fetuses for Burial." *Los Angeles Times*, October 10: A20.

Gottlieb, Jeff. 1998. "Teens Give New Life to Operation Rescue." *Los Angeles Times*, October 12, Al and A20.

Graber, Mark A. 1996. *Rethinking Abortion: Equal Choice, the Constitution, and Reproductive Policies*. Princeton: Princeton University Press.

Graglia, Lino. 1995. "Does Constitutional Law Exist?" *National Review* 47 (12): 31.

Gusfield, Joseph R. 1963. *Symbolic Crusade: Status Politics and the American Temperance Movement*. Urbana: University of Illinois Press.

Guth, James L., Lyman A. Kellstedt, Corwin E. Smidt, and John C. Green. 1994. "Cut From the Whole Cloth: Antiabortion Mobilization among Religious Activists." In *Abortion Politics in the United States and Canada: Studies in Public Opinion*, edited by Ted G. Jelen and Marthe A. Chandler. Westport, Conn.: Praeger.

Haas-Wilson, Deborah. 1993. "The Economic Impact of State Restrictions on Abortion: Parental Consent and Notification Laws and Medicaid Funding." *Journal of Policy Analysis and Management* 12 (3): 498–511.

Hack, Maureen, and Avroy A. Fanaroff. 1989. "Outcomes of Extremely Low-Birthweight Infants between 1982 and 1988." *New England Journal of Medicine* 321(24): 1642.

Haider-Markel, Donald P., and Kenneth J. Meier. 1996. "The Politics of Gay and Lesbian Rights: Expanding the Scope of Conflict." *Journal of Politics* 58(2): 332–49.

Hall, Melinda Gann. 1987. "Constituent Influence in State Supreme Courts: Conceptual Notes and a Case Study." *Journal of Politics* 49(4): 1118–24.

———. 1992. "Electoral Politics and Strategic Voting in State Supreme Courts." *Journal of Politics* 53(2): 427–46.

Halva-Neubauer, Glen A. 1990. "Abortion Policy in the Post-Webster:Age." *Publius: The Journal of Federalism* 20(3): 20–44.

———. 1993. "The States after *Roe*: No 'Paper Tigers.' " In *Understanding the New Politics of Abortion*, edited by Malcom L. Goggin. Newbury Park, Calif.: Sage.

———. 1995. "Minnesota: Shifting Sands on a 'Challenger' Beachhead?" In *Abortion Politics in American States*, edited by Mary C. Segers and Timothy A. Byrnes. Armonk, N.Y.: M. E. Sharpe.

Haney, Daniel Q. 1998. "U.S. Study Finds Abortion Pill 92 Percent Effective." *Star Telegram*, April 29.

Hanna, Mary T. 1997. "Washington: Abortion Policymaking through Initiative." In

Abortion Politics in American States, edited by Mary C. Segers and Timothy A. Byrnes. Armonk, N.Y.: M. E. Sharpe.

Hansen, Susan B. 1993. "Differences in Public Policies toward Abortion: Electoral and Policy Context." In *Understanding the New Politics of Abortion*, edited by Malcolm L. Goggin. Newbury Park, Calif.: Sage.

Harris, George W. 1986. "Fathers and Fetuses." *Ethics* 96(3): 594–603.

Harrison, Eric, and Melissa Healy. 1996. "Two Blasts Hit Atlanta Abortion Clinic: Six Injured." *Los Angeles Times*, January 17, A4.

Havemann, Judith. 1998. "Chemical Attacks Probed in 2 Other States." *Washington Post*, July 9, A2.

Hayes, Michael T. 1992. *Incrementalism and Public Policy*. New York: Longman.

Healy, Melissa. 1996. "Abortion Bill Reveals Fight." *Los Angeles Times*, March 31, A1.

———. 1998. "FBI Probing Acid Attacks at Abortion Clinics." *Los Angeles Times*, July 19, A12.

Helmer, John, and Thomas Vietorisz. 1974. *Drug Use, the Labor Market and Class Conflict*. Washington, D.C.: Drug Abuse Council.

Helton, Anne Stewart. 1987. *Protocol of Care for Battered Women*. Houston: March of Dimes Birth Defect Foundation.

Hilberman, Elaine. 1980. "Overview: The 'Wife Beater' Reconsidered." *American Journal of Psychiatry* 137(11): 1336–47.

Hillard, Paula J. Adams. 1985. "Physical Abuse in Pregnancy." *Obstetrics and Gynecology* 66(2): 185–89.

HLI Reports. 1995. Gaithersburg, Md.: Human Life International.

Hoffman, Jan. 1990. "Pregnant, Addicted and Guilty." *New York Times Magazine*, August 19, 33.

Holy Bible. King James Version. 1966. Chicago: John A. Dickson.

Hornick, Harriet L. 1993. "Mama vs. Fetus." *Medical Trial Technique Quarterly* 39 (Summer): 536–69.

Horst, Lorrie. 1991. "Important Factors in the Decision to Seek Drug/Alcohol Treatment in the Perinatal Period." M.S.W. thesis, California State University at Long Beach.

Hovey, Harold A. 1996. *State Fact Finder: Rankings across America 1996*. Washington, D.C.: Congressional Quarterly.

Hunter, James Davison. 1994. *Before the Shooting Begins: Searching for Democracy in America's Cultural War*. New York: Free Press.

Hunter, James Davison, and Joseph E. Davis. 1996. "Cultural Politics at the Edge of Life." In *The Politics of Abortion and Birth Control in Historical Perspective*, edited by Donald T. Critchlow. University Park: Pennsylvania State University Press.

Inciardi, James A. 1993. "Kingrats, Chicken Heads, Slow Necks, Freaks and Blood Suckers: A Glimpse at the Miami Sex-for-Crack Market." In *Crack Pipe as Pimp*, edited by Mitchell S. Ratner. New York: Lexington Books.

Institute for Women's Policy Research. 1996. *The Status of Women in the States*. Washington, D.C.: Institute for Women's Policy Research.

Institute of Medicine. 1975. *Legalized Abortion and the Public Health*. Washington D.C.: National Academy of Science.

———. 1990. *Treating Drug Problems*. Vol 1. Washington, D.C.: National Academy of Science.

Jackman, Jennifer, Christine Onyango, and Elizabeth Gavrilles. 1999. "1998 National Clinic Violence Survey Report." http://www.feminist.org/research/cvsurveys/1998/finaldraft.html.

Jackson, Anthony. 1995. "Action for Wrongful Life, Wrongful Pregnancy, and Wrongful Birth in the United States and England." *Loyola of Los Angeles International & Comparative Law Journal* 17: 535–613.

Jacob, Herbert. 1984. *Justice in America: Courts, Lawyers, and the Judicial Process.* Boston: Little, Brown.

———. 1996. "Courts: The Least Visible Branch." In *Politics in the American States: A Comparative Analysis*, 6th ed., edited by Virginia Gray and Herbert Jacob. Washington, D.C.: Congressional Quarterly Press.

Jacoby, Joan E. 1980. *The American Prosecutor: A Search for Identity.* Lexington, Mass.: Lexington Books.

Jenkins-Smith, Hank C. 1990. *Democratic Politics and Policy Analysis.* Pacific Grove, Calif.: Brooks Cole.

Jensen, Eric L., Jurg Gerber, and Ginna M. Babcock. 1991. "The New War on Drugs: Grass Roots Movement or Political Construction." *Journal of Drug Issues* 21: 651–67.

Jessup, Marty, and Robert Roth. 1988. "Clinical and Legal Perspectives on Prenatal Drug and Alcohol Use: Guidelines for Individual and Community Response." *Medicine and Law* 7(4): 377–89.

Jewell, Malcolm E., and Marcia Lynn Whicker. 1994. *Legislative Leadership in the American States.* Ann Arbor: University of Michigan Press.

Johnsen, Dawn. 1989. "From Driving to Drugs: Governmental Regulation of Pregnant Women's Lives after *Webster*." *University of Pennsylvania Law Review* 138 (November): 179–215.

Jos, Philip H., Mary Faith Marshall, and Martin Perlmutter. 1995. "The Charleston Policy on Cocaine Use during Pregnancy: A Cautionary Tale." *Journal of Law, Medicine, and Ethics* 23(2): 120–28.

Kandall, Stephen R. 1991. "Perinatal Effects of Cocaine and Amphetamine Use during Pregnancy." *Bulletin of the New York Academy of Medicine* 67(3): 240–55.

Kandall, Stephen R., and Wendy Chavkin. 1992. "Illicit Drugs in America: History, Impact on Women and Infants, and Treatment Strategies for Women." *Hastings Law Journal* 43: 615–43.

Kane, H. H. 1882. *Opium Smoking in America and China.* New York: G. P. Putnam's.

Kansas Department of Health and Environment. 1997. "If You Are Pregnant." Topeka: Department of Health and Environment.

Kantrowitz, Barbara, Vicki Quade, Bonnie Fisher, James Hill, and Lucille Beachy. 1991. "The Pregnancy Police." *Newsweek*, April 29, 52–53.

Karlsen, Carol F. 1989. *The Devil in the Shape of a Woman: Witchcraft in Colonial New England.* New York: Vintage.

Kearl, Kurtis J. 1983. "*Turpin v. Sortini*: Recognizing the Unsupportable Cause of Action for Wrongful Life." *California Law Review* 71 (July): 1278–97.

Kebler, Lyman F. 1908. "Soft Drinks Containing Caffeine and Extracts of Coca Leaf and Kola Nut." In *Reports of the President's Homes Commission*. Washington, D.C.: U.S. Government Printing Office.

Keyes, Alan. 1999a. "Alan Keyes on Abortion and Euthanasia." http://idt.net/~mkollar/ Intellectual%20Stimulation/thoughts/others/09.htm.

———. 1999b. "Alan Keyes Challenges America on the Right to Life." http://forerunner.com/champion/X0024_Alan_Keyes.html.

Kime, Mary Lynn. 1995. "Hughes v. State: The 'Born Alive' Rule Dies a Timely Death." *Tulsa Law Journal* 30 (Spring): 539.

Kingdon, John W. 1984. *Agendas, Alternatives, and Public Policy.* Boston: Little, Brown.

Kirn, Walter. 1998. "The Drug Once Called Speed Has Come Roaring Back as a Powdery Plague on America's Heartland." *Time*, June 22, 24–32.

Klasing, Murphy S. 1995. "The Death of an Unborn Child: Jurisprudential Inconsistencies in Wrongful Death, Criminal Homicide, and Abortion Cases." *Pepperdine Law Review* 22: 933–79.

Klein, Ethel, Jacqueline Campbell, Esta Soler, and Marissa Ghez. 1997. *Ending Domestic Violence: Changing Public Perceptions/Halting the Epidemic.* Thousand Oaks, Calif.: Sage.

Koff, Stephen 1993. "Judges Set Own Abortion Consent Rules: Some Girls Try Court Shopping." *Cleveland Plain Dealer,* January 18, 1B and 4B.

Kolder, Veronika E. B., Janet Gallagher, and Michael T. Parsons. 1987. "Court-Ordered Obstetrical Interventions." *New England Journal of Medicine* 316: 1192–96.

Koran, Gideon, Karen Graham, Heather Shear, and Tom R. Einarson. 1989. "Bias against the Null Hypothesis: The Reproductive Hazards of Cocaine." *Lancet* 2 (December): 1440–42.

Kowitz, Julie F. 1995. "Not Your Garden Variety Tort Reform: Statutes Barring Claims for Wrongful Life and Wrongful Birth Are Unconstitutional under the Purpose Prong of *Planned Parenthood v. Casey.*" *Brooklyn Law Review* 61 (Spring): 235–72.

Krieger, Lisa M. 1998. "RU-486 Abortion Pill Still Not Widely Available in the U.S." *San Francisco Examiner,* January 27, A1.

Lancaster New Era. 1997. "Killing Fetus Would be a Crime." April 30, A1.

Laswell, Harold D. 1971. *A Preview of Policy Sciences.* New York: American Elsevier.

Laudor, Michael B. 1994. "In Defense of Wrongful Life: Bringing Political Theory to the Defense of a Tort." *Fordham Law Review* 62 (April): 1675–1704.

Lavelle, Marianne. 1998. "When Abortions Come Late in a Pregnancy." *U.S. News & World Report,* January 19, 31–32.

Leff, Lisa. 1990. "Treating Drug Addiction With the Woman in Mind." *Washington Post,* March 5, E1 and E4.

Leightman, Carole Wolfson. 1982. "*Roback v. United States*: A Precedent Setting Damage Formula for Wrongful Birth." *Chicago-Kent Law Review* 58: 725–64.

Lewin, Tamar. 1998. "Report Tying Abortion to Welfare." *New York Times,* June 8, A10.

Lindblom, Charles E. 1959. "The Science of 'Muddling Through.' " *Public Administration Review* 19 (Spring): 79–88.

Lindgren, J. Ralph, and Nadine Taub. 1993. *The Law of Sex Discrimination.* 2d ed. Minneapolis: West Publishing.

Lipsky, Michael. 1980. *Street-Level Bureaucracy: Dilemmas of the Individual in Public Services.* New York: Russell Sage Foundation.

Long, Carol. 1997. "National Right to Life Political Action Committee." *NRLC 1997 Yearbook.* Washington, D.C.: National Right to Life Committee.

Losco, Joseph. 1988. "Fetal Abuse: An Exploration of Emerging Philosophic, Legal, and Policy Issues." *Western Political Quarterly* 42(2): 266–85.

Lowi, Theodore J. 1964. "American Business, Public Policy, Case Studies, and Political Theory." *World Politics* 16(4): 677–715.

——. 1972. "Four Systems of Policy, Politics, and Choice." *Public Administration Review* 32(4): 298–310.

——. 1988. "Foreword: New Dimensions in Policy and Politics." In *Social Regulatory Policy: Moral Controversies in American Politics,* edited by Raymond Tatalovich and Byron W. Daynes. Boulder: Westview Press.

Luker, Kristen. 1984. *Abortion and the Politics of Motherhood.* Berkeley: University of California Press.

"Man Charged with Raping Cousin, Trying to Kill Fetus." 1998. *Los Angeles Times,* January 15, B4.

Mathieu, Deborah. 1995. "Mandating Treatment for Pregnant Substance Abusers: A Compromise." *Politics and the Life Sciences* 14(2): 199–208.

——. 1996. "Pregnant Women in Chains?" *Politics and the Life Sciences* 15(1): 77–81.

Maurer, Christine, and Tara E. Sheets. 1997. *Encyclopedia of Associations.* 32d ed. Vols. 1 and 2. Detroit: Gale.

May, Margaret. 1978. "Violence in the Family: An Historical Perspective." In *Violence and the Family*, edited by J. P. Martin. New York: Wiley.

McBrien, Richard P., ed. 1995. *Encyclopedia of Catholicism.* San Francisco: HarperCollins.

McCall, C., J. Casteel, and N. S. Shaw. 1985. "Pregnancy in Prison: A Needs Assessment of Perinatal Outcome in Three California Penal Institutions." Oakland, Calif: Prison Match.

McDonagh, Eileen. 1994a. "Abortion Rights Alchemy and the U.S. Supreme Court: What's Wrong and How to Fix It." *Social Politics* 1(2) (Summer): 131–54.

——. 1994b. "From Pro-Choice to Pro-Consent in the Abortion Debate: Reframing Women's Reproductive Rights." *Studies in Law, Politics and Society* 14: 245–87.

——. 1996. *Breaking the Abortion Deadlock: From Choice to Consent.* New York: Oxford University Press.

McDowell, David W. 1994. "Wrongful Death–Nonviable Fetus Is Not a 'Minor Child' under Alabama's Wrongful Death Act." *Cumberland Law Review* 24: 159–76.

McDowell, Gary L. 1988. *Curbing the Courts: The Constitution and the Limits of Judicial Power.* Baton Rouge: Louisiana State University Press.

McFarlane, Judith. 1989. "Battering during Pregnancy: Tip of an Iceberg Revealed." *Women and Health* 15 (3): 69–84.

McKechnie, Jean L., ed. 1983. *Webster's Deluxe Unabridged Dictionary.* 2d ed. New York: Simon and Schuster.

McKee, Mike. 1997a. "State Settles Suit over Prison Medical Care." *Recorder*, July 30, 1.

——. 1997b. "Lawyers to Get $1.2 M in Prison Settlement."*Recorder*, August 14, 1.

McKeegan, Michele. 1992. *Abortion Politics: Mutiny in the Ranks of the Right.* New York: Free Press.

McLeer, Susan V., and Rebecca Anwar. 1989. "A Study of Battered Women Presenting in an Emergency Department." *American Journal of Public Health* 79(1): 65–66.

McNulty, Molly. 1990. "Pregnancy Police: Implications of Criminalizing Fetal Abuse." *Youth Law News* Special Issue: 33–37.

Meersman, Nancy. 1998. "Doctor: Abortion Policy Risked Woman's Health." *Union Leader*, May 23, A4.

Meier, Kenneth J. 1994. *The Politics of Sin: Drugs, Alcohol and Public Policy.* Armonk, N.Y.: M. E. Sharpe.

Meier, Kenneth J., and Deborah R. McFarlane. 1993. "Abortion Politics and Abortion Funding Policy." In *Understanding the New Politics of Abortion*, edited by Malcolm L. Goggin. Newbury Park, Calif.: Sage.

Melton, Gary B. 1987. "Legal Regulation of Adolescent Abortion: Unintended Effects." *American Psychologist* 42: 79–83.

Melton, Gary B., and Nancy Felipe Russo. 1987. "Adolescent Abortion: Psychological Perspectives on Public Policy." *American Psychologist* 42: 69–72.

Melton, Gordon J. 1989. *The Church Speaks on Abortion.* Detroit: Gale.

Moen, Matthew C. 1984. "School Prayer and the Politics of Life-Style Concern." *Social Science Quarterly* 65(4): 1070–81.

Mohr, James C. 1978. *Abortion in America.* New York: Oxford University Press.

Montgomery, Nancy. 1999. "Morning After Project a Success." *Seattle Times*, July 25, B1–2.

Mooney, Christopher Z., and Mei-Hsien Lee. 1995. "Legislating Morality in the American States: The Case of Pre-*Roe* Abortion Regulation Reform." *American Journal of Political Science* 39(3): 599–627.

———. 1996. "Why Not Swing? The Definition of Death Penalty Legislation in the American States since 1838." Paper presented at the annual meeting of the American Political Science Association.

Moore, Wayne D. 1996. *Constitutional Rights and Powers of the People*. Princeton: Princeton University Press.

Morain, Dan. 1998. "Battle Brews in GOP as Foes of Abortion Target 2 Justices." *Los Angeles Times*, January 20, A3 and A18.

Morey, Martha A., Michael L. Begleiter, and David J. Harris. 1981. "Profile of a Battered Fetus." *Lancet* 11: 1294–95.

Morrison, Patt. 1997. "Licenses and Liberties." *Los Angeles Times*, October 31, B2.

Moss, Kary L. 1990. "Substance Abuse during Pregnancy." *Harvard Women's Law Journal* 13 (Spring): 278–99.

Murley, John A. 1988. "School Prayer: Free Exercise of Religion or Establishment of Religion?" In *Social Regulatory Policy: Moral Controversies in American Politics*, edited by Raymond Tatalovich and Byron W. Daynes. Boulder: Westview Press.

Musto, David F. 1987. *The American Disease: Origins of Narcotics Control*. New York: Oxford University Press.

Nagel, Stuart S. 1973. *Comparing Elected and Appointed Judicial Systems*. Beverly Hills: Sage.

Nason-Clark, Nancy. 1997. *The Battered Wife: How Christians Confront Family Violence*. Westminster, Canada: John Knox Press.

National Abortion and Reproductive Rights Action League. 1995a. *Sexuality Education in America: A State-by-State Review*. Rev. ed. Washington, D.C.: NARAL Foundation.

———. 1995b. *Who Decides? A State-by-State Review of Abortion and Reproductive Rights*. 4th ed. Washington, D.C.: NARAL Foundation.

———. 1997a. "NARAL Factsheets: Limitations on the Rights of Pregnant Women." Washington, D.C.: NARAL Foundation.

———. 1997b. *Who Decides? A State-by-State Review of Abortion and Reproductive Rights*. 6th ed. Washington, D.C.: NARAL Foundation.

———. 1998a. "Wisconsin Abortion Providers Halt Services." Press release, May 19. Washington D.C.: NARAL Foundation.

———. 1998b. "Military Women Stationed Overseas Again Denied Access to Abortion Services by House." Press release, May 20. Washington, D.C.: NARAL Foundation.

———. 1998c. "Senate Bans Abortion Services for Military Women." Press release, June 25. Washington, D.C.: NARAL Foundation.

———. 1998d. *Who Decides? A State-by-State Review of Abortion and Reproductive Rights*. 7th ed. Washington, D.C.: NARAL Foundation.

———. 1998e. "State Legislation to Ban So-Called 'Partial-Birth' Abortion." Washington, D.C.: NARAL Foundation.

———. 1999. *Who Decides: A State-by-State Review of Abortion and Reproductive Rights*. 8th ed. Washington, D.C.: NARAL Foundation.

National Abortion Federation Annual Report. 1994. Washington, D.C.: NAF.

National Cancer Institute. 1996. *Risk of Breast Cancer Associated with Abortion*. Bethesda, Md.: NCI.

National Institute on Drug Abuse. 1992. *Drug Services Research Survey: Final Report Phase I and II*. Waltham, Mass.: Bigel Institute for Health Policy, Brandeis University.

National Right to Life Committee. 1998. "When Does Life Begin?" http://www.nrlc.org/abortion/index.html.

——. 1999. "Letter from NRLC to Congress Re: UVWA." September 30. http://www.nrlc.org./press_releases_new/093099.html.

National Right to Life Convention Handbook. 1994. "The Pro-Life Majorities." Washington, D.C.: NRL.

Nazario, Sonia. 1997a. "Orphans of Addiction." *Los Angeles Times*, November 16, A1 and A24–A28.

——. 1997b. "Healing Shattered Lives—and Families." *Los Angeles Times*, November 17, A1 and A20–A22.

——. 1998. "Searching for Alternatives." *Los Angeles Times*, January 11, A18.

Nazario, Sonia, and Michael Krikorian. 1998. "County Weighs Plan to Curb Child Abuse." *Los Angeles Times*, February 18, B1 and B8.

Nelson, Lawrence, Brian P. Buggy, and Carol J. Weil. 1986. "Forced Medical Treatment of Pregnant Women: Compelling Each to Live as Seems Good to the Rest." *Hastings Law Journal* 37 (May): 703–63.

New Mexico Attorney General. 1990. Opinion No. 90-19. October 3.

Nice, David C. 1988. "State Deregulation of Intimate Behavior." *Social Science Quarterly* 69(1): 203–11.

——. 1992. "The States and the Death Penalty." *Western Political Quarterly* 45(4): 1037–48.

Niebuhr, Gustav. 1998. "Southern Baptists Declare Wife Should 'Submit' to Her Husband." *New York Times*, June 10, A1.

North American Council on Adoptable Children. 1996. Unpublished data on special needs adoption subsidies and foster care payments.

Nossiff, Rosemary. 1995. "Pennsylvania: The Impact of Party Organization and Religious Lobbying." In *Abortion Politics in American States*, edited by Mary C. Segers and Timothy A. Byrnes. Armonk, N.Y.: M. E. Sharpe.

Novello, Antonia C., Mark Rosenberg, Linda Saltzman, and John Shosky. 1992. "From the Surgeon General, US Public Health Service." *Journal of the American Medical Association* 267(23): 3132.

NOW Legal Defense and Education Fund. 1987. *The State-by-State Guide to Women's Legal Rights*. Washington, D.C.: National Organization for Women.

Office of Population Research. 1998a. "Does Use of Emergency Contraception Cause an Abortion?" Princeton: Princeton University. http://opr.princeton.edu/ec/ecabt.html.

——. 1998b. "How Do Emergency Contraceptives Work?" Princeton: Princeton University. http://opr.princeton.edu/ec/ecwork.html.

——. 1998c. "Why Is Emergency Contraception the Nation's Best Kept Secret?" Princeton: Princeton University. http:/opr.princeton.edu/ec/eminfo.html.

Olasky, Marvin. 1992a. *Abortion Rites: A Social History of Abortion in America*. Wheaton, Ill.: Crossway Books.

——. 1992b. "Victorian Secret." *Policy Review* 60 (Spring): 30–37.

Olsen, Frances. 1989. "Unraveling Compromise." *Harvard Law Review* 103(43): 105–35.

Ooms, Theodora, and Lisa Herendeen. 1990. *Drugs, Mothers, Kids and Ways to Cope*. Washington, D.C.: American Association for Marriage and Family Therapy.

Ourlian, Robert. 1997. "Woman Offers Payment if Addicts Get Sterilization." *Los Angeles Times*, October 24, A3 and A40.

Paltrow, Lynn M. 1991. "Perspective of a Reproductive Rights Attorney." *The Future of the Children* 1: 85–92.

——. 1992. "Criminal Prosecutions against Pregnant Women." New York: Reproductive Freedom Project.

Parness, Jeffrey A. 1985. "Crimes against the Unborn: Protecting and Respecting the Potentiality of Life." *Harvard Journal on Legislation* 22: 97–172.

Pasternak, Judy. 1998a. "Meth Kids: Heartland's Tragic Tale." *Los Angeles Times*, May 29, A1 and A35.

——. 1998b. "Wisconsin OKs Civil Detention for Fetal Abuse." *Los Angeles Times*, May 2, A1 and A13.

Peak, Ken, and Frankie Sue Del Papa. 1993. "Criminal Justice Enters the Womb: Enforcing the 'Right' to Be Born Drug-Free." *Journal of Criminal Law* 21(3): 245–63.

Pearson, Jessica, and Nancy Thoennes. 1995. *The Impact of Legislation and Court Decisions Dealing with Drug-Affected Babies.* Denver: Center for Policy Research.

Peltason, James Walter. 1991. *Understanding the Constitution.* San Diego: Harcourt Brace Jovanovich.

Peretz, Paul, and Jean Reith Schroedel. 1996. "The Road Not to Travel: A Comment on Deborah Mathieu's Proposal to Mandate Outpatient Treatment for Pregnant Substance Abusers." *Politics and the Life Sciences* 15(1): 67–69.

Perko, Gary V. 1990. "*State v. Beale* and the Killing of a Viable Fetus: An Exercise in Statutory Construction and the Potential for Legislative Reform." *North Carolina Law Review* 68: 1144–58.

Petchesky, Rosalind Pollack. 1985. *Abortion and Women's Choice: The State, Sexuality, and Reproductive Freedom.* Boston: Northeastern University Press.

——. 1987. "Foetal Images: The Power of Visual Culture in the Politics of Reproduction." In *Reproductive Technologies: Gender, Motherhood and Medicine*, edited by Michelle Stanworth. Minneapolis: University of Minnesota Press.

Planned Parenthood. 1998. *Fact Sheets: Legal Questions and Answers about So-called "Partial-Birth" Abortion Bans.* http://www.plannedparenthood.org/library/abortion/legalquest.html.

Podewils, Lisa A. 1993. "Traditional Tort Principles and Wrongful Conception Child-Rearing Damages." *Boston University Law Review* 73(3): 407–25.

Poland, Marilyn L., Mitchell Dombrowski, Joel W. Ager, and Robert J. Sokol. 1993. "Punishing Pregnant Drug Users: Enhancing the Flight from Care." *Drug and Alcohol Dependency* 31(3): 199–203.

Pollitt, Katha. 1990. "Fetal Rights: A New Assault on Feminism." *Nation*, March 26, 409–18.

Public Law 99–117, October 7, 1998.

Ratner, Mitchell S. 1993. "Sex, Drugs, and Public Policy: Studying and Understanding the Sex-for-Crack Phenomenon." In *Crack Pipe as Pimp*, edited by Mitchell S. Ratner. New York: Lexington Books.

Reagan, Leslie J. 1997. *When Abortion Was a Crime.* Berkeley: University of California Press.

Reinarman, Craig, and Harry Levine. 1997. "The Crack Attack: Politics and Media in the Crack Scare." In *Crack in America: Demon Drugs and Social Justice*, edited by Craig Reinarman and Harry G. Levine. Berkeley: University of California Press.

Reproductive Freedom Project. 1994. "Legal Docket." New York: American Civil Liberties Union.

Richard, Patricia Bayer. 1995. "Ohio: Steering toward Middle Ground." In *Abortion*

Politics in American States, edited by Mary C. Segers and Timothy A. Byrnes. Armonk, N.Y.: M. E. Sharpe.

Ripley, Randall B., and Grace A. Franklin. 1988. *Congress, the Bureaucracy, and Public Policy*. 4th ed. Chicago: Dorsey Press.

Rivenburg, Roy. 1997. "Partial Truths." *Los Angeles Times*, April 2, E1 and E8.

Roan, Shari. 1996. "How Many Babies Is Too Many?" *Los Angeles Times*, May 14, A1, A16, and A17.

Roberts, Dorothy E. 1991. "Punishing Drug Addicts Who Have Babies: Women of Color, Equality, and the Right of Privacy." *Harvard Law Review* 104 (May): 1419–82.

Robertson, David B., and Dennis R. Judd. 1989. *The Development of American Public Policy*. Glenview, Ill.: Scott, Foresman.

Robertson, John A. 1983. "Procreative Liberty and the Control of Conception, Pregnancy, and Childbirth." *Virginia Law Review* 69 (April): 405–63.

——. 1994. *Children of Choice: Freedom and the New Reproductive Technologies*. Princeton: Princeton University Press.

Romney, Tiffany M. 1991. "Prosecuting Mothers of Drug-Exposed Babies: The State's Interest in Protecting the Rights of a Fetus versus the Mother's Constitutional Rights to Due Process, Privacy and Equal Protection." *Journal of Contemporary Law* 17(2): 325–44.

Rosen, Judith C. 1989. "Who Will Guard the Guardians?" In *Abortion Rights and Fetal Personhood*, edited by Ed Doerr and James W. Prescott. Long Beach, Calif.: Centerline Press.

Rosenberg, Gerald N. 1991. *The Hollow Hope*. Chicago: University of Chicago Press.

Rosenblum, Victor, and Thomas J. Marzen. 1987. "Strategies for Reversing *Roe v. Wade* through the Courts." In *Abortion and the Constitution: Reversing* Roe v. Wade *through the Courts*, edited by Dennis J. Horan, Edward R. Grant, and Paige C. Cunningham. Washington, D.C.: Georgetown University Press.

Ross, Alfred, and Lee Cokorinos. 1997. "Promise Keepers: A Real Challenge from the Right." *National NOW Times*, May, 1 and 6.

Rossum, Ralph A., and G. Alan Tarr. 1995. *American Constitutional Law*, 4th ed. Vols. 1 and 2. New York: St. Martin's Press.

Roth, Rachel. 1997. "At Women's Expense: The Costs of Fetal Rights." Ph.D. diss., Yale University.

Rozell, Mark, and Clyde Wilcox. 1996. *Second Coming: The New Christian Right in Virginia Politics*. Baltimore: Johns Hopkins University Press.

Rubenfeld, Jed. 1991. "On the Legal Status of Proposition That Life Begins at Conception." *Stanford Law Review* 43(3): 599–635.

Rubin, Alissa. 1991. "Interest Groups and Abortion Politics in the Post-*Webster* Era." In *Interest Group Politics*, edited by Allan J. Cigler and Burdett A. Loomis. Washington, D.C.: Congressional Quarterly Press.

——. 1998. "Abortion Providers at Lowest Mark since '73." *Los Angeles Times*, December 11, A45.

Rubin, Eva R. 1994. *The Abortion Controversy: A Documentary History*. Westport, Conn.: Greenwood.

Russo, Michael A. 1995. "California: A Political Landscape for Choice and Conflict." In *Abortion Politics in American States*, edited by Mary C. Segers and Timothy A. Byrnes. Armonk, N.Y.: M. E. Sharpe.

Rydell, Peter C., and Susan S. Everingham. 1994. *Controlling Cocaine: Supply versus Demand Programs*. Santa Monica, Calif: Rand Corporation.

Savage, David G. 1997. "Supreme Court Grants States a Power Surge." *Los Angeles Times*, June 29, A1, A16, and A18.

Scales, Ann, with Wendy Chavkin. 1996. "Abortion, Law, and Public Health." In *Man-Made Medicine: Women's Health, Public Policy, and Reform*, edited by Kary L. Moss. Durham, N.C.: Duke University Press.

Schacter, Jim. 1986. "Of Drugs and Death: Prosecutors Raise the Ante, Woman Accused of Contributing to Baby's Demise during Pregnancy." *Los Angeles Times*, October 1, 1 of Metro, pt. 2.

Schierl, Kathryn. 1990. "A Proposal to Illinois Legislators: Revise the Illinois Criminal Code to Include Criminal Sanctions against Prenatal Substance Abusers." *John Marshall Law Review* 23 (Spring): 393–422.

Schneider, Anne, and Helen Ingram. 1993. "Social Construction of Target Populations: Implications for Politics and Policy." *American Political Science Review* 87(2): 334–47.

Schroedel, Jean Reith, and Daniel Jordan. 1998. "Senate Voting and Social Construction of Target Populations: A Study of AIDS Policy-making, 1987–1992." *Journal of Health Politics, Policy and Law* 23(1): 107–32.

Schroedel, Jean Reith, and Paul Peretz. 1994. "A Gender Analysis of Policy Formation: The Case of Fetal Abuse." *Journal of Health Politics, Policy, and Law* 19(2): 335–60.

Schroeder, Mark G. 1995. "Media Attention Often Causes Lawmakers to Act." In *State Politics*, edited by Thad L. Beyle. Washington, D.C.: Congressional Quarterly Press.

Segers, Mary C., and Timothy A. Byrnes. 1995. "Introduction: Abortion Politics in American States." In *Abortion Politics in American States*, edited by Mary C. Segers and Timothy A. Byrnes. Armonk, N.Y.: M. E. Sharpe.

Sensibaugh, Christine Cregan, and Elizabeth Rice Allgeier. 1996. "Factors Considered by Ohio Juvenile Judges in Judicial Bypass Judgments: A Policy-Capturing Approach." *Politics and the Life Sciences* 15(1): 35–45.

Seward, Paul N., Charles A. Ballard, and Arthur Ulene. 1973. "The Effect of Legal Abortion on the Rate of Septic Abortion at a Large County Hospital." *American Journal of Obstetrics and Gynecology* 115(3): 335–38.

Shelton, Barbara J., and Derek G. Gill. 1989. "Childbearing in Prison: A Behavioral Analysis." *Journal of Obstetrics, Gynecology, and Neonatal Nursing* 18(4): 301–8.

Shepherd, Lois. 1995. "Protecting Parents' Freedom to Have Children with Genetic Differences." *University of Illinois Law Review*: 761–812.

Siegel, Barry. 1994. "In the Name of the Children." *Los Angeles Times Magazine*, August 7, 14–38.

Siegel, Loren. 1997. "The Pregnancy Police Fight the War on Drugs." In *Crack in America: Demon Drugs and Social Justice*, edited by Craig Reinarman and Harry G. Levine. Berkeley: University of California Press.

Smith, Bill. 1995. "Prosecute for Abortions, Group Says." *St. Louis Post Dispatch*, August 5.

Smith, Lynn. 1998. "The $200 Questions." *Los Angeles Times*, April 3, E1 and E8.

Smith-Rosenberg, Carroll. 1985. *Disorderly Conduct: Gender in Victorian America*. New York: A. Knopf.

Society for Assisted Reproductive Technology, American Society for Reproductive Medicine. 1995. "Assisted Reproductive Technology in the United States and Canada: 1993 Results Generated from the American Society for Reproductive Medicine/Society for Assisted Reproductive Technology Registry." *Fertility and Sterility* 64: 13–17.

Stabile, Carole. 1992. "Shooting the Mother: Fetal Photography and the Politics of Disappearance." *Camera Obscura* 28 (January 1): 179–85.

Staggenborg, Suzanne. 1996. "The Survival of the Pro-Choice Movement." In *The Pol-*

itics of Abortion and Birth Control in Historical Perspective, edited by Donald T. Critchlow. University Park: Pennsylvania State University Press.

Stammer, Larry B. 1998. "A Wife's Role Is 'to Submit,' Baptists Declare." *Los Angeles Times*, June 10, A1, A26, and A27.

Stark, Evan, Annie Flitcraft, and William Frazier. 1979. "Medicine and Patriarchal Violence: The Social Construction of a 'Private Event.' " *International Journal of Health Services* 9(3): 461–93.

State & Local Sourcebook 1999. 1999. Washington, D.C.: Congressional Quarterly.

"State Bill on Fetal Death is Mischief." 1997. *The Morning Call*, 1 May, A22.

"State Legislation on Reproductive Health in 1990: What Was Proposed and Enacted." 1991. *Family Planning Perspectives*, March–April, 82.

Stauffer, Diane M. 1986. "The Trauma Patient Who Is Pregnant." *Journal of Emergency Nursing* 12(2): 89–93.

Stern, Marcus. 1990. "In Inner City, Crack Has Scarred Mother and Child." *San Diego Union-Tribune*, June 27.

Stone, Deborah A. 1988. *Policy Paradox and Political Reason*. New York: HarperCollins.

——. 1989. "Causal Stories and the Formation of Policy Agendas." *Political Science Quarterly* 104(2): 281–300.

——. 1997. *Policy Paradox and Political Reason: The Art of Political Decision Making*. New York: Norton.

Stotland, Nada L. 1992. "Commentary: The Myth of the Abortion Trauma Syndrome." *Journal of the American Medical Association* 268(15): 2078–79.

Strickland, Ruth Ann. 1995. "North Carolina: One Liberal Law in the South." In *Abortion Politics in American States*, edited by Mary C. Segers and Timothy A. Byrnes. Armonk, N.Y.: M. E. Sharpe.

——. 1996. "The Incivility of Mandated Drug Treatment through Civil Commitments." *Politics and the Life Sciences* 15(1): 70–72.

Strickland, Ruth Ann, and Marcia Lynn Whicker. 1992. "Political and Socioeconomic Indicators of State Restrictiveness toward Abortion." *Policy Studies Journal* 20(4): 598–617.

Sugg, Nancy Kathleen, and Thomas Inui. 1992. "Primary Care Physicians' Response to Domestic Violence." *Journal of the American Medical Association* 267(23): 3157–60.

Sunstein, Cass R. 1993. *The Partial Constitution*. Cambridge, Mass.: Harvard University Press.

Sverdlik, Alan. 1997. "Blast Rocks Atlanta Abortion Clinic; At Least 7 People Slightly Injured in Explosions 45 Minutes Apart." *Washington Post*, January 17, A03.

Sward, Susan, and Bill Wallace. 1995. "Class Action Suit Filed against Women's Prisons." *San Francisco Chronicle*, April 5, A15–A16.

Tatalovich, Raymond. 1988. "Abortion: Prochoice versus Prolife." In *Social Regulatory Policy: Moral Controversies in American Politics*, edited by Raymond Tatalovich and Byron W. Daynes. Boulder: Westview Press.

Tatalovich, Raymond, and Byron W. Daynes. 1988. "Introduction: What Is Social Regulatory Policy?" In *Social Regulatory Policy: Moral Controversies in American Politics*, edited by Raymond Tatalovich and Bryon W. Daynes. Boulder: Westview Press.

——. 1993. "The Lowi Paradigm, Moral Conflict, and Coalition-Building: Pro-Choice versus Pro-Life." *Women and Politics* 13(1): 39–66.

Theodore, Joyce, Stanley K. Henshaw, and Julia DeClerque Skarrud. 1997. "The Impact of Mississippi's Mandatory Delay Law on Abortion and Births." *Journal of the American Medical Association* 278(8): 653.

Thompson, Roger. 1986. *Sex in Middlesex: Popular Mores in a Massachusetts County, 1649–99.* Amherst: University of Massachusetts Press.

Times Wire Services. 1996. "Drug Pregnancy Case Prosecutions Ok'd in South Carolina." *Los Angeles Times*, July 17, A12.

———. 1998. "Anti-Abortion Activists Hold Fetuses Burial." *Los Angeles Times*, October 12, A20.

Tin, Win, Unni Wariyar, and Edmund Hey. 1997. "Changing Prognosis for Babies of Less than 28 Weeks' Gestation in the North of England between 1983 and 1994." *British Medical Journal* 314 (January 11): 107.

Tracy, Carol, Donna Talbert, and Janice Steinschneider. 1990. *Women, Babies, and Drugs: Family-Centered Treatment Options.* Washington, D.C.: Center for Policy Alternatives, National Conference of Governors.

Tribe, Laurence H. 1990. *Abortion: The Clash of Absolutes.* New York: Norton.

Trindel, Robin. 1991. "Fetal Interests vs. Maternal Rights: Is the State Going Too Far?" *Akron Law Review* 24(3–4): 743–62.

Ulrich, Laurel T. 1982. *Good Wives: Image and Reality in the Lives of Women in Northern New England, 1650–1750.* New York: Oxford University Press.

Van Stolk, Mary. 1976. "Beaten Women, Battered Children." *Children Today,* March–April, 8–12.

Vermont Department of Social Welfare. 1980. Medicaid Policy M617.

Waldman, Steven, Elise Ackerman, and Rita Rubin. 1998. "Abortions in America: So Many Women Have Them, So Few Talk about Them." *U.S. News & World Report,* January 19, 20–25.

Walker, Gillian, Kathleen Eric, Anitra Pivnick, and Ernest Drucker. 1991. "A Descriptive Outline of a Program for Cocaine-Using Mothers and Their Babies." *Journal of Feminist Family Therapy* 3(3–4): 7–17.

Warnock, Mary. 1987. "Do Human Cells Have Rights?" *From Lecture Ormond College, Melbourne* 1(1): 1–14.

Warren, Jennifer. 1997. "Special Children, Special Needs." *Los Angeles Times*, July 27, A1 and A30–31.

———. 1998. "For Aborted Fetuses, a Question of Pain." *Los Angeles Times*, January 4: A3 and A24.

Wegner, Judith Romney. 1988. *Chattel or Person?* New York: Oxford University Press.

Wetstein, Matthew E. 1996. *Abortion Rates in the United States.* Albany: State University of New York Press.

Wexler, David B. 1996. "Some Therapeutic Jurisprudence Implications of the Outpatient Civil Commitment of Pregnant Substance Abusers." *Politics and the Life Sciences* 15(1): 73–75.

"What the Nurse Saw." 1996. *National Right to Life News*, May 20, 20.

Wilcox, Clyde. 1989. "Political Action Committees and Abortion: A Longitudinal Analysis." *Women and Politics* 9(1): 1–20.

———. 1995. "The Sources and Consequences of Public Attitudes toward Abortion." In *Perspectives on the Politics of Abortion*, edited by Ted G. Jelen. Westport, Conn.: Praeger.

Wilcox, Clyde, and Barbara Norrander. 1997. "The Causes and Consequences of State Opinion on Abortion." Unpublished manuscript. Georgetown University; University of Arizona.

Williams, Patricia. 1990. "Fetal Fictions: An Exploration of Property Archetypes in Racial and Gendered Contexts." *Florida Law Review* 42(1): 81–95.

Wilson, Janet S., and Renee Leasure. 1991. "Cruel and Unusual Punishment: The Health Care of Women in Prison." *Nurse Practitioner* 16 (February): 32–39.

Wilson, Sharon. 1994. "The Human Face of a Budget Cut: How a City Program Made a Difference, A Recovering Addict's Pleas." *New York Times*, November 20, Section 13:25.

Wisot, Arthur L., and David Meldrum. 1997. *Conceptions and Misconceptions: A Guide through the Maze of in Vitro Fertilization and Other Assisted Reproductive Methods*. Point Roberts, Wash.: Hartley and Marks.

Wlezien, Christopher, and Malcolm Goggin. 1993. "The Courts, Interest Groups, and Public Opinion about Abortion." *Political Behavior* 15(4): 381–403.

Woliver, Laura R. 1996. "Policies to Assist Pregnant Women and Children Should Include a Complete Assessment of the Realities of Women's Lives." *Politics and the Life Sciences* 15(1): 75–77.

Woloch, Nancy. 1984. *Women and the American Experience*. New York: Knopf.

Woolredge, John D., and Kimberly Masters. 1993. "Confronting Problems Faced by Pregnant Inmates in State Prisons." *Crime and Delinquency* 39(2): 195–203.

Wright, Gerald, Robert Erikson, and John McIver. 1987. "Public Opinion and Policy Liberalism in the American States." *American Journal of Political Science* 31(4): 980–1001.

Zaitchik, Alan. 1984. "Viability and the Morality of Abortion." In *The Problem of Abortion*, edited by Joel Feinberg. Belmont, Calif.: Wadsworth.

Zent, Jeff. 1998. "Minot Planning Commission Rejects Treatment Center Plan." *Minot Daily News*, August 25, B2.

List of Cases

Abrams v. Foshee, 3 Iowa 274 (1856).
American Academy of Pediatrics v. Lungren, 882 P.2d 247 (Cal. 1994).
American Academy of Pediatrics v. Lungren, 32 Cal. Rptr. 2d 546 (Cal. App. 1994).
Application of the President and Directors of Georgetown College Hospital, 331 F.2d 1000 (1964).
Atlantic Coast Line Co. v. Goldsboro, 232 U.S. 548 (1914).
Babbitz v. McCann, 310 F.Supp. 293 (E.D. Wis. 1970).
Beecham v. Leahy, 287 A.2d 836 (Vt. 1972).
Bronbrest v. Kotz, 65 F.Supp. 138 (1946).
Buck v. Bell, 274 U.S. 201–3 (1927).
Burdett v. Hopegood, 24 Eng. Rep. 485 (1718).
Carhart v. Stenberg, 11 F.Supp. 2d 1099 (D. Neb. 1998).
Christopher C. Goins v. Commonwealth of Virginia, 251 Va. 442 (1996).
Clarke v. State, 117 Ala. 1, 23 So. 671 (1898).
Cohens v. Virginia, 19 U.S. 264 (1821).
Colautti v. Franklin, 439 U.S. 379, 388–89 (1979).
Commonwealth v. Bangs, 9 Mass. 387 (1812).
Commonwealth v. Cass, 392 Mass. 799 (1984).
Commonwealth v. Lawrence, 404 Mass. 378; 536 N.E.2d 571 (1989).
Commonwealth v. Somnuk Viriyahiranpaiboon, 412 Mass. 224L 588 N.E.2d 643 (1992).
Commonwealth of Kentucky, Morant v. Connie Welch, 864 S.W. 2d (1993).
Conner v. Monkem Co., 898 S.W.2d 89 (Mo. 1995)
Cornelia Whitner v. South Carolina; and Melissa Ann Crawley v. South Carolina, 97–1562 Supreme Court of the United States 1998 U.S. Lexis 3564; 66 U.S.L.W. 3758.
Cruzan v. Director, Missouri Department of Health, 497 U.S. 261 (1990).
Curlender v. Bio-Science Laboratories, 106 Cal. App. 3d 811 (1980).
Curran v. Bosze, 566 N.E. 2d 1319 (Ill. 1990).
Delaware Women's Health Org. v. Wier, 441 F.Supp. 497 n. 9 (D. Del. 1977).
DiDonat v. Wortman, 320 N.C. 423, 427–28; 358 S.E.2d 489, 491–92 (1987).
Dietrich v. Northampton, 138 Mass. 14 (1884).
Doe v. Bolton, 410 U.S. 179 (1973).
Doe v. Bridgeton Hospital Association, 366 A.2d 641 (N.J. 1976).

Subject Index

Legal Index

Legal Index

221